"Say to This Mountain"

"Say to This Mountain"

Mark's Story of Discipleship

Ched Myers, Marie Dennis, Joseph Nangle, O.F.M.,
Cynthia Moe-Lobeda, and Stuart Taylor

Edited by Karen Lattea

ORBIS BOOKS
Maryknoll, New York 10545

Third Printing, November 1997

The Catholic Foreign Mission Society of America (Maryknoll) recruits and trains people for overseas missionary service. Through Orbis Books, Maryknoll aims to foster the international dialogue that is essential to mission. The books published, however, reflect the opinions of their authors and are not meant to represent the official position of the society.

Published by Orbis Books, Maryknoll, NY 10545-0308

Bible translations are predominantly from the New Revised Standard Version

Manufactured in the United States of America

Library of Congress Cataloging-in-Publication Data

Say to this mountain : Mark's story of discipleship / Ched Myers . . .
  [et al.] : edited by Karen Lattea
        p.   cm.
  Includes bibliographical references.
  ISBN 1-57075-100-5 (alk. paper)
    1. Bible. N.T. Mark—Criticism, interpretation, etc.   I. Myers,
  Ched.   II. Lattea, Karen.
  BS2585.2.S23   1996
  226.3'06—dc20   96-33153
                                                        CIP

Truly, I tell you,
whoever says to this mountain,
"Be taken up and cast into the sea"
—and does not doubt but believes it will transpire—
it will be done.

Mark 11:23

CONTENTS

PART III: THE DISCIPLESHIP "CATECHISM"

Appendices

INTRODUCTION

The Circle of Story

There are two kinds of stories and two kinds of readers. One kind of story aspires only to entertain or to distract its audience. Such stories assume readers who are passive spectators. In North American culture today we are most familiar with these kinds of stories and readers. Movies, political speeches, and the six o'clock news all maintain an essential distance between the "performance" and the audience. The other kind of story intends to change its audience. It invites spectators to become "spec-actors"—a term coined by popular theater practitioner Augusto Boal connoting those who are so engaged by a story that they want to become part of it. Spec-actors are open to allowing the story to challenge their own life-scripts—to let the story "read them."

The gospel of Mark, a first century C.E. manifesto of radical Christian discipleship, is such a story. It beckons readers to "have ears to hear" (4:9), and to "see" and "follow" (10:51f). This book invites readers into a process of reflecting on this gospel, a process we believe can become a journey of transformation. We as authors believe in the power of Mark's story of Jesus to turn spectators into spec-actors.

Background

Since the publication of Ched Myers's *Binding the Strong Man: A Political Reading of Mark's Story of Jesus* (Orbis, 1988) almost ten years ago, there have been numerous requests to popularize that commentary so as to make it more accessible to the lay reader. This book attempts to do that, and to make specific connections between Markan themes and the challenges of discipleship in today's world. To help with the twin tasks of *simplification* and *application*, Ched turned to a group of colleagues committed to both popular education and Christian activism.

In 1991 Ched collaborated with Stuart Taylor, Cindy Moe-Lobeda, and Marie Dennis on a resource for the Columbus quincentenary, a study booklet published by the Catholic national peace and justice movement Pax Christi titled *The American Journey, 1492-1992: A Call to Conversion.* Later, while Ched was working on *Who Will Roll Away the Stone? Discipleship Queries for First World Christians* (published by Orbis in 1994), Stuart, Cindy, Marie, and Joe Nangle collaborated on *St. Francis and the Foolishness of God* (published by Orbis in 1993). During this period, the five of us were also turning our attention toward the present project. Struggling with logistics of time, distance, and a plurality of writing styles, we more recently called upon the editorial expertise of *Sojourners* magazine managing editor Karen Lattea to help us complete the work.

Our group represents a spectrum of church traditions: Roman Catholic, Lutheran, Presbyterian, Methodist, and "free ecumenical." We live and work in Los Angeles, Tucson, and Washington, D.C. We are male and female, lay and clergy. None of us are professional academic theologians, though we all take the task of critical theological reflection seriously. We are of middle-class, European-American background, yet we are deeply committed to defecting from our dominant culture entitlements in order to participate in the work of justice and peace in solidarity with the poor in the U.S. and abroad.

Each of our life stories has been impacted by living and working with people on the underside of history, people whose lives are threatened by the continuing war against the poor. To be in relationship with these brothers and sisters is to become a divided person, tied to the worlds of both the privileged and the oppressed. We experience this conflict as a gift. Because we feel our first responsibility is to call the church of the dominant culture to discipleship, we conceive of this book's audience primarily as other European-American Christians. We welcome of course all readers interested in the gospel of Mark and questions of church renewal today.

The process of writing this book has not been easy. We have struggled with the text together, laughed and cried, challenged each other. At times differences in our interpretations were intense and painful, yet each grew from the insights of the others. We remained knit together by our deep respect for one another, by the joy and the energy we found in each other's presence, and by our shared conviction that following Jesus calls us to resist injustice and to rebuild a more just and compassionate social order as we do the gospel.

Reading the gospel again together reinforced our conviction that the Word is best reflected upon in community. We invite our readers to engage this process with others as well.

Goals of this Reading Process

Mark's story has transforming power only as it intersects with our individual life-stories and the broader collective history in which we live. We have designed a process that tries to keep moving between these three circles of story, in the belief that each should always inform the others.

In a commitment to read the whole of Mark, we divided the text into twenty-five units and grouped these into five parts corresponding to the five major narrative sections of the gospel. We think these units—presented in this book as chapters—represent reasonable "chunks" for group or individual study. A group of people meeting twice a month, for example, could finish the entire program in a year. Each chapter consists of two parts:

- **The Text in Context** offers commentary that looks briefly at all the salient themes raised by the Markan episodes.
- **The Word in Our World** draws out one thematic strand from the commentary and reflects upon it in light of our contemporary situation.

Each of the five major parts begins with an **Opening Meditation,** in recognition of the fact that it is necessary and appropriate to apprehend scripture prayerfully. Each part ends with a section titled **Our Discipleship Journey,** which offers a few practical suggestions about how readers might move toward "spec-acting."

These four aspects of our process represent the essential stages of what liberation theologians call the "hermeneutic circle":

1) our initial apprehension of the text in terms of our own concerns;
2) critical study of the text in terms of its socio-historical and narrative context;
3) reflection upon the reader's socio-historical and life-context;
4) a transformed engagement with the world.

This process continually juxtaposes the story of our world with that of scripture. In keeping with the orientation of *Binding the Strong Man,* our emphasis here is on the social, economic, and political dimensions of discipleship in the world. This does not imply that the inward, spiritual journey is not equally important to Christian practice—nor that the public and private dimensions of our faith can even be separated. It simply recognizes that in North America today there is little debate among Christians about the need for prayer, but little consensus about how to engage public issues of social, economic, and political justice.

Maps for the Journey

To navigate your way around the three circles of gospel, life-story, and history, it will help to have some basic "maps." You will find these in the **Appendices,** and we encourage you to look at them before proceeding.

Appendix 1 offers some tools for analyzing Mark's narrative, drawing upon our native competence for interpreting stories. These exercises can and should be employed on the Markan text of each reading unit, preferably before looking at the commentary. We trust that you or your group will read carefully each Markan passage before proceeding with the commentary. The aim of this book is merely to facilitate your engagement with *Mark* 's story!

Appendix 2 walks you through a process of reflection on your own life-story by mapping your family system. This is obviously an individual exercise. Creating and critically reflecting upon our geneagrams helps bring to consciousness not only issues of gender, race, and class identity, but also reminds us that broader historical events have impacted our own family, and thus our view of the world.

Appendix 3 invites you to map your immediate context using the tools of social analysis. How is power distributed in your neighborhood or place of employment or state or nation? How much do you know about your own social location? This work is best done in a group that shares the same context.

Appendix 4 affirms that we Christians regularly share and celebrate the biblical stories in a liturgical context. It offers a few supplements to certain chapters that can be used in small or large group worship. These examples may give you ideas about how to adapt other components of this book into a liturgical setting.

We also encourage you to keep a **Discipleship Journal** along this reading journey. In your journal you can chart your "inner" geography, jot down thoughts and questions, make notes, draw your "maps," and so on. This journal can be a place for you to integrate the process and articulate your commitments to the discipleship journey.

While it will quickly become evident that we have strong points of view on both Word and World, we have endeavored to make this book as accessible as possible in both language and structure. We have tried to employ inclusive language and to avoid wherever possible technical, theological, and political jargon. We are aware that gospel stories of healing have often been used in ways insensitive to the struggle of physically disabled people today to live full and independent lives. We understand these healing stories to symbolize deeper issues that address all of us, however; in Mark, "blindness" and "deafness" are narrated as *spiritual* disabilities, not physical ones. This book does not use footnotes and rarely cites sources in the text; there is a short bibliography to which readers can refer for full citations. We hope our readers will forgive us where we have failed to keep things simple.

The great prophet Isaiah promised that one day God would "destroy on this mountain the net that is cast over all peoples, the veil that is spread over all nations" (Isaiah 25:7). According to Mark, that day dawned with Jesus of Nazareth. Repudiating both the Judean ruling class and the Roman imperial system of his time, Mark's Jesus envisioned social reconstruction from the bottom up. His practice of inclusiveness and equality questioned all forms of political and personal domination. This Jesus called for a revolution of means as well as ends, enjoining his followers to embrace nonviolence and to risk its consequences. Above all, he offered the contradiction of the cross—life given, not taken—as the only power that can remove the "veil" over the nations.

Writing in the midst of the pressure and suffering generated by the Roman-Jewish war of 66–70 C.E., Mark issued a manifesto for radical discipleship. This story today still invites its audience to "turn around" (1:15) and to "see clearly" (8:25); to proclaim good news and to cast out demons (3:14f); to row against the storms of ethnic division (6:48) and to give the hungry something to eat (6:37); and to take up our cross and follow Jesus (8:34). In our world the "net over all peoples" has become a noose, and the deadly logic of domination is pushing history into a dead end. It is our hope that Mark's story will animate us to "speak the truth to this mountain" (11:23), and to live the Jesus Way of compassion and justice in the world.

I
LIBERATING SPACE FOR CHANGE

OPENING MEDITATION

The pauper's cemetery in Rabinal, Guatemala, is at first sight shocking. Located at the edge of town, it is near—but clearly separated from—the regular cemetery. Mounds of dirt, many child-sized, mark a final resting place for the poorest ones in a poor village in a poor world. A few stick crosses, some flowers and barely surviving shrubs, plus a stone or two, suggest that loved ones have not been forgotten.

At the far end of the plot is a large monument and a thirty-foot-long mound of dirt that serves as the mass grave for 101 children and 76 women massacred in the nearby village of Rio Negro in 1982. Names are inscribed on the monument with a brief description of three other massacres endured by the same small village in one year. Guatemala, with a population that is 70 percent indigenous, has long been ruled by a few very powerful and wealthy landowners and business people, and an even more powerful military, covertly supported by the United States. During the 1980s, these forces engineered the brutal elimination of more than 400 Mayan villages to perpetuate their economic, political, and cultural domination.

Every eight days the widows of Rio Negro, a few men who survived the brutality, and young people with childhood memories of horror gather to honor the dead in prayerful ritual. Just to recite the litany of the saints of Rio Negro buried together nearby is a powerful, healing act. With their decision to build the truth-telling monument, the remnant community of Rio Negro broke a decade of silence and reclaimed life from the dead.

"The messenger will appear in the wilderness" (1:3). The scene at the cemetery in Rabinal gives new meaning to the word "wilderness." It is a place defined by its exclusion, a stark space between life and death, hope and hopelessness, spirit and flesh. It is a place to meet God. Located outside of the centers of political, economic, social, or cultural power, Rabinal represents the margins of our world, a wilderness place where the need for repentance is evident and a prophetic Word is possible.

3

Chapter 1

The First Call to Discipleship
Mark 1:1-20

THE TEXT IN CONTEXT

Mark the evangelist believed that the story of Jesus was so extraordinary that he needed to invent a new literary genre. He called this "gospel," a term that brackets his prologue (1:1 and 1:15). It is an action-based hero-narrative, but, unlike Roman biographies, it draws its main characters not from the elite classes but from plain folk. Jesus is portrayed as a healer and exorcist, but, unlike popular tales of magicians common to that period, Mark's story downplays the miraculous, emphasizing instead the empowerment of Jesus' subjects ("Your faith has healed you," 5:34, 10:52).

In his work Mark drew upon many contemporary narrative styles, including various parts of the Hebrew Bible, apocalyptic literature, didactic rabbinic stories, Wisdom sayings, and even Greco-Roman tragedy. But his "gospel" represented a new voice in the literature of antiquity. Because it is a narrative, we can and should approach it with the native skills we routinely use to interpret stories. (For an exercise in applying these skills to Mark's prologue, see Appendix 1.)

Read Mark 1:1-3

The story's title is: "The Beginning of the Gospel of Jesus the Christ" (1:1). Ancient writers frequently established their credentials at the outset by appealing to recognizable authorities (think of the credits in a film's opening moments). Mark's title uses two terms that would have been familiar to his audience.

Gospel was a term associated with Roman propaganda. News of a military victory on the far-flung frontiers of the Pax Romana, or of the accession to power of a new emperor, was trumpeted as

5

"glad tidings" throughout the empire. Caesar was eulogized as a "divine man" on coins and in emperor-cults. In contrast, Mark offers decidedly non-imperial "good news" about Jesus of Nazareth, a Jewish "Christ." By using such rhetoric, Mark was engaging the struggle for hearts and minds through the popular media of the Mediterranean world.

Mark's title also echoes Genesis 1:1, suggesting that he wished to reclaim and renew the great story of God's creative activity in the world. Creation, he seems to be arguing, continues wherever the story is told and lived again. This is emphasized in 1:2, as an off-stage voice cites the Hebrew scriptures, Mark's most important legitimating authority. "Isaiah" promises a re-opening of the "Way," calling to mind the foundational narrative of Israel, the Exodus journey of liberation. "I am sending a messenger before you to guard you on the Way" (Exodus 23:20). In Mark's story, this Way will become synonymous with discipleship: As Israel followed the angel in the wilderness, we will be invited to follow Jesus.

This promise generates dramatic tension: Something is about to happen. But what—and where? The citation is in fact a combination of two prophetic texts. Verse 1:2 is a paraphrase of Malachi's warning of God's imminent appearance "in the Temple" (Malachi 3:1). This oracle portends judgment against those who oppress. It specifically indicts the Temple, which was supposed to function as a central storehouse from which the agricultural surplus of the community was to be redistributed, as a mechanism for "robbery" (Malachi 3:8-10). Jesus will echo this charge when he visits the Temple later in Mark's story (Mark 11:17; see Chapter 16).

Mark 1:3 now cites Isaiah 40:3, which announces a messenger in the wilderness—exactly where John the Baptist shows up (1:4). Through this deft editorial combination of Malachi and Isaiah, Mark has introduced a major theme of his gospel. It is the tension between two archetypically opposite symbolic spaces: Temple and wilderness—center and margins.

Read Mark 1:4-8

The action begins with John the Baptist preaching repentance (1:4-6). John's costume is symbolic, invoking the memory of the great prophet Elijah who challenged kings, as will John (read 2 Kings 1:1-17). But Elijah's story lacked "closure," since he disappeared into heaven at the Jordan (read 2 Kings 2:6-14). This "missing in action" status meant that his presence might erupt into history again—and here is John-as-Elijah at the Jordan! Moreover, Malachi promised that God would send Elijah "before the great and terrible day of the Lord" to turn the people around (Malachi 4:5f). And here is John exhorting the people to "repent"—which means "turn around"! The reader's expectations are heightened, but we are off balance. Does this story herald the beginning or the *end*?

In 1:5, Mark reports that "all of Judea and Jerusalem" came out to John in the wilderness. Here the tension between center and margins becomes explicit. According to the national myth of the Judean Temple-state, Jerusalem was center of the world, a place to which all nations would someday come to submit (see Psalm 2:6, 14:7, 48, 69:35f, 87, 102:15-22; Isaiah 4:5f, 18:7, 60:10-14). But Mark reverses directions: Salvation is being regenerated not at the center but at the margins. This is why the people as a whole must turn around!

John immediately introduces the gospel's main character: a "stronger one" who will baptize with the Holy Spirit (1:7f). This raises more expectations. But Jesus' appearance onstage is initially unremarkable. He is from "Nazareth in Galilee," an unknown village in provincial northern Palestine, further underscoring the marginal geography of this prologue. Yet it is to this obscure figure, from these doubtful social origins, in this remote place, that the divine voice speaks.

Read Mark 1:9-13

In the account of Jesus' baptism, the narrative is suddenly invaded by dramatic imagery. Jesus rises from the Jordan's waters to a vision of the "heavens rent asunder" (1:10), an allusion to another prophetic text: "Oh, that you would tear the heavens open and come down to make known your name to your enemies and make the nations tremble at your presence, working unexpected miracles" (Isaiah 64:1f).

Does Jesus' identification as "beloved Son" by the mysterious voice from heaven designate him as the messianic ruler of Psalm 2:7? Or does the descent of the dove point us rather to Isaiah's Suffering Servant: "I will put my spirit upon him, he will bring forth justice to the nations" (Isaiah 42:1)?

This heavenly intervention is the first of many instances in which Mark draws upon the symbolism of apocalyptic literature. In Mark's time, apocalyptic was the popular language of political dissent. It envisioned the "end of the world"—that is, the world ruled by the powers. Following his baptism Jesus is driven by the Spirit further out into the wilderness, where he engages in a struggle with the "ruler of this world" (1:12f). The struggle symbolizes the apocalyptic war between good (the angels and Jesus) and evil (Satan and the wild beasts). It is the first of many Markan allusions to the book of Daniel, a Jewish apocalyptic tract that exhorted resistance to Hellenistic imperialism two centuries before Mark. Daniel portrays oppressive rulers as "beasts" and speaks of angels contending with the "princes of kingdoms" (see Daniel 7:1-7, 10, 12:1).

But is there yet more to this strange temptation episode? Is it possible to interpret Jesus' journey deep into the wilderness as a kind of "vision quest"? Among native peoples still today the vision quest is at once an outward adventure beyond the margins of society; an inward passage of purification and self-encounter; and a journey "in the spirit" to discover the identity and destiny of one's people. Might Jesus be somehow interiorizing and reliving the experience of Israel? "For forty days" (1:13) is clearly meant to invoke Israel's forty years of "testing" in the wilderness.

Israel's identity commenced when it escaped from Pharaoh: "I will bring my people out of Egypt" (Exodus 3:10). Similarly, Jesus' identity has just been confirmed at baptism: "You are my son, the Beloved" (Mark 1:11). Now he, like his ancestors, must struggle in the wilderness to discover what this vocation means. Jesus re-traces the footsteps of his people to their "place of origins," the Exodus wilderness, in the hope of discovering where they went wrong. He faces again the forces that lured his people into idolatry and injustice, because to forge a different future he must confront the past. Jesus undertakes a radical quest to uncover the root-causes of his people's problems.

Read Mark 1:14-15

Jesus begins preaching "after John was arrested" (1:14), a tale of political intrigue that Mark will return to later in the story (6:14-30; see Chapter 8). Jesus takes up John's challenge to "turn around and believe the good news," but adds something startling. He claims that the "kingdom of God" has arrived (1:16; we will use the less patriarchal phrase "sovereignty of God" in this book). Much has been made of this phrase by theologians over the centuries, but few have acknowledged its most obvious background: the anti-kingship traditions of early Israel.

The Sinai covenant envisioned a decentralized style of self-governance: Because YHWH was king over Israel, royalist politics were precluded. For example, after the kings of Canaanite city-states are vanquished (see Joshua 12), the victorious military leader Gideon rejects attempts to make him king: "I will not rule over you...YHWH will rule over you" (Judges 8:22f). Instead, "judges" administer the tribal confederacy.

1 Samuel 8 narrates the decline of this system because of internal corruption and external military threats. Disillusioned with their experiment in self-determination, the people go to the great judge Samuel to demand that he "appoint for us a king to govern us, like other nations" (1 Samuel 8:5). "They have not rejected you," says God to Samuel, "they have rejected me from being king over them" (8:7).

God then instructs Samuel to warn the people about "the ways of the king," which include: forced conscription, militarism, state expropriation of labor and resources, an economy geared to the elite, and taxation (8:11-17). The grim litany concludes: "And you will be his slaves." The moral of this story: In choosing a centralized monarchy, the people freed from slavery recreate Pharaoh's society of domination.

By reasserting the sovereignty of God, then, Jesus is taking sides in the debate within the biblical tradition between those who saw the monarchy as blessed by God and those who saw it as a step backward. He seeks a renewal of the "confederate" roots of free Israel (see Chapter 4).

But Jesus is not proposing a utopian dream that can be realized only in another place (heaven) and/or time (the afterlife). The gospel leaves no room for otherworldly religion: "The time is now; the sovereignty of God is here" (Mark 1:15).

Read Mark 1:16-20

In the prologue, events unfold in a rapid sequence of prediction and fulfillment. "Isaiah" announces John, who announces the "stronger one," who announces the sovereignty of God. We expect something momentous to happen—yet in Mark's next scene Jesus is shown merely talking to some common laborers (1:16ff)! In Mark's narrative strategy, anti-climax functions to subvert our expectations, in order to open us to new possibilities. In the call of the fishermen, the sovereignty of God is realized—because Mark identifies it with the discipleship adventure.

This is the first of three invitations to follow Jesus in Mark, episodes that drive the major "plot line" of the narrative. The other two occur in the middle (8:34ff; see Chapter 11) and again at the end of the gospel (16:6f; see Chapter 25). In 1:16 we see Jesus choosing his students, a reversal of the normal practice of rabbinic recruitment in Mark's day. He encounters these men at their workplace, a family fishing business, yet calls them to abandon their trade for a new vocation.

An apt paraphrase of Jesus' invitation is: "Follow me and I will show you how to catch the Big Fish!" (1:17). In the Hebrew Bible, the metaphor of "people like fish" appears in prophetic censures of apostate Israel and of the rich and powerful:

> "I am now sending for many fishermen, says God, and they shall catch [the people of Israel]..." (Jeremiah 16:16)

> "The time is surely coming upon you when they shall take you away with fishhooks..." (Amos 4:2)

> "Thus says God: I am against you, Pharaoh king of Egypt. ...I will put hooks in your jaws, and make the fish of your channels stick to your scales..." (Ezekiel 29:3f)

Jesus is, in other words, summoning working folk to join him in overturning the structures of power and privilege in the world!

"They left their nets and followed him" (1:18, 20). In antiquity, the demand to leave the workplace would have entailed more than the loss of economic security. It represented a rupture in the social fabric of the extended family. But there is more: The verb "to leave" is used elsewhere in Mark to connote release from debt! As a later episode will make clear (10:28f; see Chapter 14), this "leaving" alludes to the discipleship community's practice of social and economic redistribution. The call to discipleship demands more than an assent of the heart; it invites an uncompromising break with "business as usual."

THE WORD IN OUR WORLD

Our world is divided as never before. Dichotomies between rich and poor people and nations are vast. Separation between racial and ethnic groups, between women and men, between the powerful and the excluded, are increasing. For example, *Forbes* magazine reported in July 1994 that the world's 358 billionaires had collectively accumulated personal capital worth more than the total income of 45 percent of the world's population—2.5 billion people!

The experience of wilderness is common to the vast majority of people in the world. Their reality is at the margins of almost everything that is defined by the modern Western world as "the good life." This wilderness has not been created by accident. It is the result of a system stacked against many people and their communities, whose lives and resources are exploited to benefit a very small minority at the centers of power and privilege. It is created by lifestyles that deplete and pollute natural resources. It is created by the forced labor of impoverished farmers who strip steep mountainsides in order to eke out an existence from infertile terrain while the most arable land produces profit for a few families. Wilderness is the residue of war and greed and injustice.

The urban wilderness is a belt of misery around cities like Lima and Mexico City or a core of poverty in the heart of Washington, D.C., or Los Angeles. These are places where people from the margins gather seeking a modicum of economic or social security and too often find just the opposite. The wilderness is the dwelling place of the world's 23 million refugees and far too many of the world's children. It is most common in the Southern Hemisphere but increasingly is found in wealthy countries in the industrialized North as well. Globalization of the economy, based on freedom without accountability, is exacerbating the spread of this wilderness. That is how the system survives: One group of people thriving at the expense of others and the earth; one belching on the other's hunger; one powerful because the others have no power.

Life in modern wilderness places such as the pauper's cemetery at Rabinal is intense, stark, fragile, bereft of comforting distraction. Survival is not assured—even the plants by the gravesites are wilted. Yet a deeper gaze reveals that this wilderness can be an empowering place.

On the margins of society, an encounter with self and truth is inevitable. Out of the Rabinals of our world have emerged people who are very clear about who they are, where life is, and what their destiny should be. These are people determined to speak the truth to the centers of privilege and control. In facing death, they have found life; on the cross of dehumanized existence, they are embracing resurrection.

One of the first steps of hope for people in such wilderness places is to understand that their situation reflects social and political forces, not the divine will. Many faith communities in such places use a tool of social analysis called the center/margins exercise to help them understand their social reality. It can be adapted to various situations, from one's local neighborhood to the world as a whole. In this exercise, social reality is portrayed as a circle whose center is defined as the place where power and access are concentrated in the hands of dominant groups and institutions. The circumference or margin of the circle is occupied by persons and groups who are dominated or oppressed.

In Mark's world, for example, the Jerusalem Temple would be placed at the center of the circle; the wilderness would lie at the margins. In our world, the industrialized, "developed" societies of the North Atlantic, Japan, and the Pacific rim countries may generally be equated with the center, with the United States at the hub. The poorer nations of the Southern Hemisphere represent the margins. "First" and "Third" worlds have been used as labels on this contemporary map of the global distribution of power.

In fact, however, we can identify centers and margins within both the "First" and the "Third" worlds. For example, one can see widespread impoverishment in New York, London, and Tokyo, and extreme wealth in São Paulo, Bangalore, and Nairobi.

While the margin has a primarily negative political connotation as a place of disenfranchisement, Mark ascribes to it a primarily positive theological value. It is the place where the sovereignty of God is made manifest, where the story of liberation is renewed, where God's intervention in history occurs.

Here the modern disciple should find much food for thought. What invitation do we hear to journey to the wilderness—to the margins? What would that mean concretely in our lives?

The first disciples were invited by Jesus to a new *location* and a new vocation. They were called to join him "on the road" in a struggle to overturn the existing order of inequality. Across the intervening centuries, this invitation has been reiterated time and again. The discipleship adventure beckons. Yet its context is the stuff of everyday life and work—ennobled by a commitment to the community and to the sovereignty of God.

Chapter 2

Jesus the Healer
Mark 1:21–2:12

THE TEXT IN CONTEXT

The first major narrative section of the gospel begins (1:16) and ends (4:36) by the shores of the Sea of Galilee. In this section Mark paints a portrait of Jesus' public ministry in and around the Galilean city of Capernaum. This series of episodes exhibits the three essential characteristics of Jesus' mission: the healing and exorcism of marginalized people, the proclamation of God's sovereignty and call to discipleship, and the resulting confrontations with the authorities.

Read Mark 1:21-28

Conflict erupts in Jesus' first public action, a dramatic exorcism in a Capernaum synagogue. Here we encounter for the first time a "miracle story." The modern debate over whether or not we can "believe" such stories is not only misplaced, it fails to address the function of this kind of narrative. The possibility of extraordinary manipulations of the physical (or spirit) world was never questioned in antiquity.

Nevertheless, the "miracle" lay not in the act, but in what the act symbolized. Mark goes to great lengths to discourage us from seeing Jesus as a mere popular magician. Not only does Jesus constantly discourage people from fixating upon his acts of healing or exorcism (see 1:44, 3:12, 5:18f, 5:43, 7:36), he actually exhorts his disciples (and the reader) to look into the deeper meaning of his actions (8:17-21).

Let us begin by noticing the significance of the setting in 1:21ff. Jesus has moved from the wilderness margin to the heart of the provincial Jewish social order—the holy time and space of a synagogue on the Sabbath. An example of how the form of an episode can help us understand its function is the way the actual exorcism is "framed" by Mark's report of the crowd's reaction:

> And they were astonished at Jesus' teaching, for he taught them as one who had authority, unlike the scribes. (1:22)

> And they were all amazed, so that they questioned among themselves saying, "What is this? A new teaching! With authority he commands even the unclean spirits and they obey him!" (1:27)

The essential conflict is thus defined as the contest over authority between Jesus and the scribal establishment, a contest which will be central to the entire story.

Sandwiched in between is an "unclean spirit" who "protests" Jesus' presence: "Why do you meddle with us?" (1:23f; see Judges 11:12; 1 Kings 17:18). However, the demon's defiance quickly turns to fear: "Have you come to destroy us?"

Who is the "we" on whose behalf the demon speaks? The function of Mark's framing device suggests that the demon's voice represents the voice of the scribal class whose "space" Jesus is invading. The synagogue on the Sabbath is scribal turf, where scribes exercise the authority to teach Torah. This "spirit" personifies scribal power, which holds sway over the hearts and minds of the people. Only after breaking the influence of this spirit is Jesus free to begin his compassionate ministry to the masses (1:29ff).

To interpret this exorcism solely as the "curing of an epileptic" is to miss its profound political impact. In contrast to Hellenistic literature, in which miracle-workers normally function to maintain the status quo, gospel healings challenge the ordering of power. Because Jesus seeks the root causes of why people are marginalized, there is no case of healing and exorcism in Mark that does not also raise a larger question of social oppression.

Read Mark 1:29-39

Jesus retreats from the synagogue to a home. Mark seems to contrast the home as safe site (5:38, 7:17, 7:24, 9:33, 10:10, 14:3) with the synagogue and Temple as places of political conflict, a depiction that no doubt reflects the experience of the early church. The story of Peter's mother-in-law offers the best test of the conclusion reached above: Isn't this miracle "just a healing," without social or symbolic meaning (1:30f)?

There are two reasons why this seemingly "minor" healing has deeper significance. First, Jesus heals in the privacy of a home and commences his public ministry only after sunset, that is, once the Sabbath is over (1:32). His action implies that there might be something controversial about openly healing on the Sabbath. This indeed turns out to be the case, for in the climactic episode of the cycle, Jesus returns to a synagogue on the Sabbath and heals a man—with dire consequences (3:1-6; see Chapter 3).

Second, Peter's mother-in-law is the first woman to appear in Mark's narrative. We are told that upon being touched by Jesus, "she served him" (1:31). Most commentators, steeped in patriarchal theology, assume that this means she fixed Jesus dinner. However the Greek verb "to serve" (from which we get our word "deacon") appears only two other times in Mark. One is in 10:45—"The Human One came not to be served but to serve"—a context hardly suggesting meal-preparation (see Chapter 15)!

The other comes at the end of the story, where Mark describes women "who, when Jesus was in Galilee, followed him, and served him, and...came up to Jerusalem with him" (15:41). This is a summary statement of discipleship: from beginning (Galilee) to end (Jerusalem) these women were true followers who, unlike the men (see 10:32-45), practiced servanthood.

In other words, both at the outset and at the conclusion of Mark's gospel, women, in a society which devalued them, are identified as the true disciples. In this "minor" healing, Mark is serving notice that patriarchal theology and the devaluation of women will be overturned!

Jesus the healer experiences the incessant press of needy masses, as indicated in the summary statement in 1:32-39. In Mark, Jesus' special attention to the "crowd" (mentioned some thirty-eight times) articulates an emphatic bias toward the disenfranchised. This is an accurate reflection of the social reality of Mark's time: Economic and political circumstances in the decade prior to the Roman-Jewish war had dispossessed significant portions of the Palestinian population. Illness and disability were an inseparable part of the cycle of poverty for the poor, as they still are today.

But Jesus needs space to contemplate too, so in 1:35 he withdraws back into the wilderness (see 6:31). This establishes a narrative rhythm of action and reflection. Yet, as integral as prayer was to Jesus' work, it was always placed at the service of the mission to liberate human life: "Let us go on to the surrounding villages that I may preach there also, for that is why I came" (1:38).

Background: Purity and Debt

We now turn to a pair of healings that engender hostility from the local authorities (1:45-2:12). The hostility cannot be attributed to a general intolerance of healers and magicians; in antiquity, healings were not uncommon and, in Hellenistic society, magicians practiced freely.

To understand the controversial nature of Jesus' healing, we must keep in mind that reading biblical narratives is a cross-cultural exercise. Our modern world view assumes that the gospel healing stories relate "supernatural" cures of medical disorders. In the ancient Mediterranean world, however, illness was perceived primarily as a "socially disvalued state," an aberrant or defective condition that threatened communal integrity.

The cultural system of late Second Temple Judaism was concerned with determining impurity or sin, not with scientific diagnoses of symptoms. Healing, therefore, was primarily a matter of "re-socializing" the quarantined or "defective" person. For example, what biblical writers called "leprosy" cannot be equated with what we know as Hansen's Disease, but rather with any kind of skin disorder. Imperfections in the "boundary" of the body were thought to mirror vulnerabilities in the boundaries of the body politic. The priestly rituals associated with cleansing symbolized a "covering over" of those vulnerabilities, not a medical cure.

Human societies order their existence by "maps" which seek to regulate and socialize bodies within the body politic. Bruce Malina and Richard Rohrbaugh, in their *Social-Science Commentary on the Synoptic Gospels*, describe these maps as "lines drawn around self, others, nature, time and space. When something is out of place as determined by the prevailing system of meaning, that something is considered wrong, deviant, senseless. ... The system of pure (in place) and impure (out of place) ... can be predicated on persons, groups, things, times, and places." Thus, according to ancient Hebrew patriarchy, menstruating women were considered "unclean" and had to be quarantined. Similarly, according to modern American racism, dark-skinned persons were considered "inferior" and had to be segregated. These are systems of power and privilege, not of logic.

The social maps of the Second Temple Judean state consisted of two mutually reinforcing codes: purity and debt. The purity code, adjudicated by priests, established what was clean and unclean in order to maintain group and class boundaries. For example, dietary laws and male circumcision distinguished Jews from non-Jews. One's purity status was determined by birth (e.g., tribal affiliation), body (male or female, disabled or "healthy") and behavior (cultic obligations).

Debt and sin were virtually interchangeable terms. The debt code, under the jurisdiction of the scribal class, regulated individual and social responsibilities, criminal behavior, and economic status. Its rules (e.g., the Ten Commandments) determined sins of commission (stealing an ox or adultery) and omission (not paying tithes or observing the Sabbath). It is important to remember that there was no differentiation between the "sacred" and "secular" in this system. Torah, to us a religious text, functioned then as the fundamental legal code.

When we begin to understand the sociocultural differences between this ancient "health care" and "criminal justice" system and our own, we can ask questions about how power was distributed within it. Who interpreted the purity or debt codes (the power of diagnosis)? Who was able to effect a change in someone's status in that system (the power of treatment)? What did "treatment" cost the one who was impure or indebted?

By paying attention to these matters, we can see why Jesus' actions provoked opposition. When Jesus engages in debate concerning scripture, he is involved in social criticism. When he challenges the Temple cult, he is subverting political authority and threatening those whose social status and national identity are bound to the Temple-state. When he clashes with priests or scribes, he is taking on senior administrators who are spokespersons for the status quo.

Read Mark 1:40-45

In ancient Israel, the leper represented the archetypal social outcast whose banishment was due to impurity. The extensive Levitical regulations regarding leprosy (read Leviticus 13-14) revolved around two stipulations:

1) the impurity was communicable;

2) a priest must preside over ritual cleansing.

Both principles are challenged here. This episode is constructed around Mark's repeated use of the Greek verb "to declare clean." The drama begins when the leper dares Jesus to assume the priestly prerogative and declare him clean (1:40). This may explain why "Jesus' guts were churning" (1:41)!

Rather than performing a ritual, however, Jesus simply touches the leper and declares him clean. According to the purity code, Jesus should have contracted the impurity; instead, Mark tells us that the declaration was effective (1:42). The purity code has been subverted by Jesus' willingness to have social contact with the leper (see 14:3). But the aftermath is the key to the story, as Jesus "snorts with indignation" and dispatches the man to the priests (1:43). The mood implied here is one of protest, not co-operation.

The man's task is to help confront the system that keeps him marginalized (1:44). He is instructed to submit to the Mosaic ritual in order to "witness against them," a technical phrase in Mark for confronting one's opponents (see 6:11, 13:9). The priests would hardly accept Jesus' authority to declare this leper clean! But the mission aborts: The leper goes public, and Jesus is forced to lie low (1:45). This sets the tone for Jesus' ministry: His healings will be interpreted either as liberation or lawless defiance depending upon one's commitment to the prevailing social order.

Read Mark 2:1-12

Jesus returns quietly to Capernaum but is soon discovered, hounded now by both the sick and the suspicious (2:1f). In this episode Mark posits an essential opposition between scribal "reasoning" and Jesus' "teaching":

2:2   Jesus was *teaching* them the Word...

2:6   The scribes were *reasoning* in their hearts...

2:7   Scribes: "Why does this man *teach* this?"

2:8   Jesus: "Why do you *reason* this in your hearts?"

The deeper issue this time concerns the debt code, under which the physically disabled held inferior status in the community because of their "flaws." Rather than simply "curing" his body, Jesus chooses to challenge the body politic by releasing him from debt (2:5, 7). The scribes object, claiming that only God can adjudicate debt (2:7). This is not a defense of God's sovereignty but of their own social power, since as interpreters of Torah they control how sin is defined. As in the previous episode, Jesus unilaterally bypasses public authority in order to liberate human life.

There are two allusions to the Hebrew Bible in this episode that will be key to Mark's gospel. Jesus justifies his action in the name of the "Human One" (2:10), the first appearance in Mark of this persona. We will see later that it is drawn from Daniel's apocalyptic vision of "true justice" (see Chapter 11). Jesus' presumptive forgiveness of sin, meanwhile, is the first of many references to the Levitical vision of Jubilee debt-release (see Chapter 3).

This story is an enacted parable of reconstructive worship in an inclusive community. A great crowd gathers in the home (housechurch!) where Jesus "preaches the Word" (2:2). The roof is torn off so that one excluded by the mainstream can be received (2:4). The "Human One" forgives sin, the man's place in the "body" is reinstated (2:12a), and the congregation glorifies God (2:12b).

THE WORD IN OUR WORLD

Jesus relentlessly critiqued the purity and debt systems of his day because they tended to segregate and exclude rather than to integrate and restore. The symbol for his confrontation of these systems was public exorcism.

In the public discourse of the modern world, demon possession is rarely acknowledged and evil is rarely evaluated with appropriate seriousness. Yet we live in a world in which a dramatic confrontation between good and evil continues daily on a grand scale. It is more visible in some circumstances than in others; some demons can be named quite readily, while others cannot. Demons are players in our own stories, too. They have shaped our attitudes toward others, our capacities for moral and ethical discernment, our "habits of the heart."

Let us consider racism and its partner, poverty, as examples. The scene these days in almost any inner-city neighborhood in the United States could invite exorcism: the National Guard in camouflage, shining spotlights from hum-vees, trying to push back the violence; drug dealing and violence around the edges of and criss-crossing through neighborhoods that are trying in heroic ways to survive; gangs attempting to fill the void left by absent family and community; kids, overgrown into men, with nowhere to go, hanging out all night and all day; kids, middle-sized and inching into the dangerous teen years when trafficking a little crack around the alley is a keen way (the only way?) to get a bike or sneakers or food; kids, little ones with nowhere to play, who stare through barbed-wire-topped iron fences at grass, golf courses, gardens, and trees of affluent neighborhoods on the "right" side of town or in the suburbs; schools underfunded or understaffed, and too often outright dangerous.

These are the impoverished places where dramatically disproportionate numbers of African Americans, Latinos, and other minorities live—not by choice, but by the normal functioning of a system that perpetually excludes them. They are gathered into ghettoes by a form of cultural evil in which the skin color of a person determines his or her access to opportunity. Racism has rooted itself in the Americas and has expressed itself in the most demonic ways. The prejudice of individuals has become the racism of a society.

Demons, we see, threaten our personal and family lives; but they operate adeptly in social structures and systems as well. There they feed on and exacerbate the impact of evil threatening individuals and families. Prejudice, for example, becomes racism; racism contributes to exclusion and poverty.

These demons, in fact, roam the world. The footprints of racism and poverty are clear: More than 1 billion people in poor countries lack access to basic health and education, safe drinking water, and adequate nutrition. One person in three lives in poverty. At the end of 1994, there were more than 11 million refugees. Even in wealthier countries, millions of people live in constant insecurity—threatened by crime, drugs, pollution, unemployment, and homelessness (U.N. Development Program figures).

Poor people make up whole classes. At the same time, they are individuals who suffer from increased susceptibility to disease, lack of access to most services and information, lack of control over resources, subordination to more powerful social and economic classes, extreme vulnerability to sudden misfortune, and insecurity in the face of changing circumstances. The poor are unemployed, underemployed, and underpaid. They are overwhelmingly people of color.

Theirs is a condition that has been created by the "purity and debt codes" of modern society. It is not the fruit of ignorance or natural disaster, but of deeply institutionalized evil. The poor became poor: because our national and global systems exploit and exclude them; because they do not have access to the means of survival and are dependent on those who do; because of the unjust ownership and distribution of land and other resources; because of regressive tax laws, exclusionary zoning regulations, unjust immigration laws, inadequate or manipulative educational systems, inaccessible health care, bloated military budgets, lack of access to credit, and usurious lending practices.

Around the world, the poor *are kept* poor: by a crushing debt burden; by falling or fluctuating prices on exportable commodities; by rising capital flight; by the economic legacies of colonialism and neocolonialism; by increasingly autonomous, intrusive, and controlling activities of transnational corporations and banks; and by a global economic system established after World War II that benefits the rich nations at the expense of the poor.

Poor people are not by definition perfect. They and their communities are responsible for their own sins and failings, as are all God's children. But the evil that perpetuates their poverty is an evil for which we are all responsible. That evil is a demon to be exorcised.

Chapter 3

Jubilee!
Mark 2:13–3:6

THE TEXT IN CONTEXT

Having challenged the priest-controlled purity system and the scribe-controlled debt system, Jesus turns to confront the Pharisees. The Pharisaic sect was a renewal movement that was rapidly gaining social power and influence in Mark's time. The Judean clerical aristocracy did not expect the masses to keep all the purity and debt regulations; such piety was for the educated and the affluent. The Pharisees, in contrast, were searching for ways to apply the traditions to all the people in their daily lives.

Unlike the priests, the Pharisees gave more emphasis to the agricultural practices and household matters relevant to village life than to Temple-centered obligations. Unlike the scribes, they argued that in addition to Torah there was an "oral tradition" given to Moses on Sinai that constituted a parallel authority. (These teachings, handed down over the centuries, began to be codified by the rabbis around 200 C.E. in the Mishnah.) After the destruction of the Jerusalem Temple in 70 C.E., Pharisaism emerged as a dominant force within Judaism, laying the groundwork for synagogue-based faith.

At the time of Mark, the Pharisees were real competitors with the Jesus movement for the hearts and minds of the disaffected. This is reflected in the next three episodes, where Jesus defends his disciples' practice and in so doing addresses issues that were important to Pharisaic practice: restrictive table fellowship, public piety, and Sabbath observances.

Read Mark 2:13-22

By way of narrative transition, Mark portrays Jesus retiring to the sea for the call of Levi (2:13f). Levi was probably a local Jew employed by a foreign "tax-farmer" who held contracts with Rome to collect imperial taxes plus a percentage. Native tax-collectors were despised by "upright" Jews for at least three reasons:

1) their job required close contact and collaboration with Gentiles;

2) they were notoriously unscrupulous bureaucrats;

3) they were representatives of the oppressive colonial administration.

Tax collectors were reminders of how the nation was "in debt-servitude" to the Roman political and economic system. Jesus again encounters someone at his workplace and invites him to transcend it. Levi's discipleship is portrayed in the very next scene (2:15). At his home we see "sinners" (that is, those who are in debt) sharing a meal with tax-collectors (that is, those who enforce the debt obligation). This is extraordinary table fellowship indeed! Only some kind of Jubilee debt-release could account for this sudden community between "class enemies" (see Background below).

In Mediterranean culture, the shared meal was the heart of social intercourse, so the Pharisees were deeply concerned about the dietary, ritual, and legal issues surrounding table fellowship. That is why they object here (2:16). Jesus' concluding maxim (2:17) identifies the "sick" with the "sinner," linking this episode to his previous attack upon the debt code. Those who think the status quo is "healthy" (because they benefit from it) will not respond to Jesus' "good news"; but the socially outcast and indebted will. This brief clash with the Pharisees anticipates a longer meal controversy later in the story, where Jesus repudiates not only exclusionary table practices but the whole basis of Pharisaic authority (7:1-23; see Chapter 9).

Jesus next excuses his disciples from a public fast day. Mark's community was probably impressed by the rigor of Pharisaic practice. Jesus, however, wishes to cut through piety to the real issue: a society in which some can afford to fast while others truly go hungry. In contrast to the economics of scarcity, therefore, he likens the sovereignty of God to a party (2:20). In his famous wineskins saying, Jesus argues that the "new" wine of the discipleship movement must not be coopted by "old" forms of cosmetic piety (2:22).

Background: The Jubilee and the Politics of Food

To understand these stories (and the following one, 2:23ff) fully, we need some biblical and historical background. Torah's Sabbath regulations sought to teach the people about their dependence upon the land and upon the "divine economy of grace." Because the earth belongs to God and its fruits are "free," the people should justly distribute those fruits instead of seeking to own and hoard them.

The word "Sabbath" first appears in the story of manna in the wilderness (read Exodus 16:15-26). This story was more than a lesson about God's sustaining love. It served as an archetypal reminder that the purpose of economic organization was to guarantee enough for everyone, *not* for surplus accumulation by the few. Human attempts to control the forces of production are to be regularly interrupted by prescribed Sabbath rest (once a week and once every seven years) for both the land and human labor (Exodus 31:12-17; Deuteronomy 15:1-7), patterned after the order of creation (Genesis 2:2).

The Sabbath cycle was supposed to culminate in a "Jubilee" every forty-ninth year (Read Leviticus 25). The Jubilee was intended as Israel's hedge against the inevitable tendency of human societies to concentrate power and wealth in the hands of the few, creating hierarchical classes with the poor at the bottom (see Ringe, 1985). In agrarian societies such as biblical Israel (or parts of the Third World today), the cycle of poverty begins when a family has to sell off its land in order to service a debt, and reaches its conclusion when landless peasants can sell only their labor, becoming bond-slaves.

The Jubilee aimed to dismantle such inequality, redistributing the wealth by:

- releasing community members from debt (Leviticus 25:35-42; Deuteronomy 15:1-11);

- returning encumbered or forfeited land to its original owners (Leviticus 25:13, 25-28);

- freeing slaves (Leviticus 25:47-55; Deuteronomy 15: 12-18).

The rationale for this unilateral restructuring of the community's wealth was to remind Israel that the land belongs to God (Leviticus 25:23) and that they are an Exodus people who must never return to a system of slavery (25:42). The extent to which Is-

rael abided by this economic discipline is a matter of much schol-
arly debate—and in capitalist religion, much skepticism. Yet Jubilee
remains at the heart of Torah, and Mark's Jesus, as he did with the
old vision of God's sovereignty, intended to renew that tradition—"here and now."

Read Mark 2:23-28

We now come to the third in a sequence of food controversies: *who
disciples eat with* (2:15f), *when not to eat* (2:18f), and now *where and
when they should eat* (2:23ff). The settings for these controversies represent what we today would call the economic sphere: In a traditional agricultural society, the table was the primary site of "consumption," the field of "production." Some background about
problems of economic justice in Mark's time will help clarify why
these issues arise specifically in relation to the Pharisees.

There was resentment among Galilean peasants about the control exercised by the Pharisaic establishment over the sowing, har-
vesting, and marketing of produce. Many poor peasants could not
afford to obey laws concerning tithing, or leaving their fields fallow
during the Sabbath year, or what they should and shouldn't plant
or eat. From their point of view, the Pharisees' adjudication of Sabbath rules had become a way of regulating the economy to Pharisaic benefit. Mark's grain-field episode thus contrasts Jesus' positive Jubilee ethic of Sabbath redistribution with the Pharisees'
proprietary ethic of Sabbath restriction.

Cutting through a field and stripping grain, the disciples
draw fire from Pharisees because of Sabbath rules regarding har-
vesting (2:23f). Jesus' justification of his disciples' practice appeals
to a (somewhat loosely rendered) scriptural story about David
(2:25; see 1 Samuel 21:1-6). As a guerrilla fighter on campaign,
David commandeered the Bread of the Presence for his soldiers, violating the holiness codes because he was in "need" (see 11:2f). But
Jesus has added something to the story: David and his followers
were hungry.

This story endorses the Jubilee notion that hungry people have
a right to food despite laws that restrict such access. It resonates
with at least two Levitical principles:

> If your kin fall into difficulty and become dependent on
> you, you shall support them.... You shall not lend them

your money at interest or provide them food at a profit. (Leviticus 25:35, 37)

When you gather the harvest in your country, you are not to gather the gleanings.... Leave them to the poor and the stranger. (Leviticus 23:22)

In Mark's narrative, "bread" (2:26) will be revealed as a symbol of community sharing in the manna and Jubilee traditions (6:33-44; see Chapter 8). The grainfield action, then, is nothing less than civil disobedience, advocating "food for people, not for profit"—or as Jesus puts it, "The Sabbath should be at the service of humanity, not vice versa" (2:27; see Matthew 12:7).

This series of eating stories can be read as a strong protest over the politics of food in Palestine. In the story of Levi, debtors and debt collectors share table fellowship. In the fasting debate, Jesus substitutes a banquet metaphor in place of ritual piety, for the poor need shared abundance, not religious abstinence. And the grainfield episode dramatizes the Jubilee ethic in an object lesson. Finally comes the clinching argument: The Human One is sovereign even over the Sabbath (2:28). This echo of 2:10 suggests that the whole sequence, beginning with the story of the paralytic, articulates Jesus' radical reinterpretation of the debt code in light of the Jubilee.

Read Mark 3:1-6

Jesus' Capernaum campaign ends where it began in 1:21, in a synagogue on a Sabbath. The Pharisees' complaint in 2:24 is a legal warning after which charges of violating the Sabbath will be pressed. The two issues of the campaign to date (public healing and Sabbath obligation; recall 1:30-34) now converge. This synagogue drama is determined political theater, for before Jesus defies the law, he challenges his audience with what seems at first to be a rhetorical question: "Is it lawful on the Sabbath to do good or harm?" (3:4). He then adds wryly, "To save life, or to kill?"—as if to contrast his own healing ministry with the authorities' concern for state security.

But this is no rhetorical question. It is a paraphrase of the great ultimatum given by Moses to the people of Israel at the edge of the Promised Land:

> See, I have set before you today life and prosperity, death and adversity. If you obey the commandments of God ... then you shall live.... But if your heart turns away and you do not hear... you shall perish. (Deuteronomy 30:15-18)

This timeless moment described by the Deuteronomist suspends the people between "heaven and earth," between history and destiny, between ancestors and descendants (30:19f). It invites the reader into its archetypal choice between life and death.

The synagogue confrontation is also a kind of trial scene: In the public glare, the authorities stand poised, ready for the suspect to "cross the line." By his Deuteronomic ultimatum, however, Jesus suddenly turns from defendant to prosecutor. In the classic tradition of civil disobedience, Jesus is breaking the law in order to raise deeper issues about the moral health of the common life: Is justice legal?

But Jesus' audience refuses to answer his challenge. The word describing his fury in 3:5 is a strong one, usually associated in the New Testament with the phrase "the wrath of God." Mark indicts their obstinacy as "hardness of heart"—in Exodus, "Pharaoh's disease." The heart was also a primary focus of the Deuteronomic tradition:

> To this day God has not given you a heart to understand, eyes to see, nor ears to hear. (Deuteronomy 29:4)

> It may be that among you someone's heart is already turning away from God ... (Deuteronomy 29:18)

> Among the nations recall in your hearts the blessing and curse I have set before you ... (Deuteronomy 30:1)

> God will circumcise your heart and the hearts of your descendants so that you will love God with all your heart and soul and so have life. (Deuteronomy 30:6)

For Mark the hearts of these descendants of Moses have gone astray. But beware: The same charge will soon enough be leveled against Jesus' own disciples (see 6:52, 8:17).

This is a watershed moment. Jesus, choosing life, heals the disabled man (3:5). The Galilean officials, choosing death, begin plotting against Jesus (3:6). From here on, these two trajectories will play out as Jesus continues his healing work against growing opposition from the authorities. This chilling development in the story attests to its political realism. We are not yet a fifth of the way through the gospel and Jesus is already marked for death. Jubilee practice may invoke the divine economy of grace, but it is, as Bonhoeffer reminds us, "costly grace."

THE WORD IN OUR WORLD

The politics of food are no less crucial and contested today than they were in Mark's time. And eating a shared meal can still be the means of crossing class and ethnic boundaries.

For example, at the height of the Cold War a group of North Americans walked across the Soviet Union as a gesture of good will, in an effort to break through threatened violence with human contact. As this small group of pilgrims moved slowly across the great Soviet expanse, they were greeted at the outskirts of each village and town with a loaf of bread characteristic of that region, as a symbol of hospitality. The act of sharing food broke the rules of the Cold War and transcended the political barriers that divide one people from another, making them enemies.

Halfway around the world, the women at Calle Real refugee camp in San Salvador during the civil war of the 1980s rose at 4:00 in the morning to take turns preparing tortillas for hundreds of people in the camp. From corn soaked and slowly ground between stones and from deft loving hands would come the most delicious nourishment. It was not easy for North American novices to mimic the process of patting the *masa* to the desired shape and thickness. But the attempt to do so built bonds across cultures. The bread of solidarity disrupted the rules of the war against the poor.

The bread of a people carries their stories well. The staff of life—whole grains, French breads, light and dark, corn or flour tortillas, rice cakes, pita bread, Afghan bread, German ryes—is burdened, or perhaps honored, with the task of representing its people's journey. Some suggest that one sign of bankruptcy in U.S. culture is our preference for white, sliced sandwich bread—devoid of taste and nutritional value, made in a factory, and wrapped in plastic. Meanwhile, "good bread" can be found only in boutique bakeries patronized by the affluent.

Breaking bread is the God-filled action of mutual nourishing. The fruit of loving labors, the life-giving product of time, earth, and human hands, becomes the reason for gathering family and friends. What happens when we gather around the table to share a meal? What draws us most obviously is the urgency to satisfy the physical demands of the body for food. Too many in our world rarely know that satisfaction.

But we are also drawn to the table by the needs of the soul. The good cook or host knows how to transform a meal into a love affair—a time of intimacy, a place for communion, a celebration of life. When we have nourished our souls as well as our bodies, we know that we have been made human again. Strangers around a table have become friends; perhaps even arguments have been settled. Hospitality has been offered and received. Life has been enlarged and enhanced. God has been present in the ordinary sacrament of a meal.

However, meals that are *just*—a prerequisite for true nourishment of the soul—are not as easy to come by. For we must take into consideration who sits around our table (how inclusive and diverse our circle is); who raises our food and how; who prepares and serves the meals and how they are treated; and what we eat. By this standard, how many of our meals do justice?

In recent decades we have witnessed dramatic confrontations with injustice at the table. In the 1960s, few acts of civil disobedience were as clear and challenging of racism as were the lunch counter sit-ins of the Civil Rights movement. In the 1970s, few social justice campaigns captured the imagination of the U.S. public as did the United Farm Workers' call for a grape boycott, a protest against unsanitary, unsafe, and brutal working conditions in the fields. And the 1980s saw a successful challenge to the Nestlé corporation's unnecessary marketing of baby formula in poor countries, placing profit above essential nourishment for millions of Third World infants.

But examples of injustice continue to plague our mealtimes. Take, for example, the simple tomato that finds its way onto our tables in dozens of ways, from salad to spaghetti sauce, and from salsa to soup. Sometimes in season we grow our own and know the joy of freshness and flavor. But now we can buy tomatoes all year, and many of them have traveled a long way before they arrive on our plates.

A first question to ask is: On whose land is the tomato grown? Who profits from the use of the land for export? Are people without sufficient food because tomatoes for export are grown on this land?

Next, consider the seeds. In recent years, tomatoes—like other plants—have been cross-pollinated to produce hybrid varieties with various characteristics. Most of the hybrids sell better; they are also patented. Who has access to the seeds and at what cost? Who will lend smaller farmers money to purchase the seeds?

To prepare for planting, the ground has to be worked. Large export-oriented operations depend heavily on machinery and on chemical fertilizers, herbicides, and pesticides. The production process becomes more capital-intensive and thus more exclusive. Can poor farmers qualify for credit even from local banks pressed to function in the free-market global economy? What is the ecological impact of burning fuel to run the tractors, and of dumping chemicals on the earth in large quantity? Whose bodies may have been sprayed or soaked with chemicals while they worked the land? What are the consequences of this exposure?

Now the tomatoes are ready to ship. First they are sprayed with a preservative, then transported thousands of miles. If they are destined to grace the counters in supermarket chains, packaging adds insult to injury, degrading the earth by overuse of chemicals, fuel, plastic, or trees. By the time the tomatoes have reached our tables, they have few vitamins, little food value, and no taste. While they add color to our salads, they have probably not done much to nourish body and soul of the farm workers who would have grown tomatoes for their own families and communities had they been able to retain their land.

To face a truth that is painful or threatening, rather than resting in comforting fantasies, requires great courage. A few hard questions might help us begin to evaluate the justice on and around our tables. Are we aware of those in our neighborhood, city, country, or world who are hungry in body or spirit? How do we respond? Is our table open, inclusive, welcoming? Is any person or the earth dying or brutalized because of how the food we consume was produced? What changes would be needed to enact the Jubilee at our own tables? How can we work to help ensure that the politics of food in our community does not exclude but rather enables a celebration of abundance, especially for those who have been marginalized?

Chapter 4

Binding the Strong Man
Mark 3:7-35

THE TEXT IN CONTEXT

Read Mark 3:7-12

The foreboding turn of events following Jesus' second synagogue confrontation has, from a plot perspective, thrown the discipleship narrative into considerable doubt. So as Jesus withdraws (3:7), Mark "regenerates" the momentum of the narrative in a summary passage that reiterates each characteristic element of Jesus' mission.

There is a discipleship vignette by the sea (3:7-9), as at the beginning of the story (1:16ff). Followers come now from Idumea in the far south of Palestine to Tyre and Sidon in the far north. They come from the center (Judea and Jerusalem) and from the margins ("beyond the Jordan"). We are next reminded that the "crowds" are still coming seeking healing (3:9f). In Mark the term "crowd" is synonymous with the disenfranchised masses: the poor, the unemployed, the displaced, the sick, the unclean. And Jesus continues to practice exorcism (3:11).

Western Christians are confused about exorcism, despite Mark's contention that it should be as fundamental to the church's vocation as preaching (3:14f). Liberals who ignore exorcism stories as "pre-psychological myth" are embarrassed by their centrality in Jesus' ministry, while modern "spiritual warfare" advocates ignore the public and political character of Jesus' exorcism. In antiquity, exorcism was not uncommon, and still today in traditional cultures shamans demonstrate the power to cast out evil spirits. Was there anything unique about Jesus' practice of exorcism?

Mark portrays Jesus in a struggle with unclean spirits over the power to "name." Though his disciples are confused about who he is (see 4:41), the demonic forces know exactly, and believe they can bring him under their control by announcing to the public who he is. Thus Jesus routinely forbids unclean spirits to "make him known" (3:12; see 1:24f).

This silencing motif, which will escalate throughout the narrative, has been understood by most modern commentators in terms of Jesus' desire to keep his true identity a secret. But as we shall see later (see Chapter 11), in Mark's story demons and humans alike may have the right name for Jesus, but if they do not follow his Way they are silenced. In contrast, those who do follow, even if they have the wrong name for Jesus, are commended for their faith (see Chapter 15).

In the tradition of the Exodus God who will not be named (see Exodus 3:2-15), Jesus refuses to accept any of the honorific "titles" given to him by opponents or friends. Instead he names himself as the "Human One" (see Chapter 11). Moreover, he turns on the demons in order to name them, as we will see in his struggle with "Legion" (5:1-20; see Chapter 6). His unmasking of oppressive authority is precisely why Jesus will shortly encounter scribal investigators from Jerusalem who try to discredit his exorcist work (3:22ff).

At issue in Jesus' confrontations with unclean spirits, then, is who has the power to frame reality. According to Mark, exorcism is first and foremost the practice of unmasking the truth of a situation. As such, exorcism is fundamental to any movement of liberation, personal or political.

Read Mark 3:13-19a

Jesus' next action begins with his ascent of a mountain, in Mosaic fashion (3:13). But unlike the old Sinai story, in which the people were not allowed to follow Moses up the mountain (see Exodus 19:16-25), Jesus summons his leadership group to meet with him there. In another demonstration of the power of naming, the disciples are commissioned to take up the mission of liberation (3:14f).

This "appointing" echoes the account of God's appointment of Moses and Aaron (1 Samuel 12:6). Jesus' naming of "twelve" is also an unmistakable allusion to the Twelve Tribes (see Genesis 49; Numbers 1). But Christians have wrongly correlated this to a supercessionist theology, as if the apostolic church somehow was replacing Israel. Quite the contrary; this action intends a renewal of the original form of Israelite self-government: the tribal confederacy.

The book of Joshua narrates how the Israelite tribes governed themselves in the Promised Land as a kind of decentralized confederacy unified under a covenant with God. Each tribe administered its own local affairs under the leadership of local political-military "judges." Hebrew Bible scholar Norman Gottwald, in *The Hebrew Bible: A Socio-Literary Introduction*, contends that Israel's intertribal, essentially egalitarian social organization represented a revolutionary alternative to the dominating, centralized rule of Canaanite city-states.

Israel's experiment in self-determination did not last, of course. The book of Judges narrates how the tribes would fall into idolatry and re-assimilate into Canaanite society: "Then God raised up judges who delivered them out of the power of those who plundered them" (Judges 2:16). 1 Samuel describes how the confederacy finally succumbed to the more conventional model of a monarchy under David, and then to a fully centralized Temple-state under Solomon (see Chapter 1). But during the Davidic dynasty the prophetic tradition kept alive the criticism of state power. Jacques Ellul points out in his book *Anarchy and Christianity* that the biblical Chronicler portrays powerful kings as idolatrous and unjust, and weak kings as good.

We have suggested that this anti-royalist tradition informs Jesus' commitment to re-establish the sovereignty of God (Mark 1:15; see Chapter 1). Mark's prologue calls for Israel to return to her wilderness origins and recover her premonarchic roots. Indeed, Jesus' appointment of twelve disciples here recalls Joshua's naming leaders on the eve of Israel's dramatic crossing into the Promised Land (see Joshua 3–4). It would seem therefore to represent a specific argument for "retribalization."

Given Jesus' declaration of "a renewed confederacy," it is no wonder that the very next episode brings officials from Jerusalem to investigate, and a homily from Jesus about revolution (3:21-29)! Nor is it any wonder that not all those commissioned on the mountain stayed loyal to the vision (the list includes "Judas Iscariot, who betrayed him," 3:19). Mark will later tell of how the leadership of this new/old movement was and is always tempted by the prevailing political models of domination (10:35-45; see Chapter 15).

This is, then, quite a moment of narrative regeneration after Jesus' rejection by the authorities in 3:1-6. Jesus' action on the mountain renews two of the most revered traditions of Israel: God's covenant with Moses on Sinai and Moses' founding of the free tribal confederacy in the wilderness. In this moment, Jesus, who has taken the torch from the prophets of Israel, prepares to pass it on to the disciples, who are commissioned to proclaim, heal, and exorcize (3:14f). Shortly they will be sent out to practice this charge—another regenerating episode that follows upon a second synagogue rejection (6:1-13; see Chapter 8).

Read Mark 3:19b-35

The next episode raises the stakes for Jesus' movement. As Jesus returns home, he is again engulfed by the crowds (3:20), and now his own family, "convinced he is out of his mind," urges him to cease and desist (3:21). To make matters worse, scribes from Jerusalem are launching a counteroffensive (3:22ff). The composition of 3:21-35 is a "sandwich," a favorite Markan technique of beginning one story, interrupting it with another, and then returning to the original story. This narrative structure establishes a relationship between the two episodes:

A 3:20f: Jesus' family comes to "get" him

B 3:22-30: scribes come to "get" Jesus

A1 3:31-34: Jesus' family summons him again

Mark recognizes that the two pillars of authority, the clan and the state, work together to domesticate people under the status quo. We will deal with both in turn.

In the ancient Mediterranean world, the kinship system rigidly determined personality and identity, controlled vocational prospects, and facilitated overall socialization. Jesus' family sought to rein him in no doubt for his own protection as well as for the sake of their reputation. In 3:31, after Jesus' clash with the scribal investigators, family members redouble their efforts to restrain him. Mark underlines this tension spatially: Contrary to what we would expect, the disciples and the crowd are "inside" the home, while the family is "outside" (3:32). Jesus understands that in order to weave an alternative social fabric, the most basic conventions and constraints of kinship must be questioned: "Who are my mother and my brothers?" (3:32). Jesus concludes the scene by redefining "family" as "whoever does the will of God" (3:35).

Meanwhile, the official investigators from the capital echo the family's accusations, if not their concern:

| family | 3:21 | "He is beside himself" |
| scribes | 3:22 | "He is possessed" |

Both the private sphere of the clan and the public sphere of the state collaborate to maintain the status quo. Smarting from Jesus' repudiation of their authority (1:22ff, 2:6ff), the scribes attempt to undermine Jesus' popular standing by charging that he is in the service of the "prince of demons." It is the predictable strategy of threatened political leaders: Neutralize the opposition by identifying them with the mythic arch-demon. In modern America this would be tantamount to calling Jesus a "terrorist." Jesus' deviant practice of exorcism, which liberates people for Jubilee and retribalization, must be dismissed as either lunatic or traitorous.

Who is "sane" in this polarized atmosphere will depend upon whose point of view we adopt, of course. Jesus masterfully turns the scribes' words back upon them, a strategy he will employ later with other Jerusalem leaders (11:27ff; see Chapter 17). He poses a riddle that suggests the inevitability of insurrection in a corrupt social order (3:24-26):

> How can *Satan* cast out Satan?
> A divided kingdom *cannot stand;*
> A divided house *cannot stand;*
> *Satan* divided in revolt against himself
> *cannot stand* but is coming to an end.

Here and elsewhere in Mark, "kingdom" (see 6:23; 11:10; 13:8) symbolizes the centralized state, and "house" (see 11:17; 13:34f) its symbolic center, the Temple. Jesus is thus returning the scribal "compliment" by aligning their social order with Satan.

Mark chooses this acrimonious debate to introduce Jesus' discourse in parables (3:23). Parables were understood in Jewish tradition as metaphorical stories with thinly veiled political meanings (see Numbers 24; Ezekiel 17; see Chapter 5). In fact, the most well-known parable in the Hebrew Bible concerned a king's abuse of power: Nathan's unmasking of David's murderousness (2 Samuel 12:1-15). Jesus' parable here makes his subversive intentions clear, likening his mission to that of a thief who "must bind the strong man in order to ransack the goods in his house" (3:27).

This will emerge as one of the gospel's master metaphors. Later Jesus will "break into" the Jerusalem Temple, "cast out" the true thieves, and put a ban on the "goods" of that house (11:15-17;

see Chapter 16). He will insist that it "cannot stand" (13:2) and ex-
hort his disciples to keep watch over the house as it awaits its true
Lord (13:34f). However unsettling this metaphor of criminal breaking and entering may seem, the tradition of the Lord's advent "like
a thief in the night" was one of the most enduring in the early
church (see Matthew 24:43; 1 Thessalonians 5:2, 4; 2 Peter 3:10; Revelation 3:3, 16:15).

The answer to the riddle of whether Satan can cast out Satan,
then, is that Jesus (a.k.a. the "stronger one" heralded by John the
Baptist in 1:8) intends to overthrow the "strong man" (a.k.a. the
scribal establishment represented by the demon in 1:24). Mark appears to have taken his cue from Isaiah's oracle: "The captives of
the strong one will be liberated; the prey of the tyrant will be res-
cued" (Isaiah 49:24f). The true political geography of Jesus' apocalyptic struggle with Satan (see 1:13) has now been revealed.

Jesus ends the debate by issuing a blanket pardon, under-
scored with the first of many solemn "Amen" sayings in Mark
(3:28). Excluded by definition, however, are those who demonize
acts of healing and justice (3:29f). As Juan Luis Segundo puts it in
"Capitalism versus Socialism," "The real sin against the Holy Spirit
is refusing to recognize, with 'theological' joy, some concrete liberation that is taking place before one's very eyes." Having rejected the
domesticating family and the dominating state, Jesus' first major
"campaign" draws to a close.

THE WORD IN OUR WORLD

The social context reflected in Mark's narrative may be alien in
form from our own, but not in substance. Our world is hardly free
of systems of domination. Today the free market has become the
strong man. Adherence to its principles is necessary for any person,
community, or nation that wishes to participate in the global economy. This system includes the public and private sector; domestic
bodies such as the U.S. Treasury and the Federal Reserve; international institutions such as the World Bank and the International
Monetary Fund; commercial banks and pension funds; advertising
agencies and the media; and stock markets and money movers responsible for the more than 3 trillion unregulated dollars that cross
national boundaries daily.

The strong man takes no prisoners and can exact a terrible
price from impoverished countries, from countries once on the

brink of "success," and even from the economies of wealthy indus-trialized countries. In sub-Saharan Africa, for example, almost half the population lives in absolute poverty. Millions of people do not have enough to eat, yet, as in many other poor countries, the strong man demands that agricultural land be used to produce export crops rather than food for domestic consumption. One of the only real social safety nets that poor countries can afford—the diversity of mixed farming to provide for basic food needs—is thereby placed at risk.

In Nicaragua, the strong man also stalks. These days if one slows down at any street corner, he or she will be immediately sur-rounded by a flock of children anxious to sell anything from candy to car mats, or to wash the car windows or guard a parked vehicle. These children are not playing—they are desperately trying to fill the ever-increasing vacuum in their family's income. Sixty percent of Nicaragua's workforce is unemployed or underemployed, but the Nicaraguan government is signing agreements to tighten belts even more around already hungry bellies.

The strong man also exacts tribute from the earth in the Philip-pines. The rural poor have been forced off the land; wood is har-vested from fragile rain forests; mangroves and fisheries are ex-ploited. An emphasis on exports, intensive extraction of natural resources, deregulation of investments, and inadequate oversight are all contributing to serious environmental degradation.

In the early 1990s, Mexico was preparing to enter the First World. A series of economic reforms convinced the strong man that Mexico was a model candidate for full and vigorous participation in the global economy. With the passage of the North American Free Trade Agreement in late 1993, it seemed that no obstacles remained for a country once on the brink of sinking into oblivion. Unfortu-nately, the advantages accrued only to a few. Between 1988 and 1994, the number of billionaires in Mexico doubled while the major-ity of Mexicans lived in worsening poverty.

On the day NAFTA was to commence, however, January 1, 1994, signs of strain began to emerge from the jungles of Chiapas, where indigenous communities had long been calling for another strategy of "development." Less than a year later, thanks largely to speculative foreign investment, Mexico's economy crashed. The miraculous model of recovery had failed—with dire consequences for Mexicans of every class.

In most poor countries, burdened by enormous external debt, important domestic economic decisions are being made to satisfy international creditors. The impact of these decisions is being felt by poor communities and families, in neighborhoods and barrios. In almost every case, the impact is profoundly negative: lost educational and health care services, unemployment, increased costs of living, and environmental destruction.

In the United States, the strong man rules almost every dimension of daily life and culture. Nowhere is he more visible than in the relentless, deliberate cultivation of desire for consumer goods. Even when products are superfluous, wasteful, and destructive of human life, we are told to buy, buy, buy. Wealthy and poor alike are trapped in a vicious cycle of increasing frustration as they search for meaning and identity in intrinsically meaningless objects.

The strong man acts incessantly in favor of the rich, while the poor are told they are worthless unless they own what is just out of reach in the ubiquitous shopping malls. U.S. workers on farms and in factories, whose jobs once were secure, are pitted against cheap labor from every corner of the world. The vulnerable are used to make the vulnerable more vulnerable.

Do we have the eyes to see this strong man, or are we too much under his influence? Do we have the courage to join Jesus in "binding" him, or are we cowed by his legitimacy and power? Do we desire to see the captives of our global house liberated, or are we too comfortable?

Chapter 5

Sowing Hope
Mark 4:1-34

THE TEXT IN CONTEXT

After his rift with the scribal authorities, Jesus again retires to the sea, this time to reflect on the state of his mission (4:1f). This is the first of two extended, parable-laced sermons in Mark (13:3-37; see Chapter 20). Here Jesus illustrates the character of God's sovereignty with images drawn from the hardship and wisdom of daily peasant life. These parables speak frankly of the obstacles to the discipleship adventure and enjoin patient hope.

The sermon begins when Jesus gets into a boat and ends when he embarks on a voyage to "the other side." Two-thirds of the sermon consists of the famous parable of the sower (4:3-8) and its "interpretation" (4:14-22), with a thematic refrain exhorting the audience to "Listen!" (4:3, 9, 23).

In the middle of the sower story, Jesus reflects on parables as a language directed toward those in denial (4:10-13). The last third of the sermon is made up of warnings against resignation to the status quo (4:24f) and two more seed parables, one about means and one about ends (4:26-32).

Parables have typically been preached in North American churches as "earthly stories with heavenly meanings." That, however, is exactly what they are not. Rather, Jesus is describing the sovereignty of God in the most concrete possible terms, using images any illiterate peasant could understand. The genius of parables is that they offer recognizable scenarios, drawing listeners in, then throw surprise twists in order to challenge listeners' assumptions about what is possible. Jesus no doubt struggled to explain his vision because it was so much at odds with the prevailing order and thus with the expectations of his audience.

In order to articulate what he stands for, therefore, Jesus begins with what the people stand on: the land itself. "A sower went out to sow...."

Read Mark 4:1-9

The sower story accurately describes the hardscrabble reality of dry-soil (non-irrigated) farming for Palestinian peasants. Small family farmers and sharecroppers barely scratched out a living from the marginal plots onto which they had been pushed by the wealthy who controlled the best arable land. The parable paints the familiar picture of a peasant farmer, free-casting seed and hoping for the best, at the mercy of pests and weeds, the elements, and the poor soil itself (4:4f). It would be no surprise to Jesus' audience that 75 percent of the seed sown would fail to yield.

This portrait is one of agrarian poverty. From a normally meager yield the small farmer had to feed the family, pay the rent, make tithes, cover market tolls and taxes, barter or pay for necessary supplies and tools, and put away enough seed for next year's crop. When not enough was produced, farmers would fall into debt. They then had to use their land to secure a loan from a wealthy landowner who, in the absence of banks, supplied surplus capital at interest. When farmers defaulted on loans, they lost their land and were forced to sell their labor.

This is how big landowners became richer while large numbers of peasants were driven off the land. The "adding of field to field until there is no one but you" was precisely the situation lamented by Isaiah in his parable of the vineyard (Isaiah 5:8), a text to which Jesus will later allude (Mark 12:1ff; see Chapter 18). The cycle of debt, loss of land, and bond-servitude was, however, precisely what Jubilee legislation sought to mitigate (see Chapter 3).

This brings us to the "punchline" of the sower parable: the "good" soil that yields a miraculous harvest (4:8). In reality, a bumper crop for a Palestinian farmer was at best six-fold. "Thirty, sixty, and a hundredfold" thus represents enough surplus to shatter permanently the cycle of indebtedness for the farmer's entire extended family, perhaps even the whole village! This is yet another indication that the sovereignty of God is about a Jubilee that will eradicate poverty and redistribute abundance—if we have "ears to hear" that good news (4:9).

Read Mark 4:10-12

This story, at its plain level of meaning, could only fire the hopes of desperate tenant farmers. But was such a scenario plausible, or is

Jesus simply spinning pipedreams? The next scene addresses the audience's inevitable incredulity (4:10). Jesus admits that for those who would welcome it, Jubilee justice is frankly a "mystery" (often mistranslated "secret"), because it is so incongruous with the dominant social and economic system they know (4:11a). On the other hand, those who fear a redistribution of wealth are "outsiders" to Jesus' mission, and to them this story represents a hard-edged parable (4:11b).

To explain the latter point, Jesus appeals to Isaiah's account of his prophetic call (read Isaiah 6). This text is about the commissioning of an apostle ("Whom shall I send...?" Isaiah 6:8), not unlike what we have just seen in Mark 3:13ff. Isaiah's marching orders, cited by Mark (Mark 4:12 = Isaiah 6:9f), are often misunderstood. They do not articulate a theology of divine predestination, but paint a portrait of a people in denial.

The more a prophet speaks the truth about a problem, the less inclined the people will be to accept the diagnosis, because if they did they would have to "turn and be healed" (Isaiah 6:10). It is repentance they resist, choosing illusions of innocence instead. Isaiah despairs of this state of affairs: "How long, O Lord?" The answer is grim: until the devastating consequences of denial run their course (6:11f). Yet there is always the "remnant" of hope, called the "holy seed" (6:13). This may be the inspiration for Jesus' sower parable.

Read Mark 4:13-23

This Isaian diagnosis opens up an allegorical level of meaning to the sower parable (4:13). "Seeing but not perceiving and hearing but not understanding" (4:12) now joins "hard-heartedness" (3:5) as the gospel's master metaphors for the condition of denial (see 8:17f). Those being sent out on mission need to understand that the seed of the Jubilary "Word" (4:14) will fall on many deaf ears before finding receptivity. This is why healing the deaf and blind will become the contrapuntal metaphor for discipleship later in Mark's narrative.

Each of the four types of "soil" in the parable will eventually be illustrated by an object lesson in Mark's narrative. Those "along the Way" who prove shallow in their commitment (4:15) fit Mark's characterization of the crowd in the gospel. They seek Jesus for healing at first, but in the end the crowds join the authorities in condemning him (see 15:8ff). The ones who "fall away" on account of persecution (4:16f) are the disciples themselves (see 14:27-50). And those whose discipleship is "choked" by wealth and privilege (4:18f) will be illustrated by the rich man (10:17-23). In contrast to the rich man, however, there is hope for the disciples, for they can also be described in terms of the good soil (4:20)—but only insofar as they practice Jubilee redistribution of "house, family and lands, a hundredfold" (10:28-30; see Chapter 14).

The sovereignty of God may be a "mystery" but it is neither esoteric nor inscrutable. To emphasize this, Jesus closes the sower discourse with the image of a lamp, indicating that parables are meant to reveal, not conceal (4:21f). At strategic points in Mark's narrative, parables lay bare the loyalties of Jesus' opponents (3:23ff, 12:1ff). The first part of the sermon concludes with one last exhortation to "have ears to hear" (4:23).

Read Mark 4:24-34

Jesus' audience is next warned to "beware" of the anti-Jubilary ideologies they hear in the world, which counsel resignation in the face of injustice (4:24). The assertion that the gulf between haves and have-nots will inevitably grow was no doubt the "realism" advanced by wealthy landowners to justify their privilege (4:25). Jesus repudiates such pessimism, as did another parable-spinner, Ezekiel (see Ezekiel 18:1-9).

Mark's audience doubtless wondered when and how the miraculous harvest promised in the sower parable would be realized. Against cynical economic "determinism," Jesus pits the patient hope of the farmer in two concluding seed parables:

> And he said: "The sovereignty of God is as if someone should scatter seed upon the ground..." (4:26)

> And he said: "With what can we compare the sovereignty of God?... It is like a grain of mustard seed which, when sown upon the ground..." (4:30f)

The sower "knows not how" growth occurs (4:27), because "the earth bears fruit of itself" (4:28), a reference to the yield in verse 20. Jesus is not advocating passivity but reasserting the divine economy of grace. Sabbath wisdom recognizes that humans must live within the limits of the land instead of seeking to control it or make it into a commodity. This wisdom is given urgency in 4:29, an allusion to Joel's prophetic oracle of divine judgment: "Put in the sickle, for the harvest is ripe" (Joel 3:13). God will vindicate those who sow justice faithfully, despite the appearances of history. Mark will have more to say about "revolutionary patience" in the apocalyptic parables of Jesus' second sermon (13:28f; see Chapter 20).

Jesus' sermon concludes with an insistence that despite the long odds, the smallest seed can indeed take root in a hostile world and flourish (4:30-32). The focus is again on the miraculous harvest, symbolized here by "the greatest of all shrubs in which all the birds of the air can make nests" (4:32).

The image of shelter-offering branches, found in tree parables throughout the Hebrew Bible, is a metaphor for political sovereignty. The earliest example is found in Judges, where Jotham criticizes Abimelech's murderous grab for power in the Israelite confederacy (read Judges 9:1-21). In this parable, the olive, fig, and vine all refuse to abandon their productive tasks to become "king." The bramble (thorns!) however says: "If in good faith you are anointing me king over you, then come and take refuge in my shade; but if not let fire come out of the bramble and devour the cedars of Lebanon" (9:15).

Ezekiel's tree parables also protest against royal domination. In Ezekiel 17, the prophet attempts to persuade Israel's rulers to remain faithful to God even though they dwell in the shadow of the "tall cedars" of the surrounding empires, and to resist the temptation to forge security through military alliances (17:11-21). God promises to raise up Israel "that it may produce branches and bear fruit, and become a noble cedar.... in the shade of its branches will nest winged creatures of every kind" (17:23).

A second parable satirizes imperial Egypt (read Ezekiel 31). Ezekiel asks Pharaoh: "Who are you like in your greatness?" (31:2; see Mark 4:30). He then reminds Pharaoh of Assyria, which also "towered high above all the trees of the field; its boughs grew large and its branches long.... All the birds of the air made their nests in its boughs" (31:5f). But Assyria's empire crumbled: "On its fallen trunk settle all the birds of the air," the prophet parodies (31:13). Here we find an echo of the ancient story of the Tower of Babel: "All this in order that no trees by the waters may grow to lofty height or set their tops among the clouds" (31:14; see Genesis 11:4).

Daniel 4 interprets King Nebuchadnezzar's dream of "a tree at the center of the earth... its top reached to heaven... and the birds of the air nested in its branches, and from it all living beings were fed" (Daniel 4:10ff). The prophet promises that the hubris of empire will be judged, and exhorts the king to "atone for your sins with justice and for your iniquities with mercy to the oppressed" (4:27).

Jesus' allusion to this tree-parable tradition in his conclusion, then, places the entire sermon firmly in an anti-imperial context. In Mark's time, Judea was once again a tiny client-state being "fed by the streams flowing from" the imperial center of Rome (see Ezekiel 31:4). And, within Palestine, Mark's community was a small, persecuted minority. What chance did followers of Jesus have against the power of the Judean Temple-state, much less against that of Rome? The parable of the mustard seed proposes exactly such a mismatch: "All the trees of the field shall know that I bring low the high tree, I make high the low tree" (Ezekiel 17:24).

With such parables, Jesus "spoke the Word to them," carefully interpreting their political allusions to his disciples (Mark 4:33f). This Jesus is no guru dispensing arcane secrets, pedantic theology, or pious platitudes. He is a popular educator using language that peasants can understand, images they can relate to from their experience, and stories which portray them as subjects of the sovereignty of God. In so doing he sows hope among them, insisting that the tall trees can be brought down and that the smallest of seeds *will* bear Jubilary fruit.

THE WORD IN OUR WORLD

Jesus' parables assume a life connected to the land. Perhaps they seem "quaint" to modern U.S. Americans because most of us are not so connected anymore. Yet when we look at the history of U.S. American people, land has always been at the heart of our story.

Many of our ancestors were landless Europeans who came to America as refugees. They saw their immigration as a new Exodus journey into the wilderness to carve out a new society in the land that God had given them as their own. But they encountered peoples and cultures that had been here for centuries. The promise of land to the west spurred wave after wave of exploration, immigration, military conquest, and resettlement that displaced hundreds of indigenous communities and created the nation as we know it. The history of the American people is first and foremost the story of a great struggle between the first Americans and the European immigrants.

There is a disturbing analogy between the story of the Israelites and our own national history. The church has accepted uncritically the story of how the ancient Israelites waged a divinely sanctioned "holy war" of genocide and cultural extermination against the original inhabitants of Canaan (see Judges 1–20). Similarly, we have refused to acknowledge what the coming of the European has done to the original inhabitants of this continent. Are we as people of faith finally ready both to critique and to reclaim what our sacred story offers us in order to construct a genuine and just theology of the land? Are European Americans ready to accept responsibility for a legacy of conquest in order to embrace the challenge of living within a multicultural society?

The people of Israel were taught to make offerings of the fruit of the land to God and to leave unharvested grain in the fields for the poor to eat. They were taught to help the orphan, the widow, the dispossessed, remembering that they too had been sojourners who had wandered without a home. They were taught to respect and nurture the land itself by allowing it to lie fallow every seventh year. And when they failed to live up to this ethic, their God would raise up prophets to call them back to justice. What does this biblical story tell us about our own stewardship of the land?

The first step in reconstructing a biblical theology and ethic of the land is to come to know the place where we ourselves stand. Will Campbell has written a book titled *Providence* that narrates the story of one square mile of Mississippi land. Beginning from the time when it was the homeland of the Choctaw Nation, he traces the story of the land through its transformation into plantations, and its uses from the Civil War to the civil rights movement, when this piece of land gave hospitality to a multiracial cooperative community that was evicted by the White Citizens Council. By telling the story of one plot of land, Campbell tells the story of the nation.

This suggests that we can understand the story of our people by looking at how our own family history is (or is not) identified with and shaped by a particular region or place. What was the relationship of your ancestors to the land they inhabited? Who lived there before them, and what happened to them? If your family was land-owning, how was the property procured, developed, subdivided, and passed on from generation to generation? Do you know much about these things? If not, what does that say about our understanding of inheritance?

The fact is that most of us know very little of the story of the land we live on, or of the contemporary demographic and economic activities that shape it. To begin to "relocate" ourselves on the land, we must begin to identify some of the political, social, and environmental issues germane to this land. What would it mean to be faithful stewards of its human and non-human residents? The heart of a biblical land ethic is to love a particular place the way the Creator loves all of creation—to seek its well-being and that of the creatures this land sustains.

The story of the land represents a spiritual as well as a political challenge. Today most of us find it difficult to answer questions about place: Where have I come from? Where am I now? Where do I belong? We are too busy living in a society in rapid flux to worry about where we stand. Our whole culture is uprooted and transient, made up of people moving quickly, abandoning one place for another. Our hearts are driven, wandering, ungrounded, cut off from a meaningful relationship with land. Many are never able to know the blessing of living on and with the land. Because we are estranged from the land, we are estranged from who God intended us to be.

But Christian spirituality has as much to do with how we stand on the earth as how we experience heaven. It is crucial that we seek to re-establish a sense of groundedness, of place, of connection to a story of land. The person whose home was on the plains may experience life differently from one who grew up with mountains on the horizon; the world view of desert people is shaped differently from that of ocean people. Think about the land where you were born or where you grew up.

If you were one of those who never had the chance to bond with a particular place, think about a special place where you have experienced communion with the land. What does that land mean to you? What feelings does it evoke? How has the geography of that place shaped the inward landscape of your soul?

The story of Israel, its tragedy and promise, is still our story as people of biblical faith. Where is the "promised land" today? Where is land harvested in ways sufficient to meet the needs of all who live on it? On what land do human beings live freely, peace-fully, and with justice? Where is the non-human world respected and honored and given the space to flourish alongside the human? Where is the Creator loved and thanked for creation's bounteous gifts? Might the "promised land" be right beneath our feet?

OUR DISCIPLESHIP JOURNEY

Mark's prologue announces God's inbreaking at the margins of the world, far from the centers of power. The center/margins model is a useful way to look at our own lives and ministries. Choose one context of your life—church, neighborhood, political party, bioregion, etc. In your journal, diagram where you think the center and margins are. Where are you located? How do you feel about this "map" of your world? Now reflect on the following:

> Can I *choose* to locate myself on or near the margins of my society? What would this mean concretely, given my present social and political realities?

Imagine taking a first step toward the margins.

> If I were to cross boundaries in this way, how would it open the wilderness within me? What are my anxieties regarding that boundary crossing? What am I avoiding by not crossing over?

Mark's Jesus invites the disciples, and the reader, into the story of discipleship. To enter Mark's story meaningfully, it is helpful to reflect on your own story. In your journal try a "River of Life" exercise. Use the image of a river to express the broad sweep of your discipleship experience. At the beginning of the river, indicate the sources of physical, spiritual, and emotional life for you. Draw streams joining the river along the way to indicate the addition of new life.

Now reflect on your own call to discipleship. Remember ordinary happenings that moved you in the right direction. If following Jesus brought dramatic changes to your life, draw the river turning sharply. Stones or rapids might indicate obstacles to discipleship that you have encountered along the way. Name important people who have accompanied and strengthened you. Reflect on the following questions:

According to Mark, discipleship is a break with business as usual and represents the overturning of power and privilege. Where do you see those dynamics in your own journey?

Has your work been a part of your discipleship journey? What steps can you take now to integrate your work and your discipleship vocation? What other steps might you take to move yourself closer to what you believe is your call as a disciple?

In Mark 3:31-35, Jesus indicates that discipleship happens in community and that family broadens beyond blood ties to "whoever does the will of God."

Where in your family or community do you see people "doing the will of God"?

Who of these people do *not* share your Christian faith, or your ethnic or class background? What beliefs, attitudes, or circumstances might inhibit you from fully honoring their equality and dignity?

What steps might you and your faith community take to relate to these people as brothers and sisters? How might you form alliances with them in the quest for justice?

Look at your geneagram (see Appendix 2). The families into which many of us were born, as well as the families we have created as adults, have been tremendous gifts from God. They have enabled us to glimpse the depth and steadfastness of God's love and to walk the paths of discipleship. Family is also where most of us were socialized. Through the family, our sense of entitlement was formed, gender-based divisions of labor were learned or not learned, racial identity and prejudice were absorbed or rejected, and class alliances were inherited.

Consider the family of which you are a part, your family of origin and/or the family you have created in adulthood. On your geneagram identify the ways in which this family has nurtured your discipleship by reflecting God's love, modeling faithfulness, teaching you the Word, raising you to challenge white privilege, etc.

Take a moment to honor and celebrate these gifts. Now identify the ways in which that family may have inhibited you from living "as if" the sovereignty of God is at hand. Share these reflections with a member or members of your faith community. How does your faith community function as a family—both empowering and constraining discipleship?

Finally, Jesus calls us to be "sowers of the Word."

Of the kinds of soil described in the parable of the sower, which best describes the context of your life? Are you "beside the Way," where birds pluck the seed from the ground? Are you rocky soil? Do you find yourself in shallow soil with no depth? Are you surrounded by weeds that choke new life? Where is the good soil in your context? What are the obstacles to an abundant harvest of fruit?

II
JOURNEY OF SOLIDARITY

OPENING MEDITATION

It is a Sunday morning in Advent in the year 1511. In a palm-roofed church in the New World, a Dominican friar named Antonio de Montesinos ascends the pulpit. His text is, "I am the voice of one crying in the wilderness."

In John the Baptist fashion, the fearless Montesinos hurls thunder at his shocked congregation. "By what right and by what justice do you hold the Indians in such cruel and horrible bondage? Aren't they dying, or better said, aren't you killing them to get gold every day? Are you not obliged to love them as yourselves? Don't you understand this, don't you feel it?" Then Montesinos makes his way through the astounded multitude. A murmur of fury swells up. "We'll denounce you to the king. You will be deported!"

One bewildered man remains silent. The son of a merchant who crossed the Atlantic with Columbus on his second voyage, this man has already made a great fortune in the colonies. He is a secular priest and *encomendero*, Bartolomé de las Casas, owner of slaves, gold mines, and vast plantations. On this day he takes another step on a journey of solidarity far more demanding and dangerous than crossing an ocean.

Las Casas reflects on the Book of Ecclesiastes (Sirach 34:20-22):

> Like one who kills a son before his father's eyes is the person who offers a sacrifice from the property of the poor. The bread of the needy is the life of the poor, whoever deprives them of it is a murderer. To take away a neighbor's living is to commit murder; to deprive an employee of wages is to shed blood.

In the light of what the Dominicans were preaching and the harsh reality he saw around him, Las Casas became convinced, as recorded in Gustavo Gutierrez's book *Las Casas: In Search of the Poor of Jesus Christ*, that what was being done to the native peoples of the Indies was "unjust and tyrannical." He recognized with horror the tragic relationship between greed for gold and death, turned his life around in repentance, sold his plantations, and freed his slaves.

Called the Apostle to the Indians, Bartolomé began a lifelong ministry that would last almost fifty years as advocate for the indigenous peoples of the Americas. In Nicaragua and Guatemala, he worked for peaceful colonization and denounced at every turn the violent conquest of native communities. What he learned with regard to the unjust treatment of the indigenous communities of the Americas ultimately helped him perceive the terrible violence being done to Africans and led him to an unequivocal rejection of black slavery. He criss-crossed the Atlantic many times, combining his pastoral work in the Americas with advocacy in the Royal Court of Spain, where he finally succeeded in having slavery banished.

When as an old man he left America for the last time, his return to Spain did not interrupt his pastoral activity on behalf of the people of the Americas. He wrote a history of the Americas from the perspective of the indigenous people, which helped to expose the tragedy of the conquest that is at the heart of American history.

Bartolomé de Las Casas is the spiritual father of every person of faith in the Americas who has struggled to cross over to the other side of humanity. His is the story of a conversion that empowered him to cross over the deep divisions in the New World—divisions of race, class, and culture. Bartolomé is most assuredly one of that great cloud of witnesses who accompany us on this journey from the center to the margins.

Chapter 6

Unmasking Oppression
Mark 4:35–5:20

THE TEXT IN CONTEXT

Mark's narrative strategy in the first major section of his story was primarily subversive of the status quo. It portrayed Jesus contending with the forces that dehumanize life. At the same time, Jesus' first campaign offered constructive alternatives: solidarity with the outcast, the creation of a discipleship community, a call for retribalization, and the practice of Jubilee. The next major section of the gospel, which opens and closes with a boat trip (4:35-42, 8:13-21), makes this constructive task its central concern.

Background: Symbolic Geography in Mark

Scholars have puzzled over the fact that in this section, Mark, otherwise the sparest of the gospel writers, is curiously redundant. He narrates two perilous crossings of the Sea of Galilee during storms (4:35-41, 6:45-53) and two feedings of hungry masses in the wilderness (6:33-44, 8:1-9). Jesus' healings, too, are neatly organized into pairs (5:21-43 and 7:24-37). And the exorcism of the Gerasene demoniac has clear similarities to the inaugural exorcism back in the Capernaum synagogue (5:1-20).

Remembering the essential relationship between form and content, we can observe Mark's narrative strategy in this section if we step away from the chronological flow of events in order to identify a pattern. We find two roughly parallel "cycles" of ministry in the first half of the gospel:

	1st cycle	2nd cycle
"Inaugural" exorcism	1:21-28	5:1-20
Paired healings	5:22-43	7:24-37
Feeding of multitudes	6:32-44	8:1-10
Incomprehension of loaves	6:51f	8:14-21

Each cycle takes place on different sides of the Sea, which Jesus and his disciples are traversing by boat trips back and forth. Let us take a closer look at this geography.

The entire first half of Mark's gospel takes place in Galilee in northern Palestine. Dominating this area's topography is the Sea of Galilee, with the Jordan River flowing roughly north-south into and out of it. In 4:35, Jesus and his disciples embark on the first of several journeys to "the other side" of the Sea, an area equated in the narrative with everything east of the Jordan (see 3:8, 10:1). From Mark's point of view, this is Gentile territory, symbolizing everything alien and threatening to the Jewish population west of the Sea.

There are four "crossing journeys" in Mark 4-8: three boat voyages to the east side of the Sea and a long, circuitous trip by land to the northwest coastal cities of Tyre and Sidon, a region also considered "foreign."

1. First crossing

Embark:	4:35f	From near Capernaum (northwest shore)
Arrive:	5:1f	Vicinity of Decapolis (southeast shore)
Return:	5:21	

2. Second crossing

Embark:	6:45	Wilderness, "Jewish" side, destination Bethsaida (northeast shore)
Arrive:	6:53	Blown off course? Disembark at Gennesaret (northwest shore)

3. Land journey

Leave:	7:24	To Tyre and Sidon
Return:	7:31	To Sea of Galilee via Decapolis

4. Third crossing

Embark:	8:10, 13	From Dalmanutha (west shore)
Arrive:	8:22	Bethsaida (northeast shore)

The function of this crossing pattern is to dramatize the fact that, despite their cultural and political "otherness," Mark's Jesus is determined to bring liberation to those on the other side.

Read Mark 4:35-41

After concluding his parables sermon, Jesus invites his disciples to embark on a voyage to "the other side" (4:35). During this crossing a storm blows up, and the boat begins to take on water (4:37). The disciples, among whom are fishermen experienced on the sea, realize they are going down. In a moment of high pathos, they scream at their dozing leader: "Master, do you not care if we perish?!" (4:38). Jesus then rebukes the storm (4:39).

Unlike Psalm 107:23-30, to which it alludes, this episode ends not with relief or triumph, but with Jesus and the disciples wondering about each other:

Jesus:	"Do you not yet have faith?" (4:40)
Disciples:	"Who then is this that even the sea and wind obey him?" (4:41; compare with 1:27)

The disciples are more unnerved after Jesus silences the storm than they were in the midst of it (4:41)! Is this due simply to their awe before a nature miracle, or might it have more to do with their dread of actually having to complete this crossing? We can answer this by seeing how this boat story (and its counterpart in 6:45-52) is drawing on archetypal symbols.

Mark consistently refers to the freshwater lake as a "sea" in order to invoke the most primal narratives in the Hebrew tradition: the Ark of Noah; the crossing of the Red Sea; and the psalmic odes to storms. But, above all, Mark draws on the tale of Jonah, the prophet who resisted the call to preach repentance to foreigners (read Jonah 1). Jonah fled from his mission, apparently because he was unconcerned with the fate of those suffering oppression under the imperial city-state of Nineveh (Jonah 4:11). Thus Jonah, like the disciples here, was caught up in a "great storm" (1:2-4).

The wind and waves in Mark's story, as cosmic forces of opposition (see Psalm 104:7), symbolize everything that impedes Jesus' attempted "boundary crossing." The enmity between Jew and Gentile was seen by most of Mark's contemporaries as the prototype of all human hostility. The separation between them was considered part of the "natural order." Mark's harrowing sea stories suggest that the task of social reconciliation was not only difficult but virtually inconceivable. No wonder, then, that in Mark's second boat episode Jesus must force the disciples to make the crossing (6:45).

Read Mark 5:1-13

On the other side is the "country of the Gerasenes" (5:1), one of the ten federated cities of the Decapolis. On the eastern frontier of the Roman empire, the region had been settled by many veterans of the imperial army who had been given conquered lands as payment for their service. It is no accident, then, that this story will be laced with military imagery.

This is the second major exorcism episode in Mark, and it is narrated in a way that corresponds to Jesus' first confrontation in the Capernaum synagogue (1:21-28; see Chapter 2):

Conflict:

Capernaum:	"Have you come to destroy us?" = scribal authority
Gerasa:	they begged him not to expel them from the country = Roman military occupation

Demoniac's challenge:

Capernaum:	"What do you want with us, Jesus... Holy One of God!"
Gerasa:	"What do you want with me, Jesus, Son of the Most High God?"

Jesus' command:

Capernaum:	Come out of him!
Gerasa:	Come out of the man!

Demon's defeat:

Capernaum:	the unclean spirit... went out of him
Gerasa:	the unclean spirits came out

Crowd reaction:

Capernaum:	they were astonished
Gerasa:	they were afraid

As soon as Jesus arrives, he is confronted by "a man with an unclean spirit" who challenges his mission (5:2). To Jewish readers the setting suggests profound impurity: cemeteries were considered off-limits according to the purity code, as were pigs (5:11). This description matches Isaiah's characterization of an idolatrous people:

"They live in tombs and spend nights in dark corners, eating the meat of pigs and using unclean food" (Isaiah 65:4).

Mark's description of the demoniac accurately depicts a condition of captivity to addiction or internalized oppression: he lives among the dead, crying out and engaging in self-destructive behavior (5:3-5). The demoniac, who could "no longer be bound" (5:3) because "no one had the strength to subdue him" (5:4), now faces the "stronger one" (see 1:7) who has vowed to "bind the strong man" (see 3:27). Here, as with the synagogue exorcism, Mark reports the unclean spirit's protest, a challenge at once indignant and afraid: "What are you doing here?!" (5:7 = 1:24). Yet Jesus is addressed not with the Jewish title "Holy One of God" but with the Hellenistic "Son of the Most High God."

Only here in Mark does Jesus turn the tables on a demonic attempt to name him (see Chapter 4). The answer Jesus receives to his demand for identification is stunning: "My name is Legion, for we are many" (5:9f; note the singular/plural subject confusion). In Mark's world this Latin term could mean only a division of Roman soldiers. Four such legions were based in Syria to control the eastern frontier, including Palestine. Yet this intimidating military force—in reality so powerful that "no one could subdue" it (5:4)—according to Mark "begged Jesus earnestly not to expel them from the country" (5:10).

This unlikely story offers a symbolic portrait of how Roman imperialism was destroying the hearts and minds of a colonized people. If the synagogue demoniac spoke "under the influence" of the scribal establishment, then the Gerasene demoniac represents Rome's military occupation of the land and its people. That this episode is a kind of political cartoon critical of Roman imperialism is confirmed by the recurring military terminology that follows. Legion begs to be sent into a "band" of pigs (5:11), a Greek term usually referring to a group of military recruits. Sarcasm is evident here, since the swine cult was popular among Roman soldiers.

Jesus "dismisses" them, and the word describing the pigs' rush down the hill connotes troops charging into battle (5:13). The political humor finds its punchline as the Legion meets the same fate as old Pharaoh's army: they are swallowed into the sea (see Exodus 14). If Jesus' first exorcism served notice that he would challenge the Judean elite's control over the people, this episode extends the struggle for God's sovereignty toward the Empire itself!

Read Mark 5:14-20

The second part to this episode turns our attention from the occupier to the occupied. The reaction to Jesus' liberative act is hostile, the people's fear induced equally by "what happened to the demoniac and to the swine" (5:16). Legion's petition is now reversed: The surrounding townspeople now "beg" Jesus to leave their neighborhood (5:17).

Their fear is better understood once we know that during this historical period struggles for self-determination had spawned Roman counterinsurgency campaigns that had reduced to rubble more than one city in the Decapolis region. This may be why they are hardly pleased to see one of their own now "in his right mind" (5:15). In political terms, this portrait attests to the power of the state to suppress opposition through fear. In psychological terms, it reminds us that those who are codependent with addictive behavior will usually resist changes in the dysfunctional system. Whether personal or political, liberation has a cost, and there will always be those unwilling to risk it.

Given this reaction, it is understandable that the former demoniac in turn "begs" to go with Jesus (5:18). But Jesus refuses, dispatching him instead to "return to his own" and spread the Good News (5:19). Who better can attest to the possibility of liberation from oppression than someone who knows it "from the inside out"? The man whose body was destroyed by the internalized pathologies of empire now goes to proclaim good news to all held captive by the imperial body politic (5:20).

THE WORD IN OUR WORLD

In the story of the Gerasene demoniac, we have seen oppression as a deadly fabric in which personal and political dimensions are intimately woven together.

Imagine our nation as a single living organism, with many parts. This organism bears the characteristics of the demon-possessed man (mightily self-destructive, out of control, isolated from community, living among the tombs, howling). Consider the following headlines:

Study Says Billboards, Strip Malls May Be Hazardous to
    Your Health

Police Break Hyper-Violent Heroin Ring, Arrest 60

Hotels Stung by Underage Drinking Crackdown

NRA Fights Ban on Assault Weapons

Virginians Carry Legal Guns to the Supermarket

Two Children Dead, Nine Injured in Machine Gun Attack
    on Elementary School

Homeless Children in America (part 1 of 4-part series)

Teen Suicide Rising

Television... The Dangerous Drug of Choice

Many Hill Freshman Are Millionaires, Disclosure Indicates

Gunman Stalks and Shoots Lesbian Couple

Industrialized World's Highest Gap Between Rich and
    Poor: USA

Infant Mortality Rising in Urban America

Are we as a people possessed? Who is crying out for deliverance? When the liberating power of God approaches, do they "beg the power of liberation to leave their neighborhood" (5:17)?

Read the text again, especially verses 3-10. Is the speaker the possessed man or the possessing demon? As a society might we be both the possessed and the demon? We have explored how we are occupied by demons. Consider now our role as occupying power, as demon.

It is staggering to consider the many nations whose natural resources, economies, governments, or militaries have been "occupied" by the United States to serve its own perceived self-interests or those of its corporate giants. El Salvador, Guatemala, Honduras, Nicaragua, and the Philippines are but a beginning. Many U.S. citizens who have been privileged to spend time with the people of these and other nations are aware both of the unfathomable suffering caused by U.S "occupation" and of the peoples' courageous resistance.

Consider too the occupation—by U.S. multinational corporations—of the borderlands between Mexico and the United States. There the land on which thousands of Mexicans live has become deadly, contaminated with the toxic waste spewed forth by plants relocated to Mexico to benefit from low-cost labor and lax environmental regulations. The costs of this borderland occupation are: some of the world's most polluted waterways, the spread of pathogenic viruses and bacteria, children born with severe mental retardation and other birth defects, wages so low that two hours of work are required to buy a gallon of milk, and outrageous or excessive corporate profit.

Mark's story speaks to the devastating effects of occupation. This may impel us to acknowledge, lament over, and struggle in solidarity with the victims of our nation as occupying force. But what if we do not repent, instead choosing the path of silence and denial? Are we possessed by the collective unconscious of our past which—unacknowleged—continues to repeat itself, just as the unacknowleged traumas of childhood continue to haunt the adult until they are unearthed, faced, and dealt with in some form of therapeutic process? Freud's conclusion that "what is unconscious is bound to be reproduced" has profound implications for our life as a body politic. "Then Jesus asked him, 'What is your name?' He relied, 'My name is Legion'" (5:9). The road to freedom from possession as oppressor and oppressed includes acknowledging our name. We are and have been Legion.

Is it possible that oppressive power brutalizes the oppressed and eventually also eats the children of the oppressors? "... Middle and rich class American modernity is now beginning to devour its own children just as it has long beat upon others," says theologian Larry Rasmussen. In this country that has occupied so many, can it be that the forces driving our oppression of other lands is now come home; that we are not only possessor, but also in many ways the possessed?

In confronting oppression, however, Jesus restored the possessed man to wholeness, to community, to self-possession, and to a contributing role. Jesus discouraged him from dependency by telling him to return home and tell the story. The story of demon possession and occupation became one of exorcism and liberation. The man was set free.

Close your eyes now and imagine that the organism (our nation) is exorcised of the possessing demons you saw. What images do you see? Imagine that peoples we "occupy" are exorcised of our oppressive power. What images do you see?

What would it mean for you and your church or community to live toward a new reality in which we as a nation were not "possessed" and did not "occupy" the resources of other nations? Make a commitment to some step in that direction. Record it in your discipleship journal.

- How do people in Mark's story respond to the option of freedom from demon possession?

- Are there any similarities between the villagers' fear of the exorcised man and our fears of what might happen to our lifestyles if oppressed peoples of the world were free?

- In many ways we fear freedom. We cling to the safety of being possessed. How do you feel when you think of being free from white privilege, from class privilege, from male privilege, from dependence on military might, from a consumer mentality?

Move now to a more personal—and perhaps more familiar—dimension. Is Jesus' power to wrestle with and defeat this demon at all related to the fact that he has faced and wrestled with his own demons (1:12-13)? The power to exorcise demons in our society is grounded partly in having the courage and faith to face the demons that possess us personally. Having done so, we will always know their power, the agony they cause, and the essential role of community in exorcising them.

Are there demons that possess or have possessed you personally? Are there things that cause you to damage yourself, to "live among the tombs," more dead than alive? What prevents you from loving fully, from being in true community? Are there things that hold you in bondage to self-interest, fear, anxiety, hopelessness, or powerlessness, preventing you from fully using your gifts to nurture life, to work toward the Beloved Community? Be honest with yourself. "Do not fear the truth, hard as it may appear. . . . it is your best friend and closest sister" (Dom Helder Camara).

Refer back to your geneagram. Are these demons rooted in your family history? Write a dialogue poem in which you face and name and talk with a demon possessing you. Then imagine Jesus and his liberating love stepping off the boat onto the shores of your life, walking up to you, asking the demon its name, freeing you, sending you back to your people to proclaim the liberating power of God. (Reflect on "A Psalm for Casting out Demons" in Appendix 4.)

Chapter 7

The Priority and Power of the Poor
Mark 5:21-43

THE TEXT IN CONTEXT

Read Mark 5:21-34

Having brought liberation to the other side, Jesus returns to "Jewish" territory (5:21). Mark's next episode is another example of the sandwich-construction that wraps a story within a story in order to compel the reader to relate the two. This tale of two women dramatizes how the poor were given priority in the ministry of Jesus.

The setting of the first half of the story is the "crowd" (5:21, 24, 27, 31). Jesus is approached by a synagogue ruler who appeals on behalf of his daughter, whom he believes to be "at the point of death" (5:23). Jesus departs with him, and we fully expect this mission to be completed. On his way, however, Jesus is hemmed in by the crowds (5:24). The narrative focus zooms in upon a woman whose condition Mark describes in detail (5:25f) with a series of descriptive clauses: she had been with a flow of blood for twelve years; she had suffered much under the care of many doctors; she had spent all her resources yet she had not benefited, but had grown worse instead.

Because the purity code mandated that menstruating women be quarantined (read Leviticus 15:19ff), it would have been highly inappropriate for a hemorrhaging woman to be in public—much less touching a "holy man"! But Mark focuses instead on the way she had been bankrupted by profiteering physicians who exploited her without healing her.

The woman's approach to Jesus is in stark contrast to that of Jairus. His approach was frontal and proprietary: He acknowledged Jesus' honor (lowering himself before him) in order to make a request. She, on the other hand, reaches out anonymously from behind in the crowd, seeking to touch Jesus covertly and somehow effect a magical cure. Jairus addresses Jesus directly, as would befit male equals, while the woman talks only to herself (5:28). Jairus is the "head" of both his family (speaking on behalf of his daughter) and his social group (the synagogue); the woman is nameless and alone. In other words, Mark is portraying two characters who represent the opposite ends of the social spectrum.

At the moment of contact between Jesus and the woman (5:29), however, the power dynamics of the story begin to be reversed. Her body is healed—the opposite of what a Jewish audience would expect, since it is Jesus who should have contracted her impurity through physical contact. Indeed, Mark tells us that power had been transferred (5:30). Does this comment signal a magical transaction, or is it a clue to the social reversals to come?

When Jesus stops to inquire what has happened, the whole narrative, which was in motion toward Jairus' house, grinds to a halt. A struggle now ensues:

Jesus: "Who touched my clothes?"
Disciples: "You see the crowd yet ask, 'Who touched me?'"
Jesus looked around to see who had done it. (5:31f)

To the disciples, this interruption is an inconvenience attributable to the anonymous crowd, with whom they are unconcerned. Jesus, however, seeks to know the human face of the poor.

The woman emerges from the margins of the story to center stage. It is now her turn to fall in front of Jesus, suggesting that she is now an equal to Jairus. Finding her voice, "she told him the whole truth"—including no doubt her opinion of the purity system and the medical establishment! Jesus then acknowledges her rightful status as "daughter" in the family of Israel (5:34), and commends the faith evidenced by her stubborn initiative. His commendation grants her a status exceeding that of Jesus' own disciples, who have been shown to be "without faith" (4:40)!

Read Mark 5:35-43

But what of the original "daughter"? Jairus is informed by some servants that she has died (5:35). The phrase "while Jesus was still speaking" functions to overlap the utterances, as if gain and loss are voiced simultaneously:

Daughter, your faith has made you well. Go in peace.

Your *daughter* is dead. Why trouble the Teacher further?

By attending to this importunate woman, Jesus appears to have defaulted on his original task. Will the story end in tragedy? Undeterred, Jesus ignores this "interpretation" of events and exhorts Jairus to believe. The shock cannot be missed: He is instructing a leader of the synagogue to learn about faith from this outcast woman (5:36)!

The scene now shifts to Jairus's household. There mourning turns to derision at Jesus' insistence that the girl only "sleeps" (5:39). Jesus is not being coy; "being asleep" will emerge later in the story as a symbol of lack of faith (13:36, 14:32ff; see Chapter 22). He throws out the onlookers and proceeds to raise the girl back to life (5:40-42). The witnesses are "beside themselves with great astonishment" (5:42), a reaction that will occur only one other time in Mark: at Jesus' resurrection (16:8).

This episode portrays Jesus in the tradition of the prophet Elisha, who raised the dead son of a woman of Shunem (read 2 Kings 4:8-37). This may help explain why Mark's story ends with Jesus' instruction to give the girl "something to eat" (5:43). For just as Elisha followed his healing of the young boy by multiplying loaves for people during a famine (read 2 Kings 4:38-44), Mark will shortly relate Jesus' feeding of the crowds in the wilderness (6:35ff; see Chapter 8).

In the art of narrative, every detail is there for a reason, and Mark's "aside" that the girl was twelve years old is a good case in point. She has lived affluently for twelve years, and is just on the edge of puberty. In contrast, the bleeding woman had suffered for twelve years, permanently infertile. This number symbolizes the twelve tribes of Israel (3:13; see Chapter 4), and represents the key to the social meaning of this doublet. Within the "family" of Israel, these "daughters" represent the privileged and the impoverished, respectively. Because of such inequity, the body politic of the synagogue is "on the verge of death."

The healing journey must, however, take a necessary detour that stops to listen to the pain of the crowd. Only when the outcast woman is restored to true "daughterhood" can the daughter of the synagogue be restored to true life. That is the faith the privileged must learn from the poor. This story thus shows a characteristic of the sovereignty of God that Jesus will later address: The "last will be first" and the "least will be greatest" (see 10:31, 43).

THE WORD IN OUR WORLD

Palestine in the first century was not exceptional in having a purity code that maintained stringent social boundaries and strata. The United States today is no less characterized by "purity codes," although our society fails to acknowledge them as such. They are the structures and belief systems that create "insiders" and "outsiders"; grant some people access to health care, education, housing, and food while others go without; and allow some to suffer while others prosper.

For some of our readers, oppression may be real through their own experience of struggling for justice. For others of us, oppression first became real when we experienced the suffering of others—perhaps of homeless people or of Central American refugees.

Consider first your personal story. Where does this woman's story become your story? When have you been the bleeding one, the broken one, the excluded, the invisible, the marginalized? Perhaps you have experienced a debilitating accident that changed your life in a single instant; the bondage of addiction; your humanity stunted by the cruelty or ignorance of others; or the horror of watching disease drain life from a loved one. Perhaps—as this woman—you have determined to be healed by reaching out to Jesus or otherwise accepting the healing power of the Spirit.

Most of us also know times when we have been afraid to seek healing. At other points we may have prayed persistently and passionately for healing of self or others, but felt no healing touch. Perhaps at some point we have been vessels of God's healing power for others. At other times, perhaps we have ignored the call to heal.

Few people in mainline denominations take Jesus as healer seriously. Imagine the implications if we—led by this woman—seriously accepted Jesus as healer of both personal and social disease. Imagine yourself approaching Jesus and touching his cloak. With this woman as your sister and guide, trust the healing power to be present. As did this sister, share your brokenness with God, "telling the whole truth" (5:33) of your pain. Pray that you might see where the healing Spirit is present. Allow the courage of the woman in this story to impel you along the path toward healing.

Consider now our larger world. Who is the hemorrhaging woman in our world today? Hear the story of Carmen.

> Carmen and her husband, Jose, have worked in Washington, D.C., since they immigrated from Nicaragua 14 years ago. They have two children, and—like many Latin American immigrants in the Washington area —they work hard. Carmen works cleaning offices and rooms in a retreat center for four 10-hour days a week. She cleans houses evenings every day except Sunday, which is her family day and the day she cleans her own house.
>
> Jose was a skilled construction worker until he became sick with kidney disease. Within six months the debilitating illness left him with practically no kidney function at all. At present he is on dialysis three times a week and unable to work. He has lost 30 pounds and feels ill most of the time. Carmen is now the family bread winner. Since their income has been cut by nearly two-thirds, Carmen has struggled to make their house payments so they will have a place to live.
>
> When their income fell below the poverty line, Carmen applied for food stamps. She hated to do it but knew that it was important for her husband and children to eat well. The social worker advised Carmen to sell her car, rent out a room in the basement of her home, and take her children out of Catholic school (even though the tuition had already been paid). Only once Carmen had followed the social worker's directions was she to reapply for food stamps.
>
> Yet she needs her car to take her husband for dialysis treatments as well as to get to her various jobs. She is fearful of renting space in her basement to strangers. She feels that her children's lives have been disrupted enough, and that to take them out of their familiar school at this point would hurt them to no purpose. So Carmen is left to struggle with no government assistance.
>
> (from "Reaganomics and Women: Structural Adjustment U.S. Style")

Jesus in our text is a healer of both the woman and Jairus's daughter. By healing first the poor woman, he beckons the entire people toward healing the deadly disease of social inequity. The Jesus who prioritized the healing of the poor woman surely wills the healing of Carmen, her family, and the millions of others marginalized and made ill by social inequity today. As Jesus' discipleship community, we share this healing mission.

If we are to put the last first today, we must deepen our understanding of the social diseases that marginalize the "least" today. The fact that the center of this story is a woman pushed into insignificance and suffering in part by the patriarchy of her context calls us to acknowledge male privilege as one of the social diseases from which healing is needed.

A chorus of voices—including sisters from centuries past and sisters on the streets of our cities—join this call. We all bleed because reality has been shaped and articulated by the perceptions and desires of men in dominant positions. Our concepts of God, our stories of God's saving action in history, our understanding of human psychology and development, our concepts of discipleship, our images of what it means to be a person of God and a worthy human being are shaped by patriarchy.

In capitalist culture billboards and magazines, televisions and movies seek to convince our thirteen-year-old sisters that they are worthless unless their bodies develop a certain way and they purchase certain products. Many women have been devastated by rape and sexual abuse. We hear the screams of our sisters in Bosnia and Herzegovina, whose bodies became battlefields.

How much of our soul has been submerged, perhaps lost forever, by centuries of oppression of women and suppression of women's stories and wisdom? What would be our understanding of God the Creator, of Christ, and of the Spirit had those understandings grown out of the experience of women and men not shaped by patriarchy and capitalism? We who are privileged women find ourselves not only at the center but also on the margins, and our task is not only to move to the margins with the poor but also to move with our sisters to the center as did the courageous woman in this story.

As disciples of Jesus, we are called to be his healing presence on earth. Consider who is marginalized in your life setting. How might you be in solidarity with them in ways which honor and respect them? How might you step aside (as perhaps did Jairus) to allow the rightful claims of the poor to be realized? What social taboos will you have to violate (as did the courageous woman) in order to be in solidarity with those on the margins?

As we begin to reorient toward this faithful healing task, we have as a guide the courageous woman of Mark's gospel who—although nameless and "powerless"—dared to claim dignity and worth. Allow her courage to move you toward healing social inequities, in spite of fear. (Reflect on "Rich Woman, Poor Woman: A Dramatic Reading for Two People" in Appendix 4.)

Chapter 8

Enough for Everyone
Mark 6:1-56

THE TEXT IN CONTEXT

At this point Mark alters his narrative rhythm in order to give us some background on each of the three major "protagonists": Jesus, the disciples, and John the Baptist. Three episodes concerning "rejected prophets" open up a central theme of the second half of the gospel: the cost of discipleship (6:1-6, 6:7-13, 6:14-29).

Read Mark 6:1-13

The series begins with Jesus' return "to his own country" (6:1). For a third time he teaches in a synagogue on the Sabbath (see 1:21ff, 3:1ff), and for a third time he encounters opposition. This time, however, it is not from the authorities but from his neighbors and kinfolk. They are suspicious of this local boy's notoriety, objecting that he has no distinguished lineage (6:3). Because of the domesticating constraints of nationality, kinship, and household expectations (6:4), the "prophet without honor" is unable to effect change there, and returns to his itinerant mission (6:5f).

For a second time Mark follows a rejection of Jesus with a discipleship commissioning story (see Chapter 4):

3:1-6: Rejection in Capernaum synagogue;

3:13-15: Jesus summons disciples, appoints them to preach and cast out demons;

6:1-6: Rejection in Nazareth synagogue;

6:7-13: Jesus summons disciples, sends them to heal, preach, and cast out demons.

71

The disciples are explicitly instructed to take only the bare necessities for travel on "the Way" (6:8-11). Mark is more interested here in Jesus' ground rules than in the mission itself, which is reported only in summary fashion (6:12f). This suggests that he is articulating something fundamental for the life of the "apostolic" church (the disciples are called apostles by Mark only in 6:30).

The point of this "dress code" is not asceticism, since Jesus has already rejected cosmetic piety (see 2:18-22). Instead, it assures that the missionaries will be dependent upon the hospitality of the people to whom they go. Rendered a "stranger at home," Jesus is instructing his community to learn to be "at home among strangers." The suggestion is simple and clear. Where the gospel is received and embraced, disciples are to remain; where it is rejected, they are to move on (6:10f). This severs evangelism from any practice of domination or conquest. How different the history of the world would have been had Christian missionaries heeded these directives!

Intruding between the departure and the return of the disciples (6:30) is the account of John the Baptist's fate at the hands of Herod. This Markan sandwich suggests that the following tragic episode is part of the disciples' "marching orders." To preach repentance one must accept the risks of persecution by the powerful.

Read Mark 6:14-30

The flashback account of John's execution belatedly explains the circumstances surrounding his arrest reported in 1:14. Mark tells us that Herod (that is, Herod Antipas, tetrarch of Galilee and Perea from 4 B.C.E. to 39 C.E.) believes that Jesus is John coming back to haunt him (6:14-16). Insofar as Jesus took up the Baptist's mantle, Herod is not wrong, of course. But the disturbing implication for the king is that the message persists despite his having gotten rid of one messenger. It is to that sordid tale that Mark now abruptly turns.

The Jewish historian Josephus, a contemporary of Mark, writes that Herod executed John the Baptist for plainly political reasons: His preaching was stirring up a popular insurrection. This has led many scholars to dismiss Mark's story of the king's moral predicament as merely pious legend. But Mark's account is hardly pious!

First, intermarriage was fundamental to the building and consolidation of royal dynasties, so John's objection that Herod should not marry his brother's wife could scarcely be more political (6:17f). Second, the half-Jew Herod conformed to Jewish law only when he deemed it politically expedient. Otherwise he aggressively promoted Hellenization, since his provincial power was dependent on the good favor of Rome. This policy was resented by Judean nationalists. By insisting that Herod be accountable to Torah (6:18), then, John was raising a volatile political issue in colonial Palestine.

Mark's portrait of Herodian court intrigue takes on the character of parody (6:19f). The king throws a dinner party for the ruling classes of Galilee (6:21). Despite this impressive gathering of political, military, and economic leaders, however, it is a young dancing girl and a drunken oath that finally determine the fate of the Baptist (6:22-25). This sardonic caricature of the murderous whims of the powerful faintly echoes the story of Esther and Ahasuerus (Esther 1–7).

John's burial prefigures that of Jesus (6:29), and on its heels Mark returns to the story of the apostolic mission, completing the sandwich (6:30). By weaving together three stories of "truth and consequences," Mark suggests a common destiny for all who preach repentance. Later Jesus will announce that the fate of "Elijah" will hold true for the "Human One" (9:11-13; see Chapter 12)—and for disciples as well (13:9-11).

Read Mark 6:31-44

As soon as the disciples have returned from their missionary journey, Jesus urges them to withdraw to a wilderness place for reflection (6:30f). But again their escape is unsuccessful, for people keep pressing upon them (6:32f). Jesus feels deep compassion for the crowds who were "like sheep without a shepherd," and proceeds to teach them until evening (6:34).

The scene bears a distinct resemblance to the appointment of Joshua as the military leader of the tribal confederacy "so that the congregation of God may not be like sheep without a shepherd" (Numbers 27:16). Mark no doubt also means to allude to Ezekiel's criticism of the ruling class of Israel as "shepherds who have been feeding themselves":

> You have not strengthened the weak, you have not healed the sick, you have not bound up the injured, you have not brought back the strayed, you have not sought the lost, but with force and harshness you have ruled them. So they were scattered, because there was no shepherd. (Ezekiel 34:4-5)

The prophet Zechariah also denounced those "shepherds" who sell their own flock to get rich (Zechariah 11:5). Jesus, on the other hand, is about to demonstrate solidarity with the "weak and the strayed."

As nightfall approaches the disciples demand that Jesus dispatch the people to buy food in the neighboring villages (6:35f). Jesus' response is blunt: "You give them something to eat." While they agonize, indignant at the prospect of having to dig into their own pockets to aid the hungry (6:37f), Jesus acts. Determining the food on hand, he organizes the crowd, offers a blessing, and distributes the loaves and fish (6:38-41). Nothing "supernatural" occurs here, except that "all ate and were satisfied" (6:42).

This episode obviously alludes to the old story of the wilderness manna, which, as we have seen, undergirds the Sabbath economics of grace (see Chapter 3). But Mark is also drawing upon the "food miracles" of Elisha during a time of famine (read 2 Kings 4:42-44). This suggests that the economic dimensions to Mark's wilderness feedings are more important than "eucharistic" symbolism. The disciples try to solve the problem of hungry masses through "market economics": sending the people to village stores or counting their change. Jesus, on the other hand, teaches self-sufficiency through a practice of sharing available resources.

This story addresses the concrete historical situation of the majority of Galilee's rural population. Hunger and poverty were widespread among those disenfranchised by a feudal system of land ownership and by an economic system that put the countryside at the service of urban interests. Jesus' parable of the sower envisioned an unprecedented harvest that would shatter the cycle of poverty in which the indentured peasant was trapped (see Chapter 5). In the wilderness feeding, this hope takes flesh in the "miracle of enough." Later Jesus will invite the discipleship community to embody this alternative economic model of cooperative consumption (10:28-31; see Chapter 14).

Read Mark 6:45-56

Now comes the second voyage to the other side. This time, however, Jesus must force his disciples to get into the boat and sail by themselves (6:45). Once again we find the hapless disciples upon a raging sea in the dead of night, straining pitiably against what must have felt like the roaring headwinds of hell (6:47f). Mark says they were "tortured at the oars," yet were losing ground. Is there a more heartbreaking portrait of the struggle of discipleship, a struggle in which we so often seem to be losing ground against the storms of history?

Jesus' walk on the sea is a moment of revelation that the disciples miss, thinking he is a "ghost" (6:48f). When they realize it is he, they are profoundly "agitated," a word suggesting that the storm now rages inside them as well. Now at last comes Jesus' response to their frightened question that concluded the first boat trip ("Who is this?" 4:41). Jesus identifies himself as the "I AM" (6:50), an extraordinary invocation of the name of the Exodus God (see Exodus 3:4).

But the disciples are "beside themselves" (6:51), and the crossing is unsuccessful (6:53). The disciples have now contracted Pharaoh's disease: hard-hearted, they don't understand the purpose of the crossing, which Mark here equates with the "loaves" (6:52). Undeterred, Jesus presses on with his healing ministry in the very marketplaces he eschewed in the wilderness (6:53-56).

THE WORD IN OUR WORLD

The wilderness feedings enact the "miracle" of a manna economy in which everyone in the community has "enough." What has our culture taught us about economics? From our earliest days we learn at home, in school, in the marketplace about economics; about working and earning and saving; about the cost of living; about responsibility and caring for family; about community and sharing.

We learn to define "success" and "failure." We learn about class and our own class identity location. We learn to define security and we learn about our relationship to things, to other people, to the world. Educational systems, the media, marketing techniques, religious traditions, family practices, and community rituals all contribute to shaping our values.

Other cultures have developed economic practices radically different from ours. The potlatch tradition, for example, was a widespread practice among the indigenous peoples of the Pacific Coast at times of significant personal change: puberty, marriage, accession to chiefdom, death. Potlatch is based on the idea that all wealth, material and symbolic, must circulate. It honors non-acquisitiveness, generosity, and redistribution of wealth. When ritual privileges are publicly transmitted to the next generation, prestigious objects are given away in a ceremony involving feasts, speeches, songs, and dancing. Traditionally, the potlatches were a means of affirming social and political prerogatives as well as placing obligations on friends and strengthening kinship ties and village solidarity. Potlatches were also used to end hostilities and to re-establish good relations.

The ritual practice of the "give-away" could happen only in a culture where great value is placed not on possessions, but on the willingness of the individual to dispossess her/himself for the greater good of the whole. This practice of sharing is not just an expression of the exceptional individual; it is a part of the culture itself.

In Mark's account of the first wilderness feeding, Jesus challenged the disciples to move beyond the predominant economic approach in order to enact an economics of sharing. This narrative issues the same challenge to disciples today. Many groups and organizations are accepting that challenge by testing new economic models that emphasize cooperation and participation rather than competition and individualism. Worker-owned businesses, cooperatives, land trusts, community-supported agriculture, community loan funds, socially responsible banking, community currencies, and the like offer the possibility of a significantly changed economic landscape.

Community land trusts are interesting examples. A land trust is a community-based organization that buys and holds land for the benefit of a community. It provides affordable access to land and housing for community residents, especially those with little income, and helps assure that the long-term use of the land for housing, business, and recreational purposes will best serve broad community needs.

Community land trusts attempt to meet the needs of residents least served by the prevailing markets. They prohibit speculation and absentee ownership of land and housing, promote ecologically sound land-use practices, and preserve the long-term affordability of housing.

Individuals, cooperatives, and families continue to own homes or other improvements located on the land and retain most of the rights and responsibilities which go with ownership. Future sales of housing units or other buildings on a piece of land-trust property will be at below-market prices because the resale price will not reflect any appreciation in land value.

The land trust retains an option to purchase buildings and other improvements on the land (should the owner wish to sell) for an amount that represents the value of the owner's actual invest-ment (original purchase price plus personal investment of labor and capital). In this way, community land trusts recognize the "social mortgage" on property—the appreciation in property value due to improved public infrastructure, services, and community develop-ment efforts (i.e., new rapid-transit stations, public recreation facili-ties, etc.).

A companion initiative to the community land trust move-ment is an innovative national project called Equity Trust, a com-mon fund that makes affordable housing available to low-income people. Equity Trust invites individual and institutional property owners to take an honest look at the source of increase in their property value, and then to pledge a percent of the "social mort-gage" to be used by the Trust to meet the housing needs of others. One Washington, D.C. family with a very modest income provides a concrete example: "The value of our home has increased signifi-cantly as a result of the new Metro [rapid transit] station in our neighborhood. We have decided that whenever we sell this home, we will give to Equity Trust 100 percent of the increase attributable to the new Metro station. We are grateful for the opportunity to be in partnership with people who need shelter."

Equity Trust also draws inspiration from the land-gift move-ment initiated by Vinoba Bhave, Mahatma Gandhi's successor in India:

> In 1951, following a national conference of village devel-opment workers, Vinoba began a walk through the Telen-gana region, at that time the scene of considerable social unrest. In the village of Pochampalli, he addressed the Untouchables (called "children of God" by Gandhi), who were the poorest and most oppressed members of the community and were consigned to that condition by so-cial discrimination and landlessness. Vinoba asked them how much land would be required to meet their needs and they responded, "Eighty acres."
>
> Vinoba then addressed the village as a whole, ask-ing rhetorically, "Who will give land to these people?" To his own surprise, a landowner stood and said, "I will"—and the Bhoodan or "land gift" movement was born. For several years, Vinoba walked from village to village, state to state, collecting land gifts. He was joined in this effort

by Jayaprakash Narayan, another leading figure of the Indian independence movement…and by hundreds of others.

Bhoodan evolved into Gramdan or "village gift." In a Gramdan village, a large percentage of land was pledged. Realizing that, even when land is redistributed, old patterns of ownership are likely to re-emerge over time, Gramdan lands were placed in village trusts, to be leased to landless families but protected for future generations and the benefit of the entire community. The Gramdan movement is one of the models on which community land trusts are based.

(from Equity Trust Inc., *Information for Prospective Participants*)

Many of the values embodied by these alternative economic models are in sharp contrast to the values of the dominant economic system in the United States. Yet, these ideas share the principles of Jesus' wilderness feedings: The survival and well-being of people and their communities take precedence over profit for a few; one person or community or nation does not walk on the backs of others to get ahead; the "development" of the human family cannot take place at the expense of the rest of creation; who we are is not measured by how we earn a living, or what possessions we have. We who are followers of Jesus must try to make these values real in our world so that there will be "enough for everyone."

Chapter 9

Lessons in Inclusivity
Mark 7:1-37

The Text in Context

"They laid the sick in the marketplaces and besought Jesus that they might touch his garment..." (6:56). This summary scene sets up the next episode, where we will see the contrast between the Nazarene who seeks out human contact with the sick and unclean in the town square, and the Pharisees who consider such public spaces so threatening that "when they come from the marketplace do not eat before they purify themselves" (7:3).

Jesus again takes on the scribal-Pharisaic coalition over the issue of table fellowship and the purity code (7:1; see Chapter 3). This is a three-part episode:

7:1-5:   Mark explains purity issues involved;

7:6-13:   Jesus responds by counter-attacking Pharisaic authority;

7:14-23:   Jesus returns to original issue of meal sharing, offering another "parable."

The deeper question here is whether the table will be a place where in-group boundaries are maintained or where the "outsider" may be embraced. This controversy story is followed by two healings that provide object lessons in the principle of inclusion (7:24-30 and 31-37).

Read Mark 7:1-13

The disciples apparently refuse to abide by certain purification rites at table (7:2). The washing of hands, produce, and utensils had nothing to do with hygiene; it concerned the symbolic removal of impurity (7:3f). These rituals, together with exclusive dietary rules, functioned politically (defining ethnic identity) and socially (who one ate with and what one ate reflected one's status in the class hierarchy).

The fact that Mark sets this debate in relation to the "marketplace" also suggests an economic dimension in the background. Pharisaic regulators were concerned that marketplace food had been rendered unclean at some stage (i.e., seed sown on the Sabbath or fruits harvested without properly separating out tithes), and sought to control such "contamination." Many Galilean peasants resented these Pharisaic "middlemen" in the processes of production, distribution, and consumption of produce.

The Pharisees are accusing the disciples of group disloyalty and are defending their own social and economic status as purity regulators. But here their charge is more specific: The disciples are ignoring the "tradition of the elders" (7:5). The "tradition of the elders" referred to a body of legal interpretation that the Pharisees claimed was handed down orally alongside the written Torah. Jesus refuses to recognize the authority of this oral law, portraying it as "human tradition" in contrast to the "commandment of God" (7:8f). He then quotes a canonical text to underline his point (7:6f = Isaiah 29:13). The allusion is germane: Isaiah's oracle denounces false prophets (29:10) and people who "cannot read" (29:12), and contends that "the wisdom of their wise shall perish" (29:14)!

Jesus then takes "case law" to illustrate how the Pharisees "abandon the commandment of God and hold fast to human tradition" (Mark 7:9). He argues in 7:10 that Torah enjoins a responsibility to provide economic support for one's aging parents (see Exodus 20:12) and conversely condemns those who would try to escape this obligation by pronouncing a curse (see Exodus 21:17). He accuses the Pharisees of circumventing this obligation by allowing people to will their estates to the Temple (declaring them *korban*, 7:11). Such vows of dedication froze one's assets until at death they were released to the Temple treasury, for which they represented an important source of revenue. But because this practice leaves one's parents financially ostracized, Jesus argues, the "vow" to the Temple becomes a "curse" upon the elderly (7:12), and "nullifies the command of God" (7:13).

Mark, who began this episode by linking the Pharisees with the Jerusalem scribes (7:1), will later indict both the scribal class and the Temple treasury as parts of an economic system that exploits the poor (12:38-44; see Chapter 19). The principle here is the same as the one we saw in earlier conflict stories: Jesus puts those who are vulnerable (in this case the dependent elderly) before the demands of institutions and the sophistry of the privileged. Mark is again trying to show how "piety" can pre-empt justice.

Read Mark 7:14-23

All groups establish boundaries to determine who is in and who is out. Boundaries can be a good thing, such as when they help protect weaker people from domination by stronger people. But while this "defensive" function is usually cited as justification for boundaries, more often the actual relations of power are the opposite: Boundaries function to separate the strong from the weak, protecting privilege and maintaining inequality. It is such boundaries that Jesus consistently challenges, as he does now with the purity strategy of the kosher diet (7:14).

"There is nothing which goes into a person that can defile; only that which comes out of a person defiles" (7:15). The next verse characterizes this saying as a parable, in which the physical body is a metaphor of the body politic (7:17). Jesus contends that the social boundaries constructed by the purity code are powerless to protect the integrity of the community. "Contamination" can only arise from within the community.

Mark's editorial comment interprets this to mean that Jesus "declared all foods clean" (7:19). That is, the kosher diet must no longer function as a culturally exclusive boundary that proscribes table fellowship with non-Jews. Mark agrees with both Luke (see Acts 10:9-16) and Paul (see Romans 14) that obstacles to building community with Gentiles must be removed. This will be confirmed by Mark's next episode in which Jesus welcomes a foreigner "to the table" (7:24-37; below).

In conclusion Jesus gives his alternative: The true "site of purity" is not the body but the heart, the traditional moral center of a person in Hebrew anthropology (7:18-20). A vice list follows, alluding in part to the prophet Hosea's denunciation of public crime in Israel: theft, adultery, and murder (7:21 = Hosea 4:2). Jesus thus redraws the lines of group identity: The ethnocentricity of the purity code is replaced by the rigor of collective ethical self-scrutiny, a radical proposition for a first-century Jew.

Read Mark 7:24-30

Having presented a healing doublet in "Jewish" territory (5:21-43; see Chapter 7), Mark now narrates a corresponding doublet in Gentile territory (7:24-37). Jesus journeys to the region of Tyre and Sidon, a coastal area considered well outside the scope of Palestinian Jewish society (7:24a). The healings that take place here serve as object lessons in the inclusivity just advocated.

The woman who falls at Jesus' feet appealing on behalf of her off-stage daughter (7:25f) reminds us of Jairus, but she represents a world remote from that of the synagogue leader. Because we are unfamiliar with what constituted social propriety in Hellenistic antiquity, we miss the scandal of this encounter. In conventional Mediterranean "honor culture," it would have been inconceivable for an unknown, unrelated woman to approach a man in the privacy of his residence. Worse, this woman is a Gentile soliciting favor from a Jew. Mark's description is emphatic: She is "Greek, a Syrophoenician by birth" (7:26).

This affront explains Jesus' initial rebuff, which modern readers may find troubling (7:27). He is responding as any normal Jewish male would, defending the collective honor of his people. Jesus' insult may echo a rabbinic saying of the time: "He who eats with an idolater is like one who eats with a dog" (see also Exodus 22:31). But the stipulation that "the children must first be satisfied" suggests a deeper symbolic issue.

The theme of eating has recurred throughout this narrative section (as in 2:15-28; see Chapter 3). The disciples go on mission "without bread" (6:8) even as Herod throws an opulent banquet (6:21). The crowds are "satisfied" in the wilderness feeding (6:36ff) yet the disciples do not understand the "meaning of the bread" (6:52). And in the controversy with the Pharisees, we are twice told that the disciples were eating bread with unwashed hands (7:2, 5; omitted in most translations).

This motif is sustained by the Syrophoenician woman's bold and surprising retort: "Yes Lord, but even the dogs under the table eat the crumbs meant for the children" (7:28). Protocol has now been strained to the breaking point as she dares to turn Jesus' words back upon him. Yet she is only defending the rights of her people to "the table."

The real jolt, however, is the story's conclusion. Jesus, who in Mark's story masters every other opponent in verbal riposte, concedes the argument to her: "For saying that you may go—the demon has left your daughter" (7:29)!

Jesus has allowed his privileged status as a Jewish male to be severely affronted by a Gentile woman for the sake of inclusivity. So must the collective identity of Judaism suffer "indignity" (from the perspective of honor culture) by seeing its traditional social boundaries opened to welcome Gentiles. As Jesus' command in 5:43 anticipated the feeding of the crowds on the "Jewish" side of the sea, so does this story prefigure the feeding of the masses on the "Gentile" side (8:1ff). Both the "children" and the "outsiders" have been "satisfied" (the word is the same in 6:42, 7:27, and 8:4, 8). Not only is "all food clean" (7:19); all are welcome at the table.

Read Mark 7:31-37

Mark anticipated that this radical message would fall on deaf ears. So it is no accident that his "telling" (7:14ff) and "showing" (7:24ff) the principle of inclusion is followed by the healing of a Gentile man unable to speak or hear! The episode comes at the conclusion of a southeastward itinerary that symbolically embraces all the Gentile territory surrounding Galilee (7:31).

This healing echoes many of the other healings in the first half of Mark, as if to "summarize" the compassionate mission of Jesus. The Decapolis was the place where the Gerasene demoniac was earlier liberated from Legion (5:19). As with the bleeding woman (5:25ff), the purity code is reversed when Jesus spits on his fingers and touches the man's dysfunctional ears and tongue (7:33; see Leviticus 15:8). As in the case of Jairus's daughter, an Aramaic healing word is used (7:34; see 5:41). And as with the leper (1:41ff), Jesus' admonitions against publicity are ignored (7:36).

The inclusive Jesus can make even Gentiles "hear" and "speak" (7:37; see Isaiah 35:5f). Yet we will soon see that his own disciples remain deaf (see 8:18). This irony begins to refocus the narrative on the real mission of Jesus: To bring people out of denial toward discipleship.

THE WORD IN OUR WORLD

The story of the Syrophoenician woman is the central object lesson in this section's argument for inclusivity. What does this sister—strong and courageous—say to us today? On whose behalf does she call for healing and exorcism? To whom does she speak? Who is her daughter? Who heeds her voice?

This woman—marginalized by race, gender, and class—taught Jesus something about the inclusivity of God's realm. Jesus comes to see more fully the radical inclusivity of the gospel he proclaims through the trust and daring of this woman. He is moved from the social norms of first-century Mediterranean "honor culture" that limited his vision and compassion. He is moved from a stance of excluding to one of including.

The cultural assumptions that place this woman on the margins because of her ethnicity and gender (and probably also her class, given that she is isolated from a male head-of-household) find their parallels in our society. We too live in a society in which status, privilege, and even the right to life are determined by class, race, gender, and sexual preference. We are called to dismantle the barriers that exclude.

One of the forces that creates barriers and holds oppression in place is privilege. Those of us in positions of privilege find it enormously difficult even to *recognize* our privilege. We assume that all people have the privilege which we take for granted, when in fact many do not.

Beginning to recognize privilege—although unsettling—is a *necessary* first step to overturning the systems and ideologies that marginalize. The following small-group exercise provides a useful tool for recognizing privilege. With a small group, perhaps from your faith community, focus the exercise on one of the following: male privilege, white privilege, class privilege, or heterosexual privilege. (If possible, choose a category according to which your group is diverse.)

Arrange chairs so that those with privilege (e.g., men, whites, the wealthy, heterosexuals) sit in an inner circle. The others sit on the outskirts of the circle. Those in the inner circle begin to name the "assets" of privilege that they "cash in on" at will. As the "assets" are named loudly and clearly, one person from the outskirts records them on large paper. After those in the inner circle are done, those on the outskirts add to the list. When the exercise is completed, all share their feelings with one another.

In order to catalyze your thinking, consider the following list of white privileges:

- When my son is fixing a friend's car radio, he is not in danger of being arrested for car theft.

- When I see paintings of God or Jesus Christ, the skin is the same color as mine.

– When I am told about our national heritage or about "civilization," I am shown that people of my color made it what it is.

– Whether I use checks, credit cards, or cash, I can count on my skin color not to work against the appearance of financial reliability.

– I can do well in a challenging situation without being called a credit to my race.

– I am never asked to speak for all the people of my racial group.

– I can swear, or dress in second-hand clothes, or not answer letters without having people attribute these choices to the bad manners, the poverty, or the illiteracy of my race.

(from McIntosh, *Race, Class and Gender*)

Where do we go from here? Jesus' example of learning from this woman and being moved by her to deeper faithfulness invites us to learn from her as well. Jesus' receptivity to her wisdom points to a critical truth: Oppressed people often have a profound analysis of social situations, and know the paths to justice. People in positions of authority need to heed them.

For example, the peasants and urban poor of El Salvador, Guatemala, Honduras, and Nicaragua knew and decried U.S. collusion in human rights abuses in their nations a decade before that complicity was acknowledged by the U.S. Congress and administration. Had U.S. authorities heeded those oppressed and resisting voices as Jesus heeded the voice of this oppressed and resisting woman, tens of thousands of lives might have been spared. Name other examples.

Similarly, it is when we finally allow ourselves to hear and heed the broken parts of our selves—rather than casting them away from our consciousness—that we can see more clearly the paths to our own inner healing.

Following Jesus' example of listening to and learning from this woman, listen for her voice in your world:

She speaks: My daughter is many. She is within you, broken and weeping and raging. She lives homeless on your streets. She is killed by your guns in Iraq, raped and tortured by your money in Central America. She goes to your schools hungry in the morning. She is the beautiful and suffocating earth. She seeks healing, liberation from the demons. Where do you see my daughter?

Sisters, know your strengths and use them for healing. My strengths were a clever mind, verbal dexterity, and an iron will. My request was granted because I used my gifts in the name of healing. Sisters, claim your strengths, honor them, and use them. What are the gifts you have been given for healing?

Sisters, brothers, don't back down in the face of injustice. Persist; in my persistence I was heard. Where will you struggle relentlessly for the healing of my daughters?

Where you sit in privilege at the expense of others, see it and defy it. I was a pagan and a woman; Jesus, compared to me, was a person of privilege. By the rules of his world, he should have turned me away. He did not.

In response to these challenges from the Syrophoenician woman, recall the group exercise on privilege. Make a commitment to be increasingly aware of privilege as you walk through daily life. Begin to point it out to your friends and associates.

Jesus must have been rattled to the core by what he learned from this woman regarding the gospel. We too may be rattled to the core as we allow our eyes to be opened. Jesus' friends and associates must have thought him nuts at times. What will people at your work and church and in your neighborhood think if you begin pointing to the privilege pervading everyday life? Do it. When fear threatens to stop you, face it squarely, and look into the eyes of this woman and this Jesus.

Chapter 10

Do We Understand Yet?
Mark 8:1-21

THE TEXT IN CONTEXT

Read Mark 8:1-12

The way for inclusive table fellowship having been cleared, Mark now narrates a second wilderness feeding story in "Gentile" territory (see 7:31). Though briefer, this episode reiterates the essential themes of the first (see Chapter 8). Jesus is again moved by the plight of the crowd: "If I should send them away hungry they will faint on the way" (8:3). Mark seems to be alluding to Psalm 107: "Some wandered in desert wastes, finding no way to an inhabited town; hungry and thirsty, their soul fainted within them" (107:4f).

But the disciples' response is once again constrained by the dominant economic system: "How can anyone find bread for all these people in the wilderness?" (8:4). So once more Mark outlines the alternative: Jesus determines how much bread is on hand and organizes the disciples to "pass it on" to the people to share (8:5f). And once more the result is that "all were satisfied," with surplus (8:8). There is indeed more than enough for the "children" and the "dogs." Jesus then completes the circuit back to Dalmanutha on the "Jewish" side of the Sea (8:10).

Given this extraordinary sharing of bread among insiders and outsiders, it is hardly surprising that the Pharisees appear again in order to "argue" with Jesus and "test" him (8:11). Their demand for a "sign from heaven" begins Mark's first interpretive epilogue, in which he invites the reader-listener to review the symbols of the first half of his gospel.

Jesus' refusal to give a sign to "this generation" (8:12) is the first important clue to a proper reading of this story. The Pharisees' demand is ironic given the fact that Jesus has just re-enacted again the great sign-story of Exodus: manna in the wilderness. The lesson here is that the true indicators of God's sovereignty are not heavenly but earthly. In Mark, "signs and wonders" are unreliable for discerning the true meaning of history (see 13:22), and the only "heavenly" spectacle seen by "this generation" will be the advent of the Human One (8:38f; see Chapter 11).

Read Mark 8:13-21

Mark has already identified the disciples as being "hard hearted because they did not understand about the loaves" (6:52). It is this mysterious business that becomes the focus of the third and final boat voyage, as Jesus departs one last time for "the other side" (8:13). But this crossing involves neither storm nor rescue—only a conversation about bread.

Jesus' warning about "the leaven of the Pharisees and of the Herodians" is the second clue in Mark's interpretive epilogue (8:15). He is referring to two powerful groups aligned against his campaign of justice and inclusion (see 3:6). The Pharisaic movement's enforcement of purity code exclusion will be opposed to the discipleship community's commitment to open table fellowship. The Herodian ruling elite, meanwhile, will promote cultural assimilation and collaboration with Rome (see 12:13-17), but neutralize any who criticize their sovereignty (as John found out in 6:14ff).

Such "leaven" threatens the "bread" that is itself the third clue. The issue here concerns a distinction between the singular and plural, so some literal translation will help:

> The disciples had forgotten to bring loaves, and had only one loaf with them in the boat... (8:14)

> And they discussed it with one another saying: "We have no loaves." (8:16)

> Jesus said to them, "Why do you discuss the fact that you have no loaves?" (8:17)

Jesus now begins interrogating the disciples—and the reader —about whether or not we have understood the meaning of his symbolic actions.

The disciples' faculties of comprehension are called into question: They have hard hearts, blind eyes, and deaf ears (8:17f). Isaiah's realism (cited back in 4:11f) that "outsiders" would resist the Jubilee gospel now applies to "insiders" as well. Mark is also alluding to Moses' censure of Israel for failing to recognize the "signs" of Yahweh, as did the Pharisees (see Deuteronomy 29:2-4). Like Moses, Jesus exhorts the disciples to "remember" (8:18; see Deuteronomy 32:7).

This is also Mark's signal to the reader to review the narrative, as Jesus reiterates the symbolic number-clues (8:19f). The five loaves and twelve baskets left over in the first wilderness feeding represent the Jewish world (the books of Moses, the tribes of Israel). The seven loaves and baskets left over in the second feeding symbolize the inclusion of the Gentile world (in Jewish numerology seven was the symbol of completion). To make this clear Mark even uses different terms for "basket"; the first feeding story uses a Jewish term and the second uses a Greek term.

"Do you not yet understand?" (8:21). It is as if Mark is warning us not to proceed with the rest of the story until we have correctly comprehended the "meaning of the loaves." The social, economic, and political implications of Jesus' Jubilee practice have been spelled out further in the double cycle of Mark 4–8. There is only "one loaf" around which the church is called to gather, and it symbolizes enough for everyone.

Do we "see"? In the realism of Mark's gospel, the answer is probably "no." His portrait of the disciples will show how incomprehension can turn to antagonism (see 8:32) and finally to defection (see 14:50). Yet Mark will open the second half of his story with a symbol of hope: the healing of a blind man (8:22-26). At that point Jesus abruptly abandons the site of boat and sea, and sets out on the boldest and most dangerous journey of all: the long march to Jerusalem.

THE WORD IN OUR WORLD

Mark's portrait of Jesus as a boundary crosser ought to disturb us, given our world of explicit and implicit apartheid, vast economic disparity, and institutionalized enmity. The imperatives to cross the stormy seas of racism, to give priority to those who are poor, and to rediscover human solidarity are urgent today. In this text Jesus warns disciples that they must be ever-vigilant about the ways in which, like leaven, the practice of exclusion and domination can subtly ruin the one loaf of community. Where has the church become infected by such leaven?

To understand the depth of this challenge to the contemporary church, we must grasp the profound shift that occurred in the year 313 C.E., when the Emperor Constantine reversed the Roman empire's policy of hostility toward Christianity. Once the church was made the official religion of the Roman empire, the perspective of the church began to shift from the bottom to the top, from the margins to the center, from those who had no power to those in power.

Since that time, this shift has shaped not only our interpretation of the scriptures but our understanding of such fundamental issues as violence, war, and social justice. What was once the dynamic core of the gospel message, the realm of God, was replaced by a different message, the defense of the status quo.

In U.S. history, our religious traditions were used to rationalize the conquest of millions of indigenous people and the enslavement of millions of Africans. The European church provided theological justification for the conquerors and tried to inculcate in those conquered a religion of passivity and fatalism. It is important to examine how Christian tradition has been misappropriated in U.S. history, in order to see the ways in which this may be happening in our contemporary context.

Jesus' warning about the leaven is intended for people of faith who are committed to understanding how the politics of domination and exclusion can infect our lives as individuals and communities. Liberation theology invites us to practice a "hermeneutic of suspicion," which means that we bring to the task of interpretation a healthy suspicion about the ways in which our self-interest might shape our reading of text or context.

How would we apply a "hermeneutic of suspicion" to the church's stance on issues of race, class, and gender? Sometimes the leaven of institutional racism is much more difficult to identify than blatant personal racial prejudice because the former is embedded in structures that are presented as colorblind. Has our reading of scripture been undermined by the leaven of the belief that capitalism is the economy of choice in the realm of God? What does it mean that the church generally understands its public mission as charity, rather than as redistributive justice? How has our common life and tradition been compromised and skewed by the influence of male privilege?

Bring the "hermeneutic of suspicion" to bear on the concrete ministries in which you or your faith community are involved. Examine some of the assumptions behind what you do. Look at what your institutional self-interests might be in this work. What is your analysis of the "problem" you are trying to solve? How do you define success or failure? To what values or texts do you appeal for your rationale? How do you see yourself as "change agent"? Who makes decisions for whom, and how is power exercised? How do you see the ones who are the objects of your concern or service and how would you characterize your relationship to them?

Look at your geneagram. How might your personal-family story have been shaped and determined by the leaven of race, class, gender, or nationalism?

As late as the 1950s, the mainstream Christian denominations were still dominant institutions in our society. But that time is past. For some in the church, this is an institutional crisis that requires a recasting of our message to be more in tune with the needs of mainstream culture. Loren Mead, author of *The Once and Future Church*, sees it differently. He suggests that the decline of the institutional church in America is an opportunity to reclaim what was painfully clear to the first Christians: that the church should be a community existing on the margins whose mission begins with those on the margins—the refugee, the abused woman, the unemployed, the homeless, the exploited land itself. Such a church faithful can be a "voice crying in the wilderness," providing an alternative to the dominant culture.

Doing Bible study or ministry in a cross-cultural context will open up and make evident certain blinders and biases that would not ordinarily be noticeable in us. Not everything that the poor tell us is the truth of the gospel, but we cannot know the truth of the gospel without listening to the poor.

People who live and work on the margins have the authority to challenge us to read reality and text from a different perspective, from the "underside" of history. This term, which appeared in the writings of Dietrich Bonhoeffer, has become a framework for critical reflection in liberation theology. How can we internalize the view from below?

At this critical juncture in Mark's story, we pause to review the lessons that we are learning as disciples. Depict your own journey as a reader through this story. Go back to the beginning of Mark's story and diagram what you have experienced using any symbols or images that convey your interaction with the text.

Where have you experienced "call" as an invitation to discipleship? Where have you been tempted in the wilderness? Where have you asked for healing or been confronted by demons? Where have you known the terror of a dangerous crossing to the other side? Whom have you met there? Who has offered or withheld hospitality? Wherever the story has impacted you as blessing, challenge, or insight, illustrate that now in a graphic depiction of your own discipleship story. Use images and issues raised in the first half of Mark's gospel.

OUR DISCIPLESHIP JOURNEY

Mark's dramatic stories of sea crossings suggest that the journey of solidarity will not be easy, neither the crossing nor the encounter with those we meet on the other side. We all recognize a border when we cross from one nation into another. But other borders define us as well: racial and ethnic borders; borders between genders and people with different sexual orientations; class boundaries evident as we move from one neighborhood into another.

A border can be a barrier that separates us or a meeting place, a wall from which we defend ourselves or a place of contact. A border can define our comfort zone as well as the limit beyond which we will not venture. A border can be a place of violence or a place of justice, respect, and the mutuality of giving and receiving. It can be a place of stereotypes or of understanding. Our experience of borders is largely defined by how we view the one on the other side.

If hospitality and respect for difference were among the social and political values at play in our world, borders would not be so critically important. But too often, political, ethnic, religious, or racial boundaries are tools for those who have wealth and power to avoid redistribution of any kind. Borders thus become instruments for exclusion and marginalization—camouflage for injustice or human rights violations. How can we challenge and overcome the oppressive use of borders that exclude, limit, or dehumanize others?

What are the borders that define our social existence? Is Jesus asking your community to cross to the other side? What might that journey look like in our lives? It may be literally going to another country and experiencing solidarity with those who speak a different language. Yet that may be easier in some ways than the task of crossing to the other side of our own community.

Maybe there are people in our congregations with whom we feel unsafe or uncertain as to how we are to relate. Perhaps there are borders even in our families, or in our deepest selves. Perhaps we are called to cross over to a part of our own humanity that we have been unable to accept or even to acknowledge.

We understand the human need for borders and boundaries that help us know who we are and who we are not. We all need safe and familiar places. But how do we view the one who stands on the other side of the border? We are constantly faced with individuals and communities who dress, speak, think, and act differently from us. Sometimes those differences are appealing to us. We feel enriched, honored, and enlivened by the encounter with those who are different. In other cases, however, we make assumptions about those who differ from us, feel threatened by them, allow fear to shape our perception.

The most dangerous aspect of these feelings is that often we are unaware of them. We marginalize the "other" without realizing it. The first step of the journey to the other side, then, is to face honestly our own feelings about the people we encounter there.

Take some time to reflect on the following questions. Write your responses in your discipleship journal:

Who were the "others" in the community of your childhood and youth? Perhaps they were poor people, homeless people, people of a different race, or unwed mothers. How did your family relate to them? Who are the outcasts in your family and what made them so?

How do you believe your family or ethnic group was viewed by those of different race, class, or religion?

What borders have you crossed in your life? What has been your experience of the other side of humanity both in your childhood and in your adult faith journey? What have those experiences taught you about crossing borders? Has this experience been mutually acceptable to those on the other side of the border? What guidelines did you have for being on the other side?

III
THE DISCIPLESHIP "CATECHISM"

OPENING MEDITATION

(A journal entry of one of the authors) Deny yourself. What do you mean deny yourself? No! I say LIVE. Mark, you've got it wrong! Life—every speck of it—was created good. You would squelch it with centuries of "deny yourself"!

Yes, I have "denied myself," in that deep and misdirected way—almost until death. And a voice within me says, "Precious sister, live." This is a true voice, clear and sweet and strong. I am not mistaken in knowing this voice to be Light, to be Life, to be God. The God that I am growing to hear does not tell me to deny my *self*.

And what of those who run after buying things, and after "looking good," and after "military might," and after being "better than"? If we would all learn to hear the voice of God that says "live" instead of building plastic castles, then the world would not know the agony in which it writhes. Of that I am sure.

Yet there is truth in what you say, Mark. A colleague told a story of her visit to Soweto two years before institutionalized apartheid ended. A small group of black people who live in Soweto, together with a small group of white people from Johannesburg, had formed a church in Soweto. They worshiped together, seeking reconciliation. My friend said, "Both the white people and the black people were conscious that they might have paid for this with their lives." So, for them, Mark, your story rings true. They were denying self, taking up a cross, and following. . . .

Perhaps the answer is that in some contexts—for example, that of the reconciling church in Soweto—to follow Jesus requires one to deny self and take up the cross; but in our context, where circumstances are not so brutal, to follow means something else. *No, this notion does not hold water.* In our land too our brothers and sisters are murdered daily by poverty; mothers lose their children at the hands of racism; people are strangled with billboards and commercials, plant closings, and mandates to inject violence and sex into television programming. Certainly we live in a culture no less broken or cruel than did Jesus, for whom living a different way led to torture and death.

Mark, I know you to be right also in a more personal way. When has my life been its clearest, truest, most deeply centered? In times of deep giving—including risking my life. Is there something significant about denying self out of love rather than out of obligation? To be a disciple in Jesus' context meant not only following the teacher's example, but also having a loving commitment to him that surpassed all other commitments. Maybe here I catch a glimpse?

Yet still, Mark, you are a paradox. (Perhaps if I accept you as paradox, rather than hungering for resolution, I will hear you more clearly.) The paradox is that I also know life to be at its truest and clearest in times of simple intimacy. My heart sings and my soul dances in spaces of touching others deeply; times when I do *not* deny myself and take up the cross, but rather relish in the wonder of simple life and love; when I unfold and swim deeper into self or into another. These too are times of knowing God.

It is in seeking my life this way that I find it. And I believe that the angels rejoice with God in those times. In seeking myself underneath the rubbish that has been piled on, in letting myself sing the glorious song of love, and freedom which is given to all creatures— in this do I find life. And God rejoices.

Chapter 11

The Second Call to Discipleship
Mark 8:22–9:1

THE TEXT IN CONTEXT

We have arrived at the midpoint of Mark's story. The first half began heralding a "Way" (1:2), and closed with a question addressed to the disciples and the reader: "Do you not yet understand?" (8:21). The second half opens "on the Way" (8:27), with yet another query: "Who do you say that I am?" (8:29a).

Do we really know who Jesus is, and what he is about? It is a shock to discover here that Peter's "correct" answer (8:29b) is silenced (8:30). This is followed by a "confessional crisis" (8:30-33) and Jesus' second call to discipleship (8:34ff), which together represent the fulcrum upon which the whole gospel balances. Mark's thesis is most clearly revealed here: Discipleship is not about theological orthodoxy but about the Way of the cross.

This section is punctuated by three "predictions" in which Jesus speaks of his impending arrest, trial, and execution by the authorities (8:31, 9:31, 10:33f). After each portent Mark indicates that the disciples have failed to comprehend. This in turn issues in three teaching cycles, each of which revolves around a paradoxical antithesis:

"Whosoever would save her life will lose it..." (8:35)

"If anyone would be first, he must be last..." (9:35)

"Whosoever would be great among you must be your servant..." (10:43)

Throughout Mark, Jesus' use of "whosoever" functions as an appeal to the audience, as if there is a blank space we are challenged to fill in with our name. This is an "interactive" story!

This triple cycle has the catechetical character of a "school of the road," as Jesus and his disciples journey from the far north of Palestine to the outskirts of Jerusalem.

Geography	Portent	Incomprehension	Teaching
1) Caesarea-Philippi	8:31	8:32f	8:34ff
2) Galilee to Judea	9:31	9:32-34	9:35ff
3) to Jerusalem	10:32-34	10:35-37	10:39ff

The "Way of the cross" will be explained by object lessons, both positive and negative. The catechism is framed by two stories in which the blind receive sight: in Bethsaida (8:22-26) and in Jericho (10:45-52).

Read Mark 8:22-26

The first half of the gospel concludes on the depressing note that the disciples' "faculties of perception" (eyes, ears, and heart) have failed them (8:18-20). It is no accident then that the second half opens with the story of a blind man, which is part of Mark's counter-narrative to the disciples' "blindness and deafness":

- Jesus heals a deaf and dumb man (7:31-37);

- Jesus heals a blind man (8:22-26);

- Jesus casts out a deaf and dumb spirit (9:14-29);

- Jesus heals a blind man who follows him (10:46-52).

These final four healings in Mark suggest that if Jesus can "make the deaf hear and the dumb speak" (7:37) and help the blind to "see clearly" (8:25), then there is hope for disciples.

"Do you see anything?" (8:23). Jesus' question to the blind man at Bethsaida has prophetic echoes. "What do you see?" asked the God of Amos (Amos 8:2) and the angel of Zechariah (Zechariah 4:2). "Sight" now emerges as a central metaphor for faith in Mark. The man's partial restoration (symbolizing the confused state of the disciples) requires a second touch by Jesus (8:24f). This two-stage healing suggests that the reader must now grapple with the second part of Mark's story in order to "see things clearly."

Read Mark 8:27-33

Since Mark's first storm episode, the issue of Jesus' identity has been lingering in the background (4:41). Now Mark turns to address it directly. The public's perception of Jesus parallels the three misinterpretations reported earlier concerning John (6:14-16). But when the disciples are asked for their opinion, Peter hails Jesus as "Messiah" (8:29).

We meet this politically loaded term for the first time since the story's title (1:1). The Messiah was understood by many Jews in first-century Palestine to be a royal figure who would someday restore the political fortunes of Israel. Based upon Mark's title and the centrality of this confession in the church, we are likely to approve of Peter's identification. But, to our chagrin, Peter is immediately silenced by Jesus (8:30), as if he were just another demon trying to "name" Jesus (see 1:25, 3:12)! Then, with the phrase, "Jesus began to teach them that it was necessary that the Human One must suffer," the story departs in a new direction (8:31).

Jesus' predictions have been used by conservatives as proof of his divine clairvoyance and dismissed by liberals as later theological interpretation. Both miss Mark's point. By "necessity" Mark means that those who pursue the justice of Jubilee will inevitably clash with the powers. Mark is also serving notice that Jesus will not enter Jerusalem as a triumphant military leader, but rather will be executed by the authorities. This subverts the expected Messianic "script," replacing it with what we might call a "prophetic script." At key points in the second half of the gospel Mark will appeal to this script: John followed it, so will Jesus (see 9:12f), and so will faithful disciples (see 13:9-13).

The first portent also replaces the term Messiah with the third person "Human One," the persona who earlier challenged the debt system and restored the Sabbath tradition of Jubilee (2:10, 28; see Chapters 2 and 3). But the name is taken from the apocalyptic vision of Daniel 7, which provides the key to understanding Jesus' second call to discipleship (see below).

"And he spoke this word plainly" (8:32). But Peter, like most of Christendom after him, refuses to accept this clear revisioning of the meaning of Messiah. The exchange thus escalates into a series of sharp rebukes, ending in Jesus' "counter-naming" of Peter (8:32f):

Peter: Jesus is Messiah
Jesus silences Peter
Jesus: Human One must suffer
Peter silences Jesus
Jesus again silences Peter
Jesus: Peter is aligned with Satan

What has poor Peter done to deserve such denunciation? The problem is that Peter remains loyal to the traditional Messianic script that affirms the "myth of redemptive violence," in which the hero prevails over the enemy through superior and "righteous" force (see Wink, 1992; Bailie, 1995; Beck, 1996). With this oldest lie Satan rules history, as nations and peoples invoke God while they destroy their enemies through "just wars" and crusades. Against this is pitted the Human One's strategy of nonviolence, which understands that the enemy is violence itself.

Read Mark 8:34-9:1

Jesus' first call to discipleship invited people to "leave" their places in the prevailing social and economic order and to "follow" him in reclaiming the vision of Jubilee and God's sovereignty (see Chapter 1). The second call now articulates the political consequences of that practice (8:34). Jesus' invitation begins where his argument with Peter left off:

"Get up and get *behind me . . .*" (8:33)

"If anyone desires to follow *behind me . . .*" (8:34)

Two conditions for discipleship are now stipulated: "Deny yourself and take up your cross."

The cross was not a religious icon in first-century Palestine, nor was "taking up the cross" a metaphor for personal anguish. Crucifixion had only one connotation: It was the vicious form of capital punishment reserved by imperial Rome for political dissidents. Crosses were a common sight when Mark wrote, since there was a Jewish insurrection under way. In contrast to Judean nationalists who were recruiting patriots to "take up the sword" against Rome, Mark's Jesus invited disciples to "take up the cross." The rhetoric of "self-denial," in turn, should be understood not in terms of private asceticism but in the context of a political trial. Under interrogation by state security forces, admitting allegiance to "Yahweh's sovereignty" would result in charges of subversion in a world where Caesar alone claimed lordship. Self-denial is about costly political choices.

Jesus next restates the matter another way. If one attempts to "save one's life" by denying Jesus and his Jubilee project (thus "being ashamed of me and of my words," 8:38a), one will lose true life (8:35). Conversely, to live and die "for my sake and the gospel" is truly to experience "life." These two choices will be dramatically juxtaposed in Mark's Passion narrative. Peter will "save himself" in the palace courtyard, only to break down after disowning Jesus (14:66-72). Right next door in the palace courtroom Jesus will confess the Human One (14:55-65)—and consequently "take up his cross" (15:25).

He then turns to an economic metaphor: Self-preservation at the cost of apostasy represents a bad investment, not a "profit" but a "forfeiture" (8:36f). We will later see Judas "sell out" for small change (14:11) at the cost of his soul (14:21). Jesus thus thrice reiterates that "gain" and "loss" should not be calculated according to the ledgers of the dominant culture. Unfortunately, most Christians have failed to experiment with the mysterious calculus of Jesus' nonviolence.

Jesus closes his homily by invoking a different vision of justice (8:38). Traditional exegesis has interpreted this verse in terms of the "Second Coming" of Jesus to secure the ultimate victory (violently, it is assumed). The key to understanding this "eschatological" scenario, however, lies in the heavenly courtroom vision of Daniel 7.

Background: Daniel's "Human One"

The book of Daniel was a manifesto of Jewish resistance written two centuries before the time of Jesus and Mark, during persecutions by the Hellenistic tyrant Antiochus Epiphanies IV. The first half of Daniel offers stories of heroism (Daniel 2–6). The second half switches to a different kind of genre—apocalyptic narrative—to make the same point. Apocalyptic was a popular, highly symbolic type of literature that often employed heavenly visions and angelic interpreters in order to offer veiled commentary on current political events.

Apocalyptic visions, commonly misconstrued by modern readers as predictions of the future, instead involve opening up another dimension to history: God's point of view. Apocalyptic dualism requires us to have a dual vision of reality in order to criticize "this age" from the perspective of "the age to come." Yet these two realms actually co-exist; we need only "eyes to see" them both.

Read Daniel 7

The prophet first "sees" oppressive rulers (the "beasts" of Daniel 7:2-8) who persecute the Jews (7:19-25). But the eyes of faith reveal what is really happening ("As I looked..." 7:9). At the center of the vision is a courtroom scene in which the "Ancient of Days" judges the beasts (7:9-12, 26f) and hands over true authority to the "saints" (7:18). Judgment is rendered on behalf of a "Human One" who makes an entrance "on the clouds of heaven" (7:13). This is the image Mark employs in his gospel (see Mark 14:62).

Daniel's apocalyptic visions assured persecuted Jews who were defendants in Hellenistic courts that there was a "higher court of true justice" in which they were being vindicated even as they were being convicted by Antiochus. Mark adopts the "bifocal" apocalyptic perspective of Daniel: There is not one courtroom in which the believer stands, but two. To be acquitted before the powers is to be "ashamed" in the Human One's court, and vice versa. This explains how Mark can present the Human One simultaneously as both defendant (8:31) and prosecutor (8:38)! Apocalyptic faith gives not only meaning but a mysterious efficacy to nonviolent suffering: To die (rather than to kill) for justice in history somehow advances the vindication glimpsed in the heavenly court.

This also helps us understand Jesus' concluding promise that "this generation will see the sovereignty of God come in power" (9:1). As we shall see (Chapter 24), it alludes to Mark's "third apocalyptic moment" of Jesus' crucifixion. Only apocalyptic faith can help us see that at the very moment the powers appear to have triumphed, Jesus' nonviolent power has begun to unravel their rule of domination.

THE WORD IN OUR WORLD

What does "deny self, take up the cross, and follow me" mean for us—Christians living in an imperial society that has stretched its political and economic arms around the globe, seizing the resources and overriding the self-determination of other peoples? What does it mean for us to deny ourselves, take up our cross, and follow the executed and living Jesus in our context as citizens of the United States? To avoid this question is to refuse to encounter the powerful challenge of this text in our contemporary world.

From our reading of the text, we see that to "take up our cross" has specific political and physical implications. Taking up the cross does *not* mean shouldering the personal burdens put before one in life and carrying on in the hope of heavenly rewards. Study of the text negates this spiritualized and privatized interpretation.

Jesus was speaking of the "execution stake" that is the consequence of posing a threat to entrenched powers. Yet this Jesus bears life for all. How is it that his call to follow him to the execution stake can be a call to life?

An understanding of the cross can be life-affirming only if it acknowledges and refutes historic abuses of the cross as symbol. For example, Jesus' call to "deny self" *as it has been applied to women* by Christian conventional wisdom—and as internalized by women —has been not a seed of life as Jesus promised (8:35b), but rather a source of bondage and repression. "Bear the cross" has been an admonition to deny one's own experience, needs, pain, pleasure, and rights. It has meant servanthood, not in the sense of *diakonia,* but in the sense of woman as man's *lesser* helper or slave. This was and is even more the case for women of color forced into slavery and servanthood by white America's assumptions of supremacy. Throughout history such abuse of the gospel and of women has had immeasurable social and human cost.

A contemporary example illustrates what Jesus' call to "deny self" does *not* mean. A homeless woman who lives at a church was troubled following a sermon about the idolatry of self-centered life. She was guilt-ridden about the time she was investing to reclaim her life from the hell of drug addiction. This woman never had a self of which she was conscious. Instead she became who others expected and demanded her to be. This led to self-contempt, which in turn led to addiction. For this woman (and so many like her), the Word of God is not to deny self and lose life, but to find life, to heal, to restore wholeness, to love self. So doing requires saying no to self-denial as conventional Christian wisdom has understood it.

When self-sacrifice is defined as negation of self it is destructive for women and others conditioned by society to "selflessness." This understanding of Christian love has been particularly shaped by European and Euro-American patriarchal traditions. Male theologians, for example, defined sin as rooted in self-assertion, pride, and will-to-power. For them, the highest form of love is this self-sacrifice, which is equated with a negation of self-love. This is exemplified in the view expressed by the theologian Anders Nygren: "Christianity does not recognize self-love as a legitimate form of love. Christian love moves in two directions, toward God and toward its neighbor; and in self-love it finds its chief adversary which must be fought and conquered."

The growing participation of more women in theological discourse has engendered radically different definitions of sin and Christian love. Many emphasize God's love of every being with unquenchable love. Created to love as God loves, we are invited to love every being, including self. Sin is understood to include negation of self, damaged personhood, brokenness. Christian love may thus be redefined to include the true self-love that heals and empowers us to love deeply, thus healing others and society. Self-love and other-love no longer are understood as opposing forces. On the contrary, self-love is the integral prerequisite to profound other-love.

The gospel invitation to deny self, then, does not refer to the negation of experience, selfhood, human rights, or physical integrity. Rather it challenges the self as the center of one's universe. It calls us out of life centered in individualism and self-interest and into life according to God's love.

The call to follow, then, is a call to walk in a path of radical love that challenges oppressive power structures. This can lead to danger and possibly to death because we live out this call in the midst of overwhelming forces of greed and violence. Mark does not suggest that suffering and death are God's will for Jesus or for disciples. Jesus' suffering is not to be "imitated." Jesus did not desire execution or see sacrifice as a virtue. He accepted (apparently with fear and trembling) his death as the inevitable *consequence* of living an all-encompassing love that challenged oppressive power structures. Suffering, in the form of loss and persecution, is thus presented as a consequence of discipleship.

To critique the Christian ethic of self-denial is as dangerous as not critiquing it. The critique can easily become a justification for serving one's self-interests first. Clearly this is not our intent. True Christian love—which entails self-love—refuses to place the self at the center of the universe. This in turn allows us to engage in struggle against historical forces that thwart the in-breaking reign of God. To "take up the cross," then, is to resist systems and structures that cause or perpetuate injustice. It is to rebuild systems grounded in justice, peace, and the integrity of creation.

Wholehearted commitment to this way *is* true life; not to choose this path is to choose death-in-life. The consequences of faithfulness to this way can be embraced only in the awareness that the end of this story is God's *yes* of resurrection life.

Where now does Jesus call you to take up the cross and follow him? Where in your life are you called to resist self-negation, the culture of violence, consumerism, or other forces of injustice? Be specific. What are the possible consequences of your following this path? What do you most fear? Remember that Mark's Jesus did not call people to walk the path of discipleship alone, but rather to do so in loving community. Who is the community that is called to be with you on this path?

To follow Jesus means not only to walk in his path but also to be in intimate relationship with him and the God to whom he prayed. It means being embraced by God's compassionate and self-giving love, to receive God's promises, and to be filled with the Spirit. How do you experience these gifts in your life as a community and as an individual?

Chapter 12

From Vision to Impotence
Mark 9:2-29

THE TEXT IN CONTEXT

Read Mark 9:2-8

The second call to discipleship is confirmed by the Transfiguration vision that immediately follows. The setting of this episode ("after six days Jesus...led them up a high mountain," 9:2) calls to mind one of the foundational stories of Exodus Israel:

> God said to Moses: "Come up to me on the mountain and stay there while I give you the stone tablets—the law and the commandments...." And Moses went up the mountain, and the glory of God settled on the mountain of Sinai; for six days the cloud covered it, and on the seventh day God called to Moses from inside the cloud. (Exodus 24:12, 16)

The Transfiguration represents the second "apocalyptic moment" in Mark's narrative. Just as Daniel's visions were explained by a man in glorified clothing (Daniel 10:5ff), so here the inner circle of disciples behold Jesus in shining white clothes, the apocalyptic symbol of martyrdom (see Revelation 3:5, 18; 4:4; 6:11; 7:9, 13).

Jesus is portrayed in conference with the two great heroes of Israel: Moses, representing the Law, and Elijah, representing the prophets (9:4). Perhaps they are encouraging Jesus, just as they themselves were exhorted by the voice of God during times of discouragement. Moses, rejected once by his own people, had to ascend the mountain a second time, but returned with his face transfigured (read Exodus 34:29-35). And Elijah, fleeing from the authorities he had challenged, was told, "Go out and stand on the mountain before God," who exhorted him to return to the struggle (read 1 Kings 19).

Peter, meanwhile, misunderstands for the second consecutive time (9:5). Still operating from a framework of tradition and triumphalism, he would institutionalize the moment by establishing a "tabernacle" for the three leaders. While constructing cults of admiration may be an age-old human religious impulse, Mark clearly disapproves of it (9:6). So Peter is again challenged, this time by the divine voice itself.

The first time a voice from the cloud intervened in Mark's narrative was at Jesus' baptism (1:11; see Chapter 1). The same testimony is now commended to the clueless disciples: "This is my beloved son" (9:7). But it is specifically Jesus' second call to discipleship that is endorsed here: "Listen to him." The episode's conclusion underscores the reliability of Jesus' teaching while dismissing Peter's attempt to institutionalize the Presence: "They looked around but no longer saw anyone but Jesus with them" (9:8).

Read Mark 9:9-13

As this group returns down the mountain we may recall what Moses saw upon his descent from Sinai (see Exodus 32). What happens here, however, is not Israel dancing around a golden calf but the disciples' deepening bafflement.

Jesus warns his companions that they won't understand the vision they have just witnessed until after the Human One has been raised from the dead (9:9). Mark tells us that the three disciples "held fast to the word" (that is, Jesus' word of the cross, 8:32) "while questioning among themselves what 'rising from the dead' meant" (9:10). This may well be Mark's instructions to the reader concerning the abrupt ending of his gospel. We will indeed "wonder" about the message that Jesus is risen (16:6); what is clear, however, is that we are still called to discipleship (see Chapter 25).

Despite having just been instructed by the voice from heaven to listen to Jesus, the three disciples are still preoccupied by the authority of the scribal class: "Why do the scribes say...?" (9:11). The belief that Elijah "must first return" to save the people from judgment would have been drawn from the closing verses of the book of Malachi: "Behold I send you Elijah the prophet...he will turn their hearts...lest I come and strike the land with a curse" (Malachi 4:5).

Its attribution to the scribes here may imply that the ruling elite understood this as a guarantee that they would be spared "the great and terrible Day of the Lord."

Jesus has bad news for this point of view, for as the gospel's prologue argues, "Elijah has come" (9:13; see Chapter 1). And as Mark narrates in 6:13ff, "Elijah" was executed by the authorities because they refused to "turn around." Mark thus closes the circle of argument begun in 8:28 concerning the "prophetic script":

A   How is it written about the Human One

B   that he will suffer and be repudiated

C   But I tell you Elijah has come

B1   and they did to him what they pleased,

A1   as it is written of him.

Jesus (also known as the Human One) and John the Baptist (also known as Elijah) share the inevitable political destiny of truthtellers.

Read Mark 9:14-29

Jesus returns from the mountain to find the rest of the disciples *also* arguing with the scribes (9:14)! Here, however, the issue is not scribal teaching but the disciples' own impotence. Though commissioned to exorcize (3:15), and successfully doing so earlier in the story (6:7), the disciples are here ridiculed by the crowd for not being "strong enough" (9:18). This is a harsh indictment for followers of the "stronger one" (1:7) committed to "binding the strong man" (3:27), and recalls the story of the Gerasene demoniac whom "no one was strong enough to bind" (5:4).

Yet they are confronting an especially insidious demon, a "spirit of silencing" who throws its victim to the ground, foaming at the mouth and paralyzed (9:17f). Jesus' response is one of frustration (9:19), which seems curious unless we see it as a hint that something broader is at stake in this story.

No sooner is the victim presented to Jesus than the demon strikes with full fury (9:20). Jesus' inquiry suggests that there may be a connection between the boy's condition and that of the "faithless generation":

How long has he had this? (9:21)

How long must I bear with you? (9:19)

The father's answer is irresistibly archetypal. The demon has silenced his son "since childhood" and aims to destroy him through "fire and water." Surely such language symbolizes the primal roots of the unresolved anguish and trauma that keeps human beings "silenced."

The next exchange is a poignant summary of the central theme of the gospel (9:23f):

Father:	If you can, have compassion and help us.
Jesus:	If you can! All things are possible to the one who believes!
Father:	I believe! Help me in my unbelief!

This exorcism story is thus revealed as a dramatization of the struggle for faith, symbolized by the vanquishing of the demon of silencing and the transformation from death to life (9:26f).

The metaphorical character of this episode is further indicated by the fact that the epilogue focuses not upon the exorcism but upon the disciples' continuing frustration with their impotence: "Why could we not cast it out?" (9:28). The structure of the story again helps interpret its meaning:

9:14-19:	the scribes and crowd accuse the disciples of impotence;
9:20-27:	Jesus interacts with the father, the boy, and the demon;
9:28f:	Jesus discusses impotence with the disciples.

This composition suggests that it is the *disciples* who are the true subjects of this story, impotent because they are "deaf and mute" to the Way of the cross. In other words, we cannot cast out demons by which we ourselves are possessed!

At the close of this story, and for the first time in Mark, Jesus exhorts the disciples to pray (9:29). But what does Mark mean by prayer? Jesus' prayer takes place in remote places (1:31; 6:46), in contrast to that of his opponents who exploit the public glare (12:40).

Jesus will invite his disciples to pray on just two other occasions. One is after his dramatic Temple action, when he urges the disciples to believe in the possibility of a world free of the exploitative Temple-state (11:23-25; see Chapter 16). The other is just before Jesus is seized by security forces, when he summons his followers to prayer as a way of "staying awake" to the Way of the cross (14:32-42; see Chapter 22). Note the similarities:

> "All things are possible to the one who believes." (9:23)

> "Amen, I tell you, whatever you ask in prayer, believe that you have received it..." (11:24)

> And he prayed... "All things are possible for you..." (14:36)

The powers rule in our hearts and in the world through the despair that persuades us that genuine personal and political transformation is impossible, and we have been socialized into such resignation "since childhood" (9:21). To pray is to re-center our consciousness around a faith that insists on the possibility and imperative of such transformation.

This episode suggests that prayer is the contemplative discipline of self-knowledge—an invitation to examine the roots of our impotence. If we wish to cast out *this* demon, we must engage in the difficult process of confronting the illusions that paralyze us and the unconscious power of repressed trauma that keeps us silenced.

THE WORD IN OUR WORLD

Perhaps we can remember times when someone we knew or loved was experiencing life so intensely, so joyously, that a kind of light radiated from their face and eyes. This is a pale analogy of what Mark is trying to describe in this story of transfiguration. In rare moments the glory of the new creation breaks in upon human life, as visible as sun beams that gradually pierce a cloud bank until more and more light streams through. Time that is thick with *chronos* becomes a *kairos* moment—transparent to that which is beyond past or present or future.

But what is this all about and what does it have to do with us? Is this just more mysticism that we can never experience ourselves?

Is it religiosity that carries us away from the world and from each other in private subjective experiences? So much of contemporary spirituality is precisely that: divorced from community and from the struggle of history. Or is this story of the Transfiguration about finding the perspective to understand what our history is really about?

Transfiguration moments happen when our stories become joined in their deepest core to the gospel story. From the mount of Transfiguration, the divine voice asks us again to listen! When we take seriously this discipleship journey, when we live in radical faithfulness, our stories begin to merge into a great Story like little drops of water that become rivulets, then streams and rivers, and finally rush into the ocean. We experience glory when we are given the grace to know that our story is inextricably related to that greater Story.

We are not alone but surrounded by a cloud of witnesses. Not just Elijah and Moses but all the apostles accompany us on this journey: Francis and Clare, Sojourner Truth, Martin Luther King and Steve Biko, Dorothy Day and Peter Maurin, Archbishop Romero, and everyone who has tried to be faithful to the gospel. That great Story is made up of thousands of individuals and communities who lived and struggled, who hoped and dreamed, who tasted success and failure, but who finally passed off the stage of history never knowing their glory, never knowing or being recognized for what they may have contributed to this history.

Take this opportunity to name some person of faith who for you is a part of the cloud of witnesses. Describe the qualities of faith and life that make that person so significant for you. You may even wish to have a dialogue with that person as you seek his or her counsel on how you are to remain faithful in your discipleship journey.

Mark's story takes us from the Transfiguration "high" on the mountaintop into the low valley of the scene portrayed in Mark 9:14-29. As we come down from the mountain with Jesus, what greets us is a chaotic scene of conflict and controversy in which the disciples have been unable to cast out a demon that endangers a young child. Each of us as Christians can probably tell a similar story of a time when we experienced failure or defeat.

What has happened when we have confronted evil or tried to solve a problem, and our best efforts have been met with defeat and failure? There is a kind of action-reflection process that is modeled by Jesus and his community, not just in this instance but in numerous places in the gospel story. It suggests that no one success or failure is final but is just a moment on the journey. Some of us by nature may find it difficult to reflect on anything before we are off to the next action or project. Others of us never seem to have enough information before we are ready to act.

But if in community we can see our common ministry as an action-reflection process, we can learn to look upon every moment, no matter how painful, as having something to teach us. In fact, failure can be a much more effective teacher than success. While success sometimes confirms our illusions of grandiosity, failure teaches us hard lessons about limits, about real motives and unexpected outcomes. Failure can mean disillusionment in the best sense: the sometimes painful process of giving up our illusions about ourselves and our world.

Ongoing evaluation is one of the most important spiritual disciplines of a faith community. The experience of failure can be a key moment for learning perseverance, for deepening our awareness of root causes, or for developing more effective strategies. Failure can teach us how to forgive ourselves and each other. Take the experience of a failure in the life of your community and reconstruct what happened. Ask yourselves: Why did it happen? What did it mean for us? What can we do about it?

Many times a bitter failure or defeat can be redeemed by some evaluation after the fact. A failure can become a code that allows us to see more clearly a core issue in the depths of our own soul or in the breadth of our society. Is this part of what Jesus was about when he called together the community in the privacy of a household to debrief the day? If we did more of that kind of reflection on ministry, we would surely deepen our analysis of the problems we face.

At an even deeper level, the text calls us to struggle with our own demons of unbelief because we cannot exorcise that by which we are still possessed. In your discipleship journal, name your addictions, confess the self-interest of your privileges. Share with one another the ways in which you are enslaved to destructive ways of living and being. Perhaps that naming will mean that we must honestly confess our powerlessness to change, to cast out the demons that possess us. This is the wisdom of 12-step programs—we begin to find the power to heal in the confession of our own powerlessness.

The most genuine expression of prayer is found in the father's heartfelt cry for compassion. "I believe! Help me in my unbelief." In prayer we journey toward the hidden places of our being where, if we are honest with ourselves, we encounter our brokenness and lack of freedom. There, in the ambiguous depths of the human heart, we encounter unbelief.

What shape does that unbelief take? For Mark, unbelief is not incorrect doctrine or an imperfect attitude. For Mark, unbelief is the despair that is dictated to us by the powers and principalities of this world. Unbelief is a life script that is fixed and says to us that nothing can really change. If we accept this life script and the despair that comes with it, the revolutionary vision and practice of the gospel are rendered impotent.

Prayer for Mark is that personal and communal struggle against this temptation to despair. It is wrestling with the demons within us that tempts us to abandon the way of Jesus. Prayer is naming and casting out the demons that silence us and make us docile before the status quo of self and society.

Without prayer and a spiritual foundation, prophetic anger becomes disconnected from love, ideals become empty routines, social analysis becomes cynicism, values lose their passion. The despair and unbelief that tempt us to hopelessness *will not* be disarmed until we name and face them together.

When Jesus asks us to deepen our prayer life in order to follow him, he is calling us to develop a spirituality of social action. Just as each person and community has a unique relationship with God, so prayer is different for each person and community. We encourage you and your community to explore and develop a prayer life that empowers your public discipleship.

Chapter 13

In Defense of the "Least"
Mark 9:30–10:16

The Text in Context

Mark's discipleship catechism now turns to the less heroic, yet perhaps more difficult, practice of the Way in daily life. For the cross is more than nonviolent resistance to the powers; it is the struggle against patterns of domination in interpersonal and social relationships as well.

The second teaching cycle is the longest of the three, addressing the following status issues: greatest and least (9:36f), outsiders and insiders (9:38-41), aggressors and victims (9:42-50), males and females (10:2-12), children and adults (10:13-16), and rich and poor (10:17-31). It exhibits certain similarities to catechetical traditions found elsewhere in the New Testament that concern questions of power in family and community life (for example, the so-called "house-tables" in Colossians 3:12-4:6).

Framing this section is the refrain that the "first will be last" and vice versa (9:35; 10:31). This is not offered as a mystical paradox. It represents a concrete ethic that begins, following Jesus' Jubilary logic, with the situation of the "least" in each of these social relationships. As previously illustrated in the story of Jairus and the bleeding woman (5:21-43; see Chapter 7), Jesus teaches that society can be transformed only from the bottom up.

Read Mark 9:30-41

The section begins with a second portent (9:30-32), followed by Jesus' exposé yet again of the disciples' "blindness-deafness." We should not miss the bitter irony in this vignette (9:33f). Their discipleship journey ("on the Way" is repeated twice) has degenerated into an internal power struggle. Worse, Mark indicts them exactly as he did the synagogue crowd back in 3:4: "But they were silent."

Presenting a child as an object lesson, Jesus now extends the second call to discipleship in different terms:

> If anyone desires to follow behind me let that one take up the cross... (8:34)

> If anyone desires to be first let that one be last among everyone and a servant of everyone. (9:35)

The church is not to be a power base for its members but a community that redistributes power to the excluded.

This point is underlined in the next episode. John boasts that he forbade an exorcist who was not "following us" to practice (9:38). Under the circumstances, never was the "royal we" more inappropriate! Behind Jesus' rebuke (9:39) is a story from the Hebrew Bible. In Numbers 11:24-30, Joshua objects to Moses that two young men who were not "officially ordained elders" in the community of Israel are exercising the prophetic spirit: "My Lord Moses, forbid them!" (Numbers 11:28). Moses' response is germane to Mark's point here:

> Are you jealous for me? If only the whole people were prophets, and God gave the Spirit to all of them! (Numbers 11:29)

"Powerful practices," argues Jesus, should be welcomed wherever they occur, for those "not against us are for us" (Mark 9:39f). By expanding the "us," Jesus undermines any attempt by the church to claim an exclusive franchise over the practice of justice and compassion. He understands the relationship between the power of monopoly and the monopoly of power! To sharpen the point, Jesus reminds "Christians" that they will often be on the receiving end of the works of mercy (9:41)!

Read Mark 9:42-50

Jesus' hardest words are reserved for those who "scandalize" the "little ones who believe in me" (9:42). The "sea" and the "unquenchable fire" (9:43) remind us of the torment of "water and fire" that the demon of silencing inflicts (9:22).

The call to amputate the offending hand, foot, and eye in verses 43-48 are by any account strange and troubling. Mark seems to be combining the Pauline metaphor of the community as "body" (see "hand, eye, foot" in 1 Corinthians 12:14-26) with the Pauline principle of not causing the "weaker member" to be scandalized (see Romans 14). But think of the modern analogy of the struggle against addiction. The process of recovery often feels like part of oneself (the addicted, codependent part) is being amputated. "Any struggle with addiction... involves deprivation," writes Gerald May in *Addiction and Grace*. "Every false prop is vulnerable to relinquishment." Such "amputation" is life-saving surgery on the cancer of our illusions and appetites.

According to Mark, our greatest individual and social addiction is the will to dominate. Disciples are called to defect from what society may see as natural, such as all the ways "little ones" are routinely victimized by patterns of hierarchy and exclusion. But to do this is to be perceived as "defective" (like the amputee) by the dominant culture. These strange sayings, then, are arguing that it is better to be deformed than to conform to what oppresses more vulnerable members of the body politic.

In a world of violence and institutionalized inequality, the choices are stark. We either embrace the "fire" of recovery (9:49) or live in the "hell" of addiction (9:48 alludes to the very last line in the book of Isaiah). Salt, used medicinally in antiquity, suggests that the goal is healing (9:49), which must include reconciliation within the community of faith (9:50).

Read Mark 10:1-16

The journey now continues south into Judea, progressing slowly but surely toward Jerusalem (10:1). Mark next turns to a setting where issues of justice and power are most often overlooked: marriage and divorce. The Pharisees engage Jesus in an argument not about the morality of divorce, but about what constitutes the legal grounds for a man to dismiss his wife (10:2).

This subject was vigorously debated between the two great rabbinic schools of the period, Hillel and Shammai. Jesus refuses to get involved in legalistic debate, however (10:3-5; see Chapter 9). Instead he addresses the system of male power and privilege in which a woman who had been "dismissed" by her husband became a social outcast with little means of supporting herself. The original vision of Genesis, Jesus argues, stipulated equality between men and women. The marriage covenant, far from delivering the woman into the power of the man, instructed the man to break with his patriarchal "house" in order to "become one flesh" with his wife (10:6-8). Jesus' conclusion in 10:9 refers to the way in which patriarchy, not divorce, drives a wedge that tears this equality asunder.

As in Jesus' previous conflict with the Pharisees, a private explanation is given to the disciples (10:10; see 7:17). It recognizes the fact of divorce, yet maintains the principle of equality. Jesus' first clause (10:11) went beyond the Jewish laws of the period, according to which a man could commit adultery against another married man but not against his own wife. But the second clause, which asserts the woman's right to initiate divorce proceedings, directly contradicted the teachings of the rabbis, who reserved that right solely for men (10:12).

No one who has endured the pain of "one flesh" being torn apart can minimize the tragedy of divorce. Yet even here Jesus refuses to overlook the actual relations of power. The woman must no longer be treated as object; she is a fully equal subject, bearing mutual responsibility.

It can hardly be accidental that Jesus follows this debate with another vignette about children, who are always the victims when parents divorce (10:13-16). For a second time in this section, Jesus brings children into the center of attention, but is here rebuked by the disciples (10:13). This provokes his indignation and he solemnly vows that what is at stake is nothing less than the "keys to the kingdom." The principle of acceptance, stated earlier in the positive, is now reiterated negatively:

Whoever receives such a child in my name receives me;
whoever receives me receives the One who sent me.
(9:37)

Whoever does not receive the sovereignty of God as a child shall not enter it. (10:15)

In both episodes Jesus' tough pronouncement to adult disciples is contrasted by his warm, physical embrace of children. Just as disciples must not "forbid" practices of liberation (9:39), they must never "forbid" children (10:14).

What is meant by this categorical challenge to "receive" the child? Most commentators offer quaint, idealizing homilies on children as symbols of "innocence and trust." On the contrary, the child in first-century Palestine represented the most powerless class. Children were the "least of the least" in the social order of antiquity, with neither status nor rights.

Throughout this section Mark has articulated the Way of the cross as the practice of solidarity with "little ones" in daily life. In every social relationship, power is unequally concentrated, and the Jubilary task is to redistribute it—even in the context of traditional structures such as marriage and the family. Mark has also undermined any "proprietary" rights that the discipleship community may wish to claim for itself. There is plenty of exemplary behavior outside our own communities of faith and plenty of problematic behavior inside them. The vocation of the church is not to render moral condemnations, but to seek justice within and without.

THE WORD IN OUR WORLD

Among the marginalized today, children still are the most vulnerable. They are the first victims of poverty, disease, displacement, war, and social disintegration. Above all, children are victimized by the breakdown of the family. This is why Jesus demands that they be embraced without qualification.

To respond to the children in our midst calls us to deal with the vicious intergenerational cycles of violence and create the possibility for a transformed future for us and for our children.

If the epidemic of sexual and physical abuse now becoming publicly visible is any indication, the roots of violence in our family system run deep. We are learning about the terrible price that is paid by those who are abused and by families who often deny that abuse has occurred.

Alice Miller has outlined the "silent drama" of abuse. It begins with the child's experience of being hurt and violated without anyone knowing it. The child cannot deal emotionally with that hurt, so he or she internalizes a sense of betrayal. This is obscured with rationalization, until finally the experience of the abuse is repressed altogether and forgotten. But the memory of the trauma lives on in the body and comes out unconsciously as anger at oneself and others.

Because of the courage of survivors, we are beginning to learn something about the path toward healing from the terrible psychological and spiritual damage inflicted on the child by sexual abuse. Christy Swanson, in "Breaking the Power of the Lie: An Ethic of Just Regard for the Adult Survivor," in Marie Fortune's book *Violence in the Family: A Workshop Curriculum*, offers the theological testimony of one survivor. She provides us with some important clues about the healing process based upon her own experience.

Swanson's reflections assume and build on the important work that Fortune has done in identifying the steps toward healing through which many survivors of physical violence move. It is a process that includes 1) truth-telling, 2) confrontation with the abuser, 3) repentance of the abuser, and 4) forgiveness and reconciliation.

Swanson says that most survivors of sexual abuse must deal with continuing denial. The ultimate healing of the wound of sexual abuse is thus found in the restoration of a sense of justice in self and relationships. The healing of survivors begins with the painful memory of what has been repressed and denied within themselves. This most often necessitates the help of a skilled and caring therapist. When memory is restored, survivors face the choice about whom to tell, given the reality of ongoing family relationships. It is very important that the silence that conceals the crime be broken and, in many cases, the abuser confronted with the truth. But no requirement for confrontation should be placed on survivors. The survivor must answer the question: Based on my own need for healing, whom do I need to tell?

Forgiveness and reconciliation are possible only where there is no denial and only after true repentance has taken place. "Forgiveness" that is offered an abuser who remains in denial is "cheap grace." Those who seek to support survivors must reject this. If the truth is acknowledged and true repentance comes about, however, reconciliation can happen if and when survivors are ready and willing to resume the relationship. But Swanson makes it clear that the healing of survivors is not dependent on anyone else's repentance.

Survivors can make a commitment to the truth as a cornerstone of their relationships, no matter what others decide to do. Living out the truth becomes a way of loving. With anger at injustice as an emotional resource, survivors are no longer circumscribed by whom they love but by how and if they love in a way that promotes the selfhood of all. In doing so, survivors love themselves and their denying family members most deeply.

Swanson calls on the church to provide accompaniment for survivors as they take steps along this spiritual path to healing. Support will be needed by survivors as they move through the stages of grief, as they learn to trust again in spite of profound betrayal, and as they continue to deal with the reality of denial and the brokenness of family.

The church best offers support for the spiritual formation of survivors by its belief in the liberating power of the truth. In all our actions we must give testimony to a God who listens to the grief and rage of survivors. The church can work toward healing by being willing to grieve and rage alongside survivors, knowing that their grief and anger hold the promise of new life.

Mark's gospel holds a vision of society, church, and family that is based on access and acceptance. To become like a child is to acknowledge the place and condition of the most vulnerable ones in our midst—our children. To be in compassionate solidarity with children is to confront the roots of violence in our society. This includes speaking out against the patriarchal mindset that promotes male privilege and legitimizes an abuse of power which often leads to violence against women and children. To construct a truly nonviolent life, we must weed out the structures and practices of violence at their roots in the most basic levels of human community. As parents, families, or communities of faith, we must rededicate ourselves to the struggle to convey God's blessing of children, so that children may have the life that they deserve.

How can you celebrate what your community already does to place children at the center of its life and concern? In what ways can your community of faith go further to enact what Jesus teaches us about children in these gospel scenes? Our challenge as discipleship communities is to channel our passionate love for our children into a public agenda for action, not just on behalf of our own children but for all children. How might this gospel vision be calling you into the larger community to struggle against systems that marginalize children, and to combat the violence to which they are most vulnerable?

Return to your geneagram and review it from the perspective of this chapter. Make notations of the places in your family story where you find divorce or profound alienation in relationships, physical or sexual abuse, addiction, destructive scripts, and any other trauma, oppression, or form of violence. How have these been passed on? What impact do they continue to have? Remember that you are in control of what happens and how or if you should share with others a story of childhood trauma.

It is the hope of parents to provide for their child a better world than the one they may have had as children. And yet we end up reproducing some of the patterns of violence that afflict the experience between generations. In your own family history, what vicious cycles are you called to break? What do you think you can do to interrupt these cycles and introduce new dynamics of healing?

Chapter 14

Repentance as Reparation
Mark 10:17-31

THE TEXT IN CONTEXT

To close the second cycle, Mark narrates the only discipleship rejection story in the gospel (10:17-30). The structure of the episode reveals its central concern:

A   rich man's question about eternal life (10:17)

B   rich man cannot leave possessions and follow (10:22)

C   Jesus' teaching, disciples' reaction (10:23-27)

B1   disciples have left possessions and followed (10:28)

A1   answer to eternal life question is given to them (10:30)

Here the first-last antithesis (10:31) is further defined in terms of economic class.

Read Mark 10:17-22

The action begins "on the Way." From his direct approach we can tell that the man is socially powerful; he wants something and is willing to give deference in exchange (10:17f). But Jesus flatly refuses to return the compliment, immediately alerting us to a certain tension in the story. This is heightened by the fact that although this man seems to have an ultimate theological concern ("eternal life" appears only in this episode in Mark), Jesus' response strikes us as uncharacteristically conventional.

He cites the "short list" of the Decalogue, leaving out the first four "theological" commandments whose meaning was not a matter of debate for Jews, in order to focus upon the six "ethical" commands (10:19; see Exodus 20). A closer reading, however, reveals that the last commandment—"Do not covet what belongs to your neighbor" (Exodus 20:17)—has been replaced by "Do not defraud." This Levitical censure appears in a section of Torah that concerns socioeconomic conduct in the Sabbath community:

> You shall not defraud your neighbor; you shall not steal; you shall not keep for yourself the wages of a laborer. (Leviticus 19:13)

With this deft bit of editing, Jesus reveals that he is more interested in how this man became so affluent than in his pious claims.

Let us return to the man's original inquiry. The problem is that his question assumes he can inherit eternal life. The root of this verb in Greek is the term for a parcel of land—and we will soon learn that this gentleman "possessed many properties" (10:22). It seems that he is assuming that eternal life, like property, must be inherited! Like many beneficiaries of a socioeconomic system, he envisions religion as a mere reproduction of his own class entitlement.

Indeed, in first-century Palestine, land was the basis of wealth. The estates of the rich grew in several ways. Assets were sometimes consolidated through the joining of households in marital or political alliances. At other times expropriated land was distributed through political patronage. But the primary mechanism was acquiring land through the debt-default of small agricultural land holders, as we saw in the discussion of the parable of the sower (see Chapter 5). This is how socioeconomic inequality had become so widespread in the time of Jesus. And it is almost certainly how this man ended up with "many properties."

The tiny landed class took great care to protect its entitlement from generation to generation. As Jesus later suggests in a parable about the struggle over deeded land, in which insurgent tenants try to wrest the "inheritance" from the absentee landlord, this was often a bloody business (Mark 12:1ff; see Chapter 18). Mark has given us a concise portrait of the ideology of entitlement. And Jesus is clear that the "propertied" create and maintain their surplus through "fraud"—the result of illegitimate expropriation of their neighbors' land.

Yet Jesus does not directly dispute the man's improbable contention that he has "kept the whole law" (10:20), even though it flies in the face of Jesus' own assertion that "there is no one good but

God" (10:18). Instead, Jesus "looked at the man and loved him," for he is about to deliver some hard truth (10:21).

This is the kind of compassion that refuses to equivocate. "You lack one thing." The verb implies that it is the rich man who is in debt—to the poor he has defrauded. "Get up," pleads Jesus, using the verb associated in Mark with healing episodes. "Sell what you have and give to the poor." The man must dismantle the system from which he derives his privilege. According to Jesus' Jubilary logic, by redistributing his ill-gotten surplus he stands to receive true "treasure in heaven" (this term differs from the others used to describe wealth in this episode).

"And come follow me." Jesus is not inviting this man to change his attitude toward his wealth, or to treat his servants better, or to reform his personal life. He is asserting a precondition for his discipleship: economic restitution. The man's piety collapses; stung, he whirls and slinks away. Mark matter-of-factly explains why: "For he had much property" (10:22). In the context of the class inequality, Jesus' message of repentance means reparation, the Jubilary practice of redistributive justice.

Read Mark 10:23-31

Mark wishes the reader to know that this story means exactly what it says, and so has Jesus driven the point home with a lyrical little verse whose point is sharpened with the razor's edge of absurdist humor:

> How difficult it will be for those with riches to enter the sovereignty of God!
>
> Children, how difficult it is *to enter the sovereignty of God!* It is easier for a camel to go through a needle's eye than for the rich to enter the sovereignty of God! (10:23-25)

Mark's joke about the camel and needle has of course been twisted by commentators anxious to avoid its sting, an infamous attempt being the medieval assertion that there was a small gate in Jerusalem through which camels could enter only "on their knees"! In fact, Jesus' image invoked the largest known animal and the smallest known aperture in order precisely to denote the impossible. His humorous sarcasm is captured for us by Frederick Buechner's contemporary analogy: It is like getting "Nelson Rockefeller through the night deposit slot of the First National City Bank"!

With each repetition of the point, Mark's disciples grow increasingly astonished, culminating in their protest: "Who then can be saved?" (10:26). Their consternation reflects their assumption that wealth was a sure sign of God's favor—a perception that also prevails in American piety. Indeed, Christendom has been so anxious that Jesus here might be saying something exclusive or critical about the rich that it has missed the fact that this terrifying triplet is *not* about the rich at all. These assertions, each in the indicative mood, are about the sovereignty of God as that time and place in which there are no rich and poor. By definition, then, the rich cannot enter—at least not with their wealth intact. Reparation is the only way "in."

Jesus acknowledges that for us the notion of a genuinely new social order based upon economic equality seems truly "impossible" (10:27). Certainly in the culture and religion of capitalism any economic model that has been predicated upon redistributive justice has been considered high heresy. For the same reason, the Levitical Jubilee tradition has been the subject of considerable skepticism by modern theologians (see Chapter 3).

The biblical vision of Jubilee, however, was neither a utopian prescription nor an eschatological hope; it was a practical hedge against the inevitable concentration of wealth and power within the community of Israel. This vision originates not from social idealism but from the revealed character of God. The dependent poor were to be released from debt because "I am your God who brought you out of the land of Egypt" (Leviticus 25:35-38). Land was to be returned because "the land is mine, and you are but aliens who have become my tenants" (25:23-28). This vision obviously represents the antithesis to systems that promote wealth concentration; nevertheless, Jesus not only insists that redistributive justice is possible, he implies that without it we cannot speak of the sovereignty of God.

Peter finally understands, and boasts that the discipleship community has done what the rich man could not: "left" and "followed" (10:28; see Chapter 1). As he did with the rich man, however, Jesus neither confirms nor denies Peter's claim. Instead, he issues yet another universal invitation ("Truly no one who has...") to give up private entitlements of household (the basic productive economic unit), family (patrimony and inheritance), and land (the basic unit of wealth; 10:29). He assures the reader that those who experiment with such Jubilee economics will receive (not inherit) abundant sufficiency from the new community of production and consumption (10:30).

This allusion to the divine economy of grace suggests that the "hundredfold" harvest promised in the sower parable (4:8) was not a pipedream offered to poor peasants but the concrete result of wealth redistribution. Surplus is created when "private" wealth is restructured as a community asset. Jesus adds pointedly that this "miracle" of multiplication through sharing, already enacted in the earlier wilderness feedings (6:35-42; see Chapter 8), will occur not in some remote hereafter but "now, in this time." With characteristic realism, he adds that this practice will invite "persecutions." The matter of eternal life, however, is left for "the age to come" (10:30).

This is the answer to the rich man's question—though he did not stick around to hear it. This, the one discipleship rejection story in Mark, illustrates another point of Jesus' sower parable. The wealthy may "hear the word, but the anxieties of this age, the love of riches, and the lust for everything else choke the word, so that it proves unfruitful" (4:19).

Instead, the promise of "eternal life" is made to those trying to respond to the vision of economic justice. The episode and section as a whole conclude with a simple reiteration of Jubilee logic: "Many that are first will be last, and the last first" (10:31).

The Word in Our World

Mark's portrait of the rich man seems to suggest that he is "possessed by his possessions." Today we would call this the addiction of affluence. Perhaps it is because economic greed is the most difficult and pervasive of human addictions that Mark emphasizes Jesus' love for the rich man. But love speaks the truth. "Recovery" from this addiction must be expressed as reparation.

Few subjects in the gospel are as difficult to address as is the subject of wealth. The trouble with wealth is that it is so insidious. We hardly know how to define it. Yet its pursuit is one of the primary goals of our lives, unless we take Jesus' counsel seriously.

How does wealth exhibit itself in our society? One distinguishing characteristic is the opportunity to make decisions about the direction of your own life and the lives of your loved ones. Where and when and into what circumstances we were born often determines whether we can make choices in life and, if so, which ones.

Few of God's children have ever experienced making the following choices. Take a while to read them slowly and to interpret them in the context of your own life or your family's life.

Have I ever had the opportunity to choose:

- where I will live

- how I will earn a living

- where my children will go to school

- what I will wear today

- whether I will eat today

- where I will eat today

- where I will sleep tonight

- whether I will have central heating or air conditioning

- whether I will buy medicines prescribed for me or my family

- whether I will make use of mental health or psychological care

- whether I will save money and how much I will save

- whether I will have a telephone

- whether I will have a television or cable television service

- where I will go on vacation

- how I will make my home or office more beautiful or more comfortable

- whether I will repair what is broken in my home or surroundings

- whether I will own a car

- what to do with my inheritance?

Often it is difficult to differentiate between necessities and luxuries. In fact, the very definition of "necessity" varies widely according to the context of our lives. Food, clothing, shelter, recreation, and security, for example, are basic human needs. But how we interpret the satisfaction of these needs in our own lives may provide contemporary content for this gospel story.

Food, for example, was already explored in our reflection on "just meals" (see Chapter 3). But in a world where the diets of pets in wealthy households are significantly better than the diets of many children in poor households, something is terribly wrong. No one who has lived in a poor country can enter a First World supermarket without being overwhelmed with anger and sadness. Ordinary middle-class people in the United States can easily spend more money on a single meal in a moderately upscale restaurant than the majority of people in the world spend in a week to nourish their families.

Hunger for the privileged is a state of eager anticipation of the next culinary delight. Hunger for the poor is a feared and constant companion, the root of sickness, mental and physical dullness, exhaustion.

Clothing also has a vastly different connotation for the rich and the poor. Is the breach between the children of God unbridgeable when one wears a $10,000 designer watch while the other's calloused feet have no protection from the bitter cold? When the fashion show of the one insults the nakedness of the other who picks through plastic bags of cast-away clothing? What would Jesus say to the rich young man in our own times when the social pressure to "look right" can drive a teen-ager to peddle drugs for $100 sneakers or kill for a leather jacket?

Shelter is another familiar sign of wealth or poverty. The word itself brings to mind the countless homeless people in the United States alone—many of them families. In most U.S. cities, single-family homes worth a million dollars or more house two, three, or four people in space enough for two, three, or four families. In the same cities, poor families crowd into one- or two-room apartments. And space is not the only contrasting component of shelter for the rich and the poor. Safe, beautiful, convenient, and private—common characteristics of "home" for the rich—rarely define "home" for the poor.

Vast disparities in the extent and substance of security also exist. Health and life insurance, savings and investments, job security, even personal safety are too often available only to those who are well off. But security can also (perhaps better) be found in extended family, community, neighborhood, and in knowing who you are and what values guide your way. These, sadly, are frequently sacrificed in the fast pace of the wealthy Western world.

Integral to the achievement of economic justice is a process of "conscientization" of those who live privileged lives. We are encouraged to believe that wealth and privilege just "happen"—by good luck or hard work or the will of God. But the reason riches are incompatible with the discipleship journey is that they are predicated upon injustice. Affluence represents a monstrous barrier between peoples.

Imagine a "stick figure" divided into two halves down the middle. The figure represents you. One side represents the "you" that is located in a competitive, consumer society—an honest "you" that has worked hard to provide for your loved ones a reasonably (or very) comfortable life. This "you" hears Jesus' invitation to the rich young man as "not so good news." Reflect on this side of you, naming your feelings and emotions.

The other side of the stick figure represents the "you" that, like the rich young man, wants to respond. This side of "you" has seen suffering and the tremendous injustice that causes it. This side of "you" has recognized your participation in the injustice and is ready to accept Jesus' invitation to change. Reflect on this side of you, naming your feelings and emotions.

Wealth and poverty, however, are not only personal realities. We live in a world in which the vast majority of people barely survive, while a smaller and smaller minority live extremely well. Mark's story about the rich young man must also be interpreted in our own times as an invitation to transform the systems and structures that create wealth and poverty, that maintain privilege within our own society or in our world.

Chapter 15

Leadership and Service
Mark 10:32-52

THE TEXT IN CONTEXT

Read Mark 10:32-45

The third and last cycle of the discipleship catechism again begins "on the Way," finally revealed as headed to Jerusalem (10:32). This snapshot of the discipleship community will be important to remember at the end of the story. Just as here Jesus "goes before" followers who are amazed and afraid, so at the empty tomb we are told that Jesus "goes before" disciples who are traumatized and afraid (16:7f).

The final portent is the most specific in its anticipation of the Passion drama: The Human One will be "handed over" by his community to the Sanhedrin, then to the Roman authorities, and after torture and ridicule, will be executed (10:33). Again Jesus promises that "after three days he will rise" (10:34), the meaning of which remains a mystery to the disciples (see 9:10). Do they yet comprehend the Way? The final episode of the catechism demonstrates that they do not, as Mark's caricature turns dark.

Along with Peter (8:32; 9:5) and John (9:38), James now joins in the rejection of Jesus' Way (10:35ff). Mark has implicated the whole inner circle! They look forward to a Messianic coup, and aspire to "first and second Cabinet positions" in the new regime (10:37; see Psalm 110:1). After two cycles of teaching about solidarity with the "least," we can feel Jesus' exasperation, as in characteristic fashion he turns the question back on them. Can they embrace his "baptism" and "cup," which in the symbolism of the story refer to the Way of the cross (10:38)? Mark cannot resist sarcasm: "No problem," answer the Zebedee boys (10:39a).

Jesus explains wearily that leadership in the sovereignty of God is not appointed executively; it is achieved only through an apprenticeship of the cross (10:39f). The dialectic between power and powerlessness here is ironic. Jesus can guarantee that his disciples will suffer, but cannot grant their request to rule (10:40). Indeed, in this story it will not be disciples who end up on Jesus' right and left hand, but two rebels—at the crucifixion (see 15:27). Mark's caustic tone peaks in Jesus' subsequent teaching:

> You know how it is among the "so-called" ruling class, their practice of domination, the tyranny of the "great ones." Oh but this is not so among you! (10:42f)

This section has proved repeatedly that the disciples neither "know" what they want (10:38) nor understand the practice of Jesus (10:41).

Now comes the final invitation to "whosoever" in the discipleship catechism (10:43f), imagining a new style of leadership "from the bottom up." Jesus' role reversal between the "great" one and the "slave" is a direct attack on the status hierarchy of the ancient world. This completes Jesus' challenge to conventional understandings of power: personal, social, economic, and now political. The alternative Way is embodied by the Human One, who proposes to overturn the debt system once and for all by giving his life: a servant who will "buy back" the lives of all who are truly enslaved (10:45).

The fact that the male followers of Jesus are clueless in this section makes it all the more significant that at the beginning (1:31) and end (15:41) of Mark's story it is women who demonstrate the quality of servanthood advocated here by Jesus. Is Mark implying that in a patriarchal system only women are fit to exercise leadership? This would be the most subversive proposition of all—for antiquity and modernity alike!

Read Mark 10:46-52

There is one more polemical role reversal to shock our propriety, and one more blind man healed to give us hope. On the outskirts of Jericho, the last stop before arriving in Jerusalem, we encounter a poor, blind beggar sitting "beside the Way" (10:46). Bartimaeus will provide a dramatic contrast to the previous two stories of "non-discipleship"—the rich man and the ambitious disciples—and will symbolize for Mark the "true disciple."

Unlike the rich man, Bartimaeus is landless and disabled; he is a victim of the system, not its beneficiary. Unlike the disciples, he dares not approach Jesus directly with his request. He inquires not after the mysteries of eternal life or the top posts in the new administration, but after mercy, despite those who would silence him (10:47f). While the rich man walked away from the call to discipleship, Bartimaeus gives up what little he has (the cloak he casts off represents the tool of his panhandler's trade; 10:50). And Mark intentionally parallels his petition with that of the disciples:

> Jesus said to the disciples, *"What do you want me to do for you?"* They answered, "Grant us to sit on your right and left hand in glory!" (10:36f)

> Jesus said to the blind man, *"What do you want me to do for you?"* He answered, "Master, that I might see again!" (10:51)

Jesus cannot answer the rich man's question because he will not make reparation. Jesus cannot grant the disciples' request because it is based on delusions of grandiosity. But Jesus can help the beggar because Bartimaeus knows he is blind.

At the beginning of Mark's discipleship catechism, Peter calls Jesus by the "correct" name but resists the Way of the cross (8:29ff). At the end Bartimaeus "followed Jesus on the Way" (10:52) even though he called him by the "wrong" name (10:47f; the title "Son of David" will be repudiated by Jesus in 12:35-37; see Chapter 19). The first have become last, and the last first. The moral of the catechism: Only faith-as-discipleship "makes us well."

THE WORD IN OUR WORLD

Jesus' "catechism of the cross" reveals the two kinds of power that are in conflict in our hearts, our families, our communities, and our world. It contends that the primal structures of domination can be overthrown only by the practice of personal and political nonviolence. But this Way contradicts all our orthodox notions of social and economic security, and has been all too rarely embraced by Christians throughout history.

Still, many have experimented with this truth. Recently in Washington, D.C., for example, Roman Catholic Bishop Thomas Gumbleton received the Builder of Bridges award for his pastoral concern for gays and lesbians. Those attending the award ceremony had the unusual and edifying experience of honoring a true servant leader, not only for his prophetic support for gay men and lesbians, but for many activities which place Bishop Gumbleton in the ranks of all those Christian ministers who have lived Jesus' words: "Whoever wishes to become great among you must be your servant..." (Mark 10:43).

The very fact that a U.S. bishop in the Roman Church would merit the title "servant leader" draws one's attention. To be sure, prophets have arisen from the ranks of the Catholic hierarchy in our times, such as Oscar Romero and Helder Camara. However, in the North American Catholic Church today, to be a bishop ordinarily signifies a position of careful orthodoxy and extraordinary power. Prophetic types need not apply.

The name Bishop Thomas Gumbleton, on the other hand, has been synonymous with issues of peace for several decades. He has spoken and acted on behalf of nonviolence as a member of the Catholic peace group Pax Christi. More recently, Gumbleton has engaged in justice issues, such as those connected with gay and lesbian persons. It is in this area, perhaps, where Gumbleton exercises the most notable, and risky, prophetic ministry, given the reticence of Roman Catholic theology regarding homosexuality. While official church documents call for pastoral attention on behalf of gays and lesbians, the practice of so many in that tradition has been homophobic. Now we have a bishop who publicly supports homosexuals in their struggles for justice within and outside of the church.

In this, Bishop Gumbleton exhibits that necessary quality of leadership which is summed up in the word "maturity." The true servant leader has the capacity to take risks, to try something new, not paralyzed by the fear of failure. The servant leader possesses the ability to listen well. Gumbleton listened to his mother's agonized question about another of her sons, Dan, who is gay: "Is Dan going to hell?"

Another quality of servant leadership is knowing when to lead and when to follow. Bishop Gumbleton has shown a willingness to set aside his own agenda and schedule when necessary, such as when he journeyed to Central America on two days' notice to stand with a woman seeking to discover the truth about her slain husband.

Another bishop described Gumbleton as someone who has turned a highly competitive spirit into an overriding passion for peace based on justice. This is a final quality of the servant leader— a capacity for anger. Unless there is some alienation from the world as it is, a sense that things can and should be better, no leadership can emerge. One glimpses this anger when Gumbleton speaks about unjust situations. He has the capacity to take risks and make the prophetic gesture in order to drive home his point.

At the awards ceremony honoring Thomas Gumbleton for his work on behalf of gays and lesbians, the several hundred people gathered gave him a prolonged standing ovation. Good-willed people recognize and celebrate this rare gift of servant leadership.

In every area of discipleship the temptations of competitiveness, of jealousy, or of protecting one's turf arise. An examination of conscience is in order for all who would follow Jesus.

Ask yourself:

Am I walking toward Jerusalem, in the sense that I am less interested in power now than when I began my discipleship journey?

Am I willing to "lose my life" in the sense that Jesus meant it—truly living for values beyond and greater than myself?

Am I open to the idea that those who would lead should content themselves often with following?

Do I believe that leadership must always include service?

Do I feel that gradually, over time, my eyes are being opened to new ways of being human—less interested in status, position, titles and more concerned about "the other," especially the needy?

If I am a man, do I truly cherish the discipleship gifts of women?

Have I ever had the experience of being "silenced," as Peter was, when I misunderstood the servant nature of discipleship?

Do I understand that suffering has the possibility to purge, to humble, and to save?

Do I engage in futile competition with other disciples of Jesus?

Do I have a triumphant spirit in working for social change? Would I use political power to effect the good I desire? Is this Jesus' way?

In working for social change, do I relate more with the Jesus portrayed on the mount of Transfiguration than with the Jesus on the mount of crucifixion?

In seeking to expel the demons of this world, do I rely only on human resources without turning to prayer?

Do I see all the struggles for social righteousness as examples of the ageless and apocalyptic contest between the powers of light and the powers of death?

Do I believe that the transformation of the world will be accomplished ultimately from the bottom up?

Am I inclined to impose what I see as "the good" in areas of social change?

Am I convinced that God's reign ultimately depends on God and not on me?

Make a list of all the activities in your life: home, work, social circles, church, leisure. Judge each against the questions raised above. Pay particular attention to your work setting, because many disciples do not consider this a principal arena for efforts to build the reign of God. List the good and bad aspects of your work setting. Are you contributing to those aspects of your workplace that reflect Jesus' values? Are you doing something about those aspects that contradict Jesus' values?

OUR DISCIPLESHIP JOURNEY

> Then Jesus said to him, "What do you want me to do for you?" The blind man said to him, "My teacher, let me see again."
>
> —Mark 10:51

Moral courage has its source in the capacity to perceive through the eyes of God's love, to feel for the other and the self with divine compassion, and to know divine grief and wrath over injustice. We all have rare moments of seeing clearly, moments when we know profoundly that every human being and, indeed, every living thing is sacred.

In these moments of light we comprehend that all people are created in the image of God to live as part of God's love, justice, and peace. All are created for abundant life. Yet how brief and intermittent are these moments! Usually our vision is dulled by the details of daily life, the tasks before us, our fears or desires.

In your mind, walk through your daily or weekly routine. Think slowly and deliberately about the people whose lives regularly touch your own. Think about the places you go—home, work, school. Do you commute to work in a car or on public transportation? Do you travel often? What information do you receive about the world we live in, and through what media? Do you read newspapers, listen to radio talk shows, watch television? Are you on the Internet?

Now think about what or whom you see as you move around. Do you interact with homeless people or beggars? Do you live with poverty? What do you know about Rwanda, Afghanistan, Chiapas, East Timor, or about Native Americans, inner-city schools, global warming, or labor conditions in the plants that manufacture your clothes?

One of the characteristics of the age in which we live is that we no longer can say, "We didn't know." Ordinary people have access to information hitherto hidden. When an angry mob surrounded the cathedral in San Cristobal las Casas, in Chiapas, Mexico, communities around the world knew what had happened almost instantaneously. When a young man was killed in Indonesia for speaking out about the abuse of child labor, groups in Washington, D.C., received a fax within hours with specific details about the assassination. We all watched the Soviet Union disintegrate, troops land in Somalia, and the pro-democracy movement in China under attack in Tiananmen Square. In some ways we are overloaded with information and images. But do we *see*? And do we *understand*?

Do we ask *why*? Are we critical of our sources of information? Do we demand clear pictures, honest images, truth? Through what lens do we look at the reality around us? Do we question the bias of our own line of vision? Are we willing to open our minds and hearts to the implications of what we see?

What does the world look like from the perspective of the poor and those on the margins? How can we locate ourselves in order to find out?

Jesus gives sight beyond seeing. How often have we reflected upon the gifts of the Spirit, especially wisdom, understanding, and knowledge? Have we the courage to accept these gifts that give us frightening yet healing insights about the way our world looks?

We pray: Jesus, "let us see again." Let us see through your eyes of love, so that we might follow you on the Way.

IV
JESUS THE QUESTIONER

OPENING MEDITATION

Jesus' entry into Jerusalem was dramatic public liturgy that set the stage for a final round of questions. Neither religious nor state authorities would remain unchallenged by this One who moved into their centers of power with an alternative authority.

Liturgy is ritual that surrounds and symbolizes an action of deep significance, often carrying many levels of meaning. Few locations in the modern world can equal the capital of the United States, Washington, D.C., as a fitting place for public liturgy in our own times. As you read the following examples, recall the public liturgies that have taken place in your own town or city.

On the 40th anniversary of the bombings of Hiroshima and Nagasaki, at the height of the nuclear arms race, 30,000 people brought the Peace Ribbon to Washington, D.C. The Ribbon was a graphic representation of what hundreds of thousands of people from around the world "could not bear to think of as lost in a nuclear war." Comprised of thousands of segments on which were painted, embroidered, sewn, dyed, and patched the fears of an era, the Ribbon wound around the Pentagon, across the Potomac River, around the Lincoln Memorial, down the Mall past the Washington Monument, around the U.S. Capitol building, back down the opposite side of the Mall, around the Ellipse by the White House, back by the Vietnam Memorial, and across the river again to the Pentagon—literally encircling the symbols of power in a powerful country. The message of this striking public liturgy was clear: Stop building and threatening to use nuclear weapons.

On the Wednesdays of Lent a few years later, when the U.S.-supported war in Nicaragua was raging, people of faith, including heads of communions, bishops, and hundreds of members of the different denominations, gathered at the U.S. Capitol building in Washington, D.C. In their hands they held simple white wooden crosses on which were written the names of the Nicaraguan men, women, and children killed in the war. Following a time of prayer on the steps of the Capitol, the group slowly moved inside to the

Rotunda, another symbolic center of global power. There, some engaged in civil disobedience by kneeling in prayer in the center of the Rotunda. They were promptly arrested. The message of this public liturgy was also simple and clear: Stop U.S. support for the war in Nicaragua.

On the night before the U.S. war against Iraq was scheduled to start, 10,000 people gathered at the invitation of *Sojourners* for a time of prayer in the Washington National Cathedral. They filled the massive edifice and spilled out onto the grounds. After the service, they walked in a candlelight procession down Massachusetts Avenue and past the White House, then gathered at Metropolitan AME Church a few blocks away from the White House for a night-long vigil. Their message: Don't start this war against Iraq.

A few days later, after the war had begun, hundreds of religious leaders and people of faith gathered again, this time at the invitation of Pax Christi USA, for a time of prayer and for another procession to the White House to say: We shall not be silent. Stop the war!

Not long thereafter, as Congress gutted programs for the poor, homeless people and advocates for the homeless built a shanty town in the middle of a main street on Capitol Hill. At another moment of that campaign activists served a meal to poor children on the lawn of the U.S. Capitol building. Where will we find shelter? What will our children eat?

We have grown accustomed to the symbolic arrangement of our churches. In most, the community listens to the Word proclaimed from a lectern and gathers around a table on which is shared the Bread of Life. Jesus' entry into Jerusalem suggests that our liturgical actions may also at times belong in the public square. Have you ever participated in such a liturgical act?

Chapter 16

"Say to This Mountain"
Mark 11:1-25

THE TEXT IN CONTEXT

Jesus' long march to Jerusalem takes Mark's story from the margins of Palestinian society to its center. Arriving at the suburb of Bethany (11:1), Jesus prepares to enter the Holy City not as a reverent pilgrim demonstrating allegiance to the Temple but as a subversive prophet challenging the foundations of state power.

Mark 11–12 narrates Jesus' second "campaign of direct action." In the first campaign in Galilee (1:20–3:35) he confronted the status quo with his powerful actions of exorcism and healing. Now he takes on the Temple system and its stewards, the Jerusalem clerical establishment. This campaign, like the first, will culminate in polarization and rift, and will conclude with Jesus' withdrawal to further reflect upon his mission in a second sermon about revolutionary patience (13:1ff; see 4:1ff).

Read Mark 11:1-11

The Jerusalem narrative commences with the so-called "Triumphal Entry" (11:1-10). But it is a misnomer, for this carefully choreographed political street theater is designed to repudiate Messianic triumphalism.

The scene would have been loaded with political significance for Mark's original readers. Jesus marches into the city accompanied by an army of peasants (11:7f), whose rapturous cries escalate the acclaim of Bartimaeus (10:47f) into a full-blown revolutionary chant: "Blessed be the kingdom of our Father David" (11:10). Images from the parade called to mind several biblical precedents: the colt signifying triumphant Judah (Genesis 49:11); the return of the Ark to Israel (1 Samuel 6:7ff); the declaration of Jehu as upstart king (2 Kings 9:13); a royal processional hymn (Psalm 118:25f). And the fact that the parade began "near the Mount of Olives" (11:1) would have brought to mind the final apocalyptic battle between Israel and its enemies spoken of by Zechariah (read Zechariah 14:1-5).

This theater also alludes to more recent events. It recalls the victorious military procession of Simon Maccabaeus, the great guerrilla general who liberated Palestine from Hellenistic rule some two centuries before. According to 1 Maccabees 13:51, Simon entered Jerusalem "with praise and palm branches... and with hymns and songs." And there was an incident of Messianic posturing contemporary to Mark as well. Midway through the Judean revolt against Rome (66–70 C.E.), according to the Jewish historian Josephus, the guerrilla captain Menahem had marched through Jerusalem heavily armed and "like a king," in an unsuccessful attempt to become the sole leader of the rebel provisional government (see Chapter 20).

But Mark uses all of these popular Messianic images precisely in order to subvert them. This is the point of the odd story about "commandeering" a colt, which occupies fully half the parade narrative (11:2-6). Mark is consciously reorganizing the symbolism of this parade around a different Zecharian image which is expressly anti-military:

> Shout aloud, daughter of Jerusalem! Lo, your king comes to you; triumphant and victorious is he, humble and riding upon... a colt, the foal of a donkey. He will cut off the chariot from Ephraim and the war horse from Jerusalem... and shall command peace to the nations. (Zechariah 9:9f)

This king, who has already rejected Hellenistic power politics (10:42ff), enters Jerusalem quite unarmed—though just as dangerous.

Jesus' "nonviolent siege" will not follow the Messianic script that equated national liberation with the rehabilitation of the Davidic Temple-state. When Jesus comes to the Temple it is not to defend it, but to disrupt it. He will soon expressly disassociate himself from Davidic ideology (12:35-37; see Chapter 19). And for the moment, the parade culminates in yet another Markan anti-climax: Jesus marches into the Temple, looks around—and leaves (11:11).

Read Mark 11:15-19

The composition of the famous "Temple Cleansing" is another Markan sandwich. The action in the sanctuary (11:15-19) is framed by the curious tale of the cursing of the fig tree (11:12-14, 20-25). The masterful symbolism of the latter interprets the dramatic feat of the former, which we will look at first.

After his brief reconnaissance in 11:11, Jesus returns to launch his action in the Temple court marketplace. His target is the entrepreneurial class, whom he "drives out"—the verb most commonly used by Mark for exorcism. The "buying and selling" refers to the trade in birds and animals as well as wine, oil, and salt used for Temple sacrifices.

Jesus would have been neither surprised nor indignant at the existence of this marketplace per se, as some suggest. Commercial activity was an entirely normal aspect of temple cults in antiquity. Indeed the Temple was Jerusalem's dominant economic institution, upon which most of the city depended. The issue for Jesus was rather the way in which the political economy of the cult had become oppressive to the poor.

The highly profitable Temple commercial interests were controlled by the high priestly families. Jesus singles out two street-level representatives of these financial powers: "money changers" and "pigeon sellers" (11:15). The former group presided over currency exchange and transaction, since all money brought by pilgrims had to be converted into Jewish or Tyrian coin before Temple dues and tithes could be paid. With revenues pouring into Jerusalem from Jews all over the Mediterranean world, these banking interests wielded considerable power.

The latter group refers to those who trafficked in the staple commodity by which the poor met their cultic obligations. A sacrificial offering of doves was needed, for example, in the purification of women and the cleansing of lepers (Leviticus 12:6, 14:22; see Luke 2:22-24). Jesus thus "overturns" the stations used to make a profit off those condemned to second-class citizenship.

Mark next reports that Jesus "forbade anyone to carry any goods through the Temple" (11:16), suggesting some kind of ban on further activities for that day. Is it reasonable to believe that Jesus really accomplished this feat? After all, Judean security police and a Roman garrison stood close by to protect the orderly function of the Temple. We can best interpret this episode as a narrative of symbolic direct action signaling intent toward an end. We might say that Jesus "shut down" the Temple no more—but no less—than a modern nonviolent blockade temporarily "shuts down" the Pentagon.

Such bold action obviously required strong justification, and this is forthcoming in Jesus' "teaching," which cites two great prophetic traditions (11:17). Jesus first appeals to Isaiah's vision of what the Temple ought to represent: a refuge for all peoples, especially the foreigner and the dispossessed (read Isaiah 56:3-8). But he then invokes Jeremiah to illustrate what the Temple has in fact become. The metaphor "den of thieves" comes from one of the bitterest attacks upon the Temple system in Hebrew prophecy (read Jeremiah 7:1-14). This oracle warns against "trusting in... the Temple of the Lord" and insists that unless justice is practiced toward "the alien, the orphan, and the widow," the Temple will be destroyed. According to Jesus this ultimatum now obtains, and he will shortly give an object lesson about how the Temple exploits the poor (12:41ff; see Chapter 19).

Read Mark 11:12-14, 20-25

We return now to the cursing of the fig tree that frames this action. On his way into Jerusalem, Jesus condemns a tree which is unable to relieve his "hunger" (11:12-14). The fact that it is not the "time" for figs signals to the reader that this is a symbolic action. It seems to be an enactment of Micah's lament over the apostasy of Israel:

> Woe is me! For I have become one for whom... there is no first-ripe fig for which I hunger. The faithful have disappeared from the land, and there is no one left who is upright. (Micah 7:1f)

After the Temple exorcism the disciples find that the fig tree has "withered to its roots" (11:20f). In the Hebrew Bible, the fig tree was a symbol of peace, security, and prosperity in Israel. The fruitful fig tree was a metaphor for God's blessings, while a withering tree symbolized judgment (see Jeremiah 8:13; Isaiah 28:3f; Joel 1:7, 12). Mark also seems to have had in mind Hosea's judgment oracle:

> Because of the wickedness of their deeds, I will drive them out of my house... all their officials are rebels ... their root is dried up, they shall bear no fruit." (Hosea 9:15f)

Jesus' curse, then, is a political parable: The "officials" who profit from the "house" must be "driven out." "Fruitless," the Temple-state is not destined for restoration but will "dry up."

But the Temple represented the very heart of the Judean social order. What could take its place? Because it was believed that God resided in the Temple, such talk and action by Jesus would provoke a crisis regarding God's presence among the people. This is why Jesus immediately follows his actions with an exhortation to his disciples to "Believe in God!" (11:22). That is, they must recover a theology of the Exodus God who is not domesticated under the status quo.

Jesus goes on to urge them to believe in a world liberated from the Temple-state (11:22-25). Jesus assures his disciples that this great monolith, known in the tradition as the "mountain of the house," can be overthrown (11:23). To "be taken up and cast into the sea" recalls Jesus' exorcism of Legion in 5:9-13. Faith is here defined as the political imagination that insists on the possibility of a society freed from the powers, whether Roman militarism or the Judean aristocracy (11:24).

The "House of Prayer" now abandoned, Jesus concludes his homily by offering the community a new symbolic center. It is not an institutional site but a moral one: the practice of mutual forgiveness within the community (11:25). This citation of the central petition of what Matthew and Luke know as the "Lord's Prayer" represents Jesus' final rejection of the Temple-based debt system.

Jesus' action in the Temple fulfills Malachi's threat of judgment alluded to at the beginning of Mark's story:

> The Lord whom you seek will suddenly come to his Temple.... I will be a swift witness against those who oppress. ... You are cursed because you are robbing me (Malachi 3:1, 5, 9).

And he has enacted his own parable, putting a ban on the "strong man's" goods because the "house is divided and cannot stand" (Mark 3:24-27).

THE WORD IN OUR WORLD

Mark's story about Jesus entering the Temple, the center of Jewish society, and overturning the tables there might be interpreted in our own time as an invitation to transform the systems and structures that create wealth and poverty within our society or our world. The mountain Jesus called "movable by faith" is a fitting metaphor for the global economy, which is increasingly intransigent despite the fact that it is not working for the majority of the world's inhabitants.

An interesting contemporary example of "mountain moving" is the worldwide effort to transform international financial institutions, especially the World Bank and the International Monetary Fund (IMF), primary guardians of the global economy. After years of an increasingly urgent clamor from poor countries about the destructive projects and policies of these institutions and after a decade of escalating concern about the burden of debt owed by poor countries to these multilateral institutions, a broad-based, diverse, transnational, and effective coalition of citizens emerged in the mid-1990s to demand change.

For fifty years the World Bank and the IMF (known as the Bretton Woods Institutions for the location in New Hampshire of their founding conference) have been major players in the global economy. Established in 1944 as a source of international development financing, the World Bank has more than 175 member countries, all of which must first be admitted to the IMF. A country's voting power in the Bank is proportional to its financial contribution.

The World Bank is the largest single source of international development money, lending each year in the range of $20 billion to poor countries around the world. For years the Bank has facilitated projects, often tremendous in scale, that brought electricity, water, transportation, and other apparent "basics" of life to millions of people. But these often came at great cost to the environment and to indigenous ways of life, and with significant benefit to contractors from wealthy countries who built the roads and dams and irrigation projects and wells.

Its partner organization, the IMF, was created to oversee the exchange of currencies between countries, but quickly began to monitor the balance of payments and related internal economic policies of member countries. The IMF in practice developed an "entrance exam" for participation in the global economy. A poor country would have to restructure its economy according to the rules of free market capitalism—demonstrating its ability to control inflation, reduce the role of the central government (through, for example, privatization of state-owned enterprises and cuts in services for citizens), improve tax collection, devalue its currency, open its markets to foreign products, and emphasize production for export.

A passing grade opens a poor country's door for new loans, grants, and investment from the World Bank, as well as for other international funds from national governments like the United States and private banks. A failing grade keeps that door tightly shut.

For years, the cost of IMF approval had been gutted social programs (including health care and education), unemployment, higher regressive taxes, and decreased food production for domestic consumption. The benefit of lowered inflation could not soften the devastating effect on the poor.

In more than fifty years of doing business, the Bretton Woods Institutions have been significantly reformed more than once. The World Bank especially has adjusted to the changing global reality. Its mission evolved from one of rebuilding Europe and Japan following World War II to one of supporting large-scale engineering projects in so-called "developing" countries; from an emphasis on nutrition, population, and poverty in the 1970s to an emphasis on "adjusting" the economic policies of poor countries like Nicaragua and the Philippines in the 1980s and early 1990s.

In the last years of the twentieth century, people and their organizations around the world are demanding that the World Bank and the IMF change once again. Critics claim that major changes toward accountability, transparency, and participation are needed inside the Bretton Woods Institutions, between these institutions and other financial institutions, and between the Bretton Woods Institutions and the poor people in whose interests they are supposed to serve. Programs of the Bank and the IMF should promote the economic and political empowerment of the poor; the poor, especially women, should participate in the planning and implementation of all lending operations of the World Bank and the IMF; policies and programs promoted by the Bank and the IMF should be people-centered and evaluated by their success in alleviating poverty and hunger in an environmentally sound manner.

Citizens' groups have carefully scrutinized World Bank and IMF policies, programs, and projects. Harsh structural adjustment programs that harm the poor through cuts in public health and educational services, restrictions on credit, and an emphasis on production for export rather than domestic consumption are being particularly challenged. Critics have articulated proposals for loan conditionality tied to efficient management of scarce resources; reduced spending for unnecessary military personnel and equipment; and local promotion of development that is sustainable, equitable, accountable, participatory, and self-reliant. Rather than demanding that debtor countries service their debts even at the expense of the most basic needs of their people, the Bretton Woods Institutions have been pressed to acknowledge their role in creating the debt crisis and to take real steps to lift the burden of debt from the backs of the poor.

Slowly these mammoth institutions have begun to move. The World Bank sought ways to mitigate the negative effects of cuts in social spending. The World Bank and regional development banks made information much more readily available. They engaged in some fruitful dialogue with non-governmental organizations and to some extent with local communities in borrowing countries. The World Bank established an independent mechanism of accountability called the Inspection Panel and initiated a proposal for a comprehensive strategy of debt relief. All were positive steps. Some mountains could be moved.

Changes, however, have tended to be much more on the level of program or project than policy or system. The IMF—the ultimate guardian of the free-market mountain—is most reluctant to change. The closer the critique comes to the economic system itself, the more difficult the dialogue becomes. Governments may be encouraged to maintain some social spending and even to cut wasteful military spending, but no challenge to the opening of markets or export-oriented production is tolerated. Other mountains have not yet budged!

Chapter 17

Turning the Question Around
Mark 11:27-33, 12:13-17

THE TEXT IN CONTEXT

The significance of Jesus' Temple action is not lost on the Jerusalem aristocracy. They understand that he is directly challenging their authority, but do not feel they can act against him because of the unpredictable political allegiances of the masses (11:18). Mark now turns to a series of three conflict stories between Jesus and these ruling parties: the argument over John's baptism (11:27-33), the parable of the vineyard (12:1-12), and the dispute over Caesar's coin (12:13-17). In these episodes Jesus will repudiate both partners of the Judean-Roman colonial condominium in Palestine.

On either side of the parable are stories identical in structure: Jesus is approached by opponents who challenge him with a question concerning political authority (11:28; 12:13f). Jesus in turn poses a counter-question in which he compels his antagonists to declare first their own loyalties concerning divine authority:

Was the baptism of John from heaven or merely human?
(11:30)

Whose inscription and image is on this coin?...Give then to Caesar what is Caesar's, and to God what is God's.
(12:16f)

We will look at both these vignettes here and examine the political parable they frame in the next chapter. These show how Jesus, when faced with the "entrapment" strategies of hostile leaders, refuses to react defensively. Instead, he demonstrates the power of "interrogatory theology" to lay bare the real intentions of his opponents.

153

Read Mark 11:27-33

For obvious reasons, the next time Jesus is in the Temple the "chief priests, scribes, and elders" go on the offensive against him (11:27). The appearance of this group, representing the Sanhedrin as the highest ruling body in Judea, is foreboding, since it was mentioned in Jesus' portents as the very coalition that would put the Human One on trial (8:31; 10:33).

They insist that Jesus justify why he has done "these things" in the Temple, a clear reference to the previous day's action (11:28). Unruffled, Jesus turns the scenario around: "I will ask you a question; answer me and I will answer you" (11:29). The issue of John's baptism ingenuously refocuses the exchange on a matter in which they are vulnerable (11:30). The Judean authorities cannot eulogize the murdered prophet John, because they had opposed him and no doubt consented to his imprisonment (11:31). Neither, however, can they publicly denounce him because of his enormous popularity, which no doubt skyrocketed after his martyrdom (11:32).

This public relations nightmare is, of course, precisely the same dilemma they face with Jesus, who, the story has made clear, aligned himself with John! So when the authorities equivocate, Jesus walks. He refuses to become a defendant on their terms. Instead, he relentlessly prosecutes the assumptions of those in power. In this Jesus is a model for all those who commit "civil disobedience" as a positive political act, breaking the laws of the state in order to question their moral underpinnings.

Read Mark 12:13-17

Skipping over the vineyard parable for the moment, we turn to the infamous episode concerning taxes. This text has been the long-standing object of misinterpretation by those who would impose "two-kingdom" theological doctrines upon it. Instead, we ought to read this dualism in terms of apocalyptic "bi-focal vision" (see Chapter 11). As the rhetorical parallel with the baptism episode shows, the issue is not one of compatibility between the claims of "heavenly" and "human" authority, but of conflict.

During the time at which Mark wrote his gospel, the late days of the Judean revolt, the question of whether or not to pay tribute to Rome was indeed a "test" (12:13, 15) that divided Judean nationalists from collaborators with Rome's colonial occupation (see

Chapter 20). "Do we pay or don't we?" (12:15). As far as Jesus is concerned, the question is not his but theirs, so he forces them to "own up" to their collaboration by producing a coin. The image and inscription on this Roman coin now become the center of the story (12:16).

The image of Caesar alone should have settled the matter, since no true Judean patriot would have used such idolatrous currency (the revolutionary provisional government in Palestine minted its own coins). And the inscription, which extolled Caesar as the "August and Divine Son," would have settled it for Christians, since that is the identity of Jesus. The choice then between the rival authorities of God and Caesar articulated in 12:17 could scarcely be stated more sharply. There are simply no grounds for reading the "render" statement as an exhortation to pay the tax. Jesus, who does not himself carry the coin, escapes the trap by challenging his antagonists to reveal their own political allegiances. It is this that provokes their incredulity—something no neat doctrine of obedient citizenship would have done!

Most of the episodes in Mark's gospel are composed around questions to, by, or about Jesus, from beginning (1:24) to end (16:3). Jesus is presented not as a sage who explains life's mysteries but as the great interrogator of public and private arrangements of privilege and power. His queries lay bare the "inner conflicts" of disciples and opponents alike (2:8; 8:16f; 9:33f; 11:31). Sometimes they are sharply rhetorical: "Can Satan exorcise Satan?" (3:23), or "What will the owner of the vineyard do?" (12:9). At other times they are wrapped in metaphor: "Is a lamp brought indoors to be put under a basket?" (4:21), or "Should wedding guests fast while the bridegroom is with them?" (2:19).

Jesus' questions challenge the assumptions of both the dominant culture ("How can the scribes say...?" 12:35) and of his own disciples ("Do you not yet understand?" 8:21). Above all, they query our biblical literacy: "Have you never read...?" (2:25; 12:10), and "Is it not written...?" (9:12; 11:17). Even when in legal jeopardy and cornered in a public showdown, Jesus acts as prosecutor, not defendant: "Is it lawful to do good or to do harm on the Sabbath?" (3:4). So skillful is he at turning the question around that in the end, Mark tells us, "no one dared anymore to press questions to him" (12:34).

Jesus' pedagogical strategy is to break the spell of credulity that the social order casts over its subjects and so to force a crisis of faith. He engages the disciple-reader with disturbing and disrupting quandaries that animate toward change, rather than with logically satisfying answers that pacify. Might this suggest that the church's own theological discourse should be less declarative and more interrogatory?

The Word in Our World

Doubt about the world is a necessary condition to joining the struggle to transform it. To that end, Jesus practiced what the modern popular educator Paulo Freire calls "conscientization." Freire believes that there are two fundamental approaches to education. The first is the banking method, which assumes that the teacher has all the essential information to deposit in the pupil, who is an empty vessel to be filled up with knowledge. In the other approach, the teacher provides a framework for thinking, for creative and active engagement around questions that are a part of the real-life context of the pupil, who actively engages in the process of learning. The teacher, who also learns, raises questions like who, what, why, and how. A good teacher, according to Freire, would much rather help students learn how to ask the right questions than give them the answers.

Literacy is more than the ability to read and write. It is the ability to interpret the world, to bring critical questions to bear on the social context of one's life. Questioning may be the most basic tool we need for the discipleship task of social transformation.

Perhaps the most famous example of "turning the question around" comes in Dr. Martin Luther King Jr.'s "Letter From a Birmingham Jail." The circumstances of Dr. King's reply to criticism by liberal white clergy of his 1963 campaign for civil rights in Birmingham are well-documented. The clergy had publicly urged local blacks to withdraw from demonstrations initiated by Dr. King at lunch counters in stores around that city, calling them "unwise and untimely." They went on to invoke their own religious authority against civil disobedience. From jail, where King had chosen to go by leading the sit-ins, he turned the criticism around with scathing paragraphs such as this:

> I must make two honest confessions to you, my Christian and Jewish brothers. First, I must confess that over the last few years I have been gravely disappointed with the

white moderate. I have almost reached the regrettable conclusion that the Negro's great stumbling block is not the White Citizen's Council-er or the Ku Klux Klanner, but the white moderate who is more devoted to "order" than to justice, who prefers a negative peace which is the absence of tension to a positive peace which is the presence of justice, who constantly says "I agree with you in the goal you seek, but I can't agree with your methods of direct action," who paternalistically believes that he can set the timetable for another man's freedom.

It is our responsibility as citizens of a democracy to question authority, to probe with our questions the discrepancy between rhetoric and reality, between stated values and practice. Every political organization knows the power of defining the questions in framing the public debate.

"Speaking truth to power" has never seemed so relevant or necessary as in our times. Yet the power structures of this world seem resistant to the prophetic utterance or even the right question. Take, for example, the question posed by peace groups during the Gulf War of the early nineties: Is military action against Iraq the only course of action? Or look at the questions asked more recently of the World Bank and the International Monetary Fund: After fifty years of development efforts, how is it that conditions in the two-thirds world remain the same or worse than ever? Governments and the lending institutions did not want to hear such queries; they ridiculed them as naive, irrelevant, insubordinate.

Those in power do not like to be questioned. Yet asking the right question has always served the cause of righteousness. The very fact that power is challenged makes for more healthy human equations. Some of the questions we might pose to our world:

If communism has been defeated by a better economic system, capitalism, why is there not a noticeable improvement in quality of life throughout the world?

Who gives the United States the right to "police" the globe?

Why are powerful countries dismissive of the United Nations?

Why are more and more women and children living in poverty?

Why is it that only rich people can get elected to public office in the United States?

How do we account for the growing gap in the United States between very wealthy people and those with moderate incomes? And how do we account for the continued increase in domestic poverty?

With the United States facing such financial difficulties, why is spending on military personnel and weapons not cut severely?

Why is the United States the only industrialized country which imposes the death penalty? And why is it that it is imposed overwhelmingly on people of color?

Why is there such disproportion among our school systems, even in the same city or region?

Why do so many of our churches simply mirror the dominant culture?

Why is it that the overriding agenda of the institutional churches appears to be self-preservation?

How do we justify the tremendous investment portfolios of religious institutions?

Just as Jesus questions the world, so does he question us. Perhaps because we have eyes that do not see and ears that do not hear, his questions open up painful and awkward uncertainties. In Mark's gospel, we encounter a Jesus who is portrayed not as the answer to our questions, but as the question to our answers.

Chapter 18

Revising the Song of the Vineyard
Mark 12:1-12

THE TEXT IN CONTEXT

Read Mark 12:1-12

We examined earlier how Jesus' deft use of parables was highly po-litical (3:23, see Chapter 4; 4:30-32, see Chapter 5). The parable he spins here to the authorities is no exception.

Jesus bases it upon Isaiah's "love song for the vineyard" (Isa-iah 5:1ff). This oracle begins by recalling the hard labor of a frus-trated farmer who cleared, cultivated, and invested in land (5:2). But the song turns to a first-person lament at having to abandon land that will not yield (5:3-6).

Isaiah makes it clear at the end of 5:6 that this is an allegory:

The vineyard of Yahweh Sabaoth is the house of Israel
and the people of Judah God's chosen planting;
God expected justice, but found bloodshed,
integrity, but heard only a cry of distress. (5:7)

Taking this cue, interpreters of Jesus' version of the parable have immediately concluded that it, too, is an allegory about the death of Jesus, the "beloved son" of Mark 12:6. But in both the case of Isaiah and the case of Mark the parables are not merely allegorical, for like the seed parables of Mark 4, they also reflect the lived experience of the people to whom they are addressed.

Palestinian farmers struggled to cultivate the land's rocky soil, often losing their battle with the elements for subsistence. More often, however, farmers were driven off their land by unnatural economic forces, specifically the concentration of agricultural hold-ings in the hands of a few land barons (see Chapter 5). This is why

Isaiah's love song turns into an angry indictment of the rich, "who join house to house, who add field to field, until there is room for no one else" (Isaiah 5:8), and who live in luxury (5:11f) and "call evil good and good evil" (5:20).

Jesus reappropriates Isaiah's song, revising it in order to renew the prophetic attack. To Isaiah's description of the land he adds that the owner "let it out to tenants" and then "went into another country" (Mark 12:1). This change is key, for Mark's readers knew that most members of the Jewish ruling class were also absentee-landlords. Like the sower parable, this story is all about role-reversal. The sower tale, told to and about peasant sharecroppers, invites them to imagine a situation in which they control the surplus they extract through their labor (see Chapter 5). Conversely, the vineyard tale, told to and about the Jerusalem authorities, challenges actual landowners to imagine life from the bitter perspective of rebellious tenants.

These "tenants" feel rage at having to hand over the fruits of their labor to the agent of the absentee landlord, and so decide to resist violently all who come to extract the surplus (12:2-5). Finally, they conspire to "own" the land, correctly assuming that if they can kill the "heir" the deed will pass to them (12:6-8).

Two levels are operating simultaneously here. At the literal level, the story is an accurate depiction of the violent struggle between disenfranchised sharecroppers and oppressive overlords, which often resulted in peasant revolts that were in turn inevitably crushed by superior forces mustered by the owners (12:9). At the allegorical level, the parable is about the ruling class (12:12). According to Isaiah, the vineyard belongs to God; similarly Leviticus insists that God is the only true landowner: "The land shall not be sold in perpetuity, for the land is mine; with me you are but aliens and tenants" (Leviticus 25:23).

Jesus' rhetorical question in 12:9 is tantamount to saying: How does it feel to be on the other side of the landowner's violence? This is the surprise twist of the parable: casting owners as tenants. It thus indicts the ruling class for the brutal murder of all those "sent by the true owner"—a long line of prophets. And it convicts them of conspiring to "own" (for commercial profit) what is God's gift to all. This parable further undermines both the economic and political pretensions of the authorities who are already plotting against Jesus.

In conclusion, Mark switches metaphors, citing Psalm 118:22 (12:10f). Its reference to "builders" and "cornerstones" will take on ironic significance later when Jesus predicts the dismantling of the

Temple-state "stone by stone" (13:2), and in the subsequent legal charge against him that he called for the demolition and "rebuilding" of the sanctuary (14:58). But again the authorities, who understand perfectly Jesus' challenge, are unable to arrest him—because of popular support for his criticism of them!

THE WORD IN OUR WORLD

Both Isaiah's and Jesus' parables of the vineyard protest the politics of land distribution in their time. Today millions of people around the world and in the United States continue to be displaced by the growing consolidation of land ownership in the hands of the rich and of corporate interests.

Not many years ago Nobel Peace laureate Rigoberta Menchu applauded a highly criticized politician in her native Guatemala because "he was dealing with the overriding problem of our society —land." Guatemala's bitter thirty-year war has centered on a people's right to the land and its yield. Some 100,000 Mayan peasants have lost their lives at the hands of a brutal military in that small nation because they laid claim to their ancestral heritage, the land. Land is the basic reality of all nations, defining boundaries, causing wars, producing wealth.

Mark's parable about the tenant farmers repeats itself in our day. The history of the United States is one of imperialism: To protect and expand its territory, the United States has engaged in aggressive activities. When the U.S. was thirteen small colonies on the eastern seaboard, Manifest Destiny—the belief that America was to stretch from "sea to shining sea"—drove its "foreign" policy during the first decades of its history. In pursuit of that policy, the indigenous peoples who had lived for centuries on the vast expanses west of the Allegheny Mountains were nearly eliminated.

Texas and the Southwest were taken from Mexico in a highly questionable military action. A civil war was fought in part to prove that no state could leave the Union once having joined it. Cuba and the Philippines were invaded and Hawaii annexed under this expansionist vision. More recently, the United States sent troops to the Dominican Republic, Panama, and Grenada, and supplied others in Nicaragua and El Salvador when it was determined that U.S. interests were threatened.

Too often religion in the United States has blessed this fixation on its territory. Where was the prophetic outcry when U.S. troops made their Christmas attack on Panama, for reasons that are still disputed? Who spoke up when the Marines waded ashore in Grenada to "liberate" that little island? Do we have the courage to proclaim that God is the true owner of the land? "What then will the owner of the vineyard do" (Mark 12:9)?

The story of people on the land within the United States has unfolded with restless movement and struggle. Land was taken from the Native peoples and given to European immigrants. Many of the latter carved out small farms. Today those farms are passing out of existence, having been bought up by agribusiness companies. The children of slaves left poverty in the South for the promise of Northern cities; today many of their children's children are crowded into unlivable spaces in inner cities. Merchants and professionals migrated to the cities, then abandoned them in the "flight" of the middle class to the surrounding suburbs. Today some suburban residents are returning to the cities and displacing lower-income residents by "gentrifying" old neighborhoods.

What migrations did your ancestors experience before and during this century? Did any of your family move from rural to urban centers? What migrations have you experienced in your lifetime? Think about the causes behind these moves.

Chapter 19

Arguing Scripture
Mark 12:18–13:2

THE TEXT IN CONTEXT

Read Mark 12:18-27

Jesus continues his argumentation with the authorities as the Sadducees take up the attack. The Sadducees were the most conservative of the ruling groups. The historian Josephus wrote that they had "the confidence of the wealthy alone, but no following among the populace." They rejected the notion that the dead were resurrected, and in order to ridicule Jesus pose an absurd scenario (12:19-23). Assumed here is the practice of levirate marriage, in which a deceased man's brother was obligated to marry his wife if no male heir was produced (read Deuteronomy 25:5-10). This practice was the vehicle for perpetuating the patriarchal family system and for passing on the household estate.

The Sadducean objection, of course, is that there would be no orderly way to determine which of the seven brothers would "own" the woman in the alleged afterlife. Against their instrumental attitude toward women and the whole system of class succession, Jesus asserts a vision of the world transformed. The woman will not "belong" to any of the men because in the resurrected life there is no patriarchal marriage (12:25). Jesus next contends that the blessing of posterity will be guaranteed not by structures of male succession but by the promise of God, as the lineage of Abraham, Isaac, and Jacob attests (12:26f).

The Sadducees, holding privileged positions in this life, deny the possibility—in this world or the next—of any social arrangement other than the one from which they benefit. Jesus, on the other hand, attacks the presumption that the "world of the resurrection" will simply reflect the prevailing relations of power. By invoking

163

Moses and the burning bush, he appeals to the God who cannot be named (read Exodus 3:2-14). This implies that "ultimate reality," far from legitimating the status quo, subverts it with the vision of transformed human relationships. Jesus is emphatic, pointing out that the Sadducees "are wrong" to begin and end his argument, and accuses these highly literate men of ignorance of "the scripture and the power of God" (12:24).

Read Mark 12:28-40

Concluding the Jerusalem narrative are a series of clashes with the scribes, the arch opponents of Jesus. The section begins with a challenge to interpret the great commandment, which was a central debating point among the rabbis (12:28). Jesus knows the "orthodox" answer: the Shema (12:29f; see Deuteronomy 6:4). But he boldly attaches to it a citation from the Levitical code of justice, implying that to love God is to refuse to exploit one's neighbor (12:31; read Leviticus 19:9-17).

According to Mark's narrative, exploitation is precisely what is perpetuated by the system the scribes uphold. Thus, even though this scribe appears to agree in theory, even citing Hosea 6:6 in approval (12:33), Jesus stops short of embracing him (12:34a). He has learned to be suspicious of flattery (see 10:17, 12:14)! The sovereignty of God demands more than orthodoxy and intellectual assent; there must be the practice of justice. Having silenced his critics, Jesus turns to go on the offensive against the scribal class (12:34b).

In the Temple again, Jesus finally addresses the question of Davidic Messianism directly (12:35-37). Here "sonship" has to do not with genealogy, but with political ideology. The scribes assumed that the Messiah would act to restore the Davidic monarchy, and that this would further aggrandize their own position. But citing Psalm 110, Jesus reverses the equation: Even David is subordinate to the sovereignty of God. Jesus has no interest in rehabilitating the old dreams of Davidic empire, for it is the politics of domination that is the problem.

Jesus now instructs the crowd in critical thinking, warning against the pretense of the scribal class, whom he portrays as solely concerned with the maintenance of their social status and privilege (12:38f). This is the antithesis of his call to be "last" and "servant" (see 10:43f). These are hard words, and they get harder.

Scribal affluence is attributed to "devouring widows' houses under the pretext of long prayers" (12:40). This probably refers to the practice of legal trusteeship, in which the estates of deceased men were given to scribes to administer because the widow was deemed unfit to run such affairs! In compensation the trustee received a percentage, and embezzlement and abuse were not uncommon. As in the earlier dispute over *korban* (7:9ff) and the Temple action, Jesus criticizes "piety" as a mask for "robbery."

Read Mark 12:41–13:2

The final Temple episode provides Jesus with an object lesson concerning the exploitation of widows (12:41-44). Jesus sits "opposite" the treasury (12:41), the same antagonistic stance he will shortly take toward the Temple building as a whole when he speaks of its demise (see 13:2). Ever class-conscious, Mark emphasizes the contrast between the large contributions placed in the till by the rich and the meager sums by the poor (12:41f). Infuriated by a widow who has been made destitute by her tithing obligation, Jesus summons his disciples for another solemn teaching (12:43f).

His comment here has long been trivialized as a quaint commendation of the superior piety of the poor, when in fact it is a scathing indictment. He considers this an example of "the devouring of a widow's house": "She has put in everything she had, her whole sustenance!" The Temple, like the scribal class, no longer protects the poor, but crushes them. His attack on the political economy of the Temple and its stewards complete, Jesus exits the Temple grounds for the last time in disgust (13:1).

There is an intentional symmetry between the disciples' awe at the Temple edifice Jesus has just repudiated ("Teacher, look!" 13:1) and their earlier surprise at the cursed fig tree ("Master, look!" 11:21). Key social institutions are always "bigger than life," and indeed Herod's Second Temple was considered one of the architectural wonders of the ancient Mediterranean world. Moreover, it determined all aspects of the Judean universe: cosmology, politics, and economics. Thus when Jesus calls for its utter destruction (13:2), it is no wonder that the disciples respond with terrified questions about the "end of the world" (13:4)! And to articulate his alternative vision, he must turn to the language of apocalyptic (see next chapter).

THE WORD IN OUR WORLD

Jesus engages the authorities in arguments over scripture because the latter routinely used the Bible to support their position in society. To combat this Jesus uses "scripture against scripture," and so must we today.

Consider the woman who is the subject of the debate in Mark 12:18ff. Wherein lies her worth as a human being in the eyes of these Sadducees? She is property, valued only as a source of children for the original husband. What has it meant for half of humankind to be valued as the property of the other half, and for women's worth to be found only in child-bearing?

Let us reflect upon a disturbing question: What do we do with "texts of terror" (those parts of scripture that appear to support the abuse of one group of people by another)? For example, the Bible has been used throughout church history to denigrate and subjugate women. Consider the following.

> Let a woman learn silence with all submissiveness. I permit no woman to teach or to have authority over men; she is to keep silent. For Adam was formed first, then Eve; and Adam was not deceived, but the woman was deceived and became a transgressor. Yet woman will be saved through bearing children, if she continues in faith and love and holiness, with modesty." (1 Timothy 2: 11-15)

That such texts have been interpreted in a oppressive, patriarchal tradition in the church is evident from the following citations from famous theologians:

> It was necessary for woman to be made, as the Scripture says, as a helper to man not, indeed, as a helpmate in other works, as some say, since man can be more efficiently helped by another man in other works; but as a helper in the work of generation.... As regards individual nature, woman is defective and misbegotten, for the active force in the male seed tends to the production of a perfect likeness in the masculine sex; while the production of woman comes from defect in the active force or from some material indisposition, or even from some ex-

ternal influence; such as that of a south wind, which is moist, as the Philosopher [Aristotle] observes."

— Thomas Aquinas, *Summa Theologica*

It is a great favor that God has preserved woman for us—against our will and wish, as it were—both for pro-creation and also as a medicine against the sin of fornication.... she is... an antidote and a medicine; we can hardly speak of her without a feeling of shame, and surely we cannot make use of her without shame. The reason is sin. In Paradise that union would have taken place without any bashfulness, as an activity created and blessed by God. It would have been accompanied by a noble delight, such as there was at that time in eating and drinking. Now, alas, it is so hideous and frightful a plea-sure that physicians compare it with epilepsy or falling sickness. Thus an actual disease is linked with the very activity of procreation. We are in the state of sin and of death. Therefore we also undergo this punishment, that we cannot make use of woman without the horrible pas-sion of lust and, so to speak, without epilepsy.

— Martin Luther, *Lectures on Genesis*

How are we to respond to biblical texts such as 2 Samuel 12–13 that treat women or others as property to be used and abused? The Bible has been used to sanction many other forms of oppression and injustice as well, including slavery, "just wars," the conquest of the Americas, the persecution of the Jews, the dehu-manization of gay and lesbian people. By exploring ways to face texts used to abuse women, we also develop guidelines for dealing with other "texts of terror."

This, however, is a terribly difficult dilemma to which Chris-tians have chosen varied responses.

One common option is to ignore the "texts of terror." We ig-nore the rape of Tamar, the "holy war" against the Canaanites, the silencing of women—and hope texts like these will cease to shape our collective sense of right and wrong. But reality defies that hope. These texts, ignored and unquestioned, continue to imply that some people have fewer human rights and less value than others.

A second common option is to decide tacitly that some parts of the Bible are "true" and others are not. We lose a great deal in this choice, for we then choose as "true" that with which we agree, and we cease to be challenged by that which is troubling. Scripture becomes justification for our perspective, rather than the life-changing Word of God.

Another option, perhaps less common, is to conclude that the Bible does not reveal the God of saving love and cannot guide our lives.

Mark's Jesus guides us in a different direction! He too sees the use of scripture to oppress. His response, however, is none of the above; he does not ignore the oppressive text cited by the Sadducees, or reject the text, or walk away from scripture. Rather, he refutes the use of scripture to justify oppressive social structures—in this case the objectification of women—by using scripture itself, and he returns scripture to the service of liberation. In other words, Mark's Jesus employs scripture to subvert the oppressive use of scripture!

Scripture—as the story of God's liberating love and the call to live according to it—compels us to face and reinterpret the abusive texts. Jesus sets the precedent for this approach! But *how* do we approach the Bible in this way? This question deserves to be explored deeply over a lifetime.

We suggest a starting point: Face head-on the difficult texts. Do so by appealing not to specific texts in isolation but rather to the Bible as a whole, considering its overall truth claims. Texts that seem to subjugate must be tested against the central biblical demands for love and justice. Texts which contradict those central claims are not normative for contemporary Christian life.

Then explore the factors that may have caused the text to be written as it was. Keep in mind the huge cultural gulf between ourselves and these ancient texts; many troubling texts are less problematic when understood in their *own* socio-historical context. Or perhaps a New Testament text is based upon the writer's untenable interpretation of the Hebrew Bible, such as in the passage from Timothy quoted above. An interesting rationale for texts of terror is offered by Michael Lerner in *Jewish Renewal*. He suggests that the Hebrew Bible contains two voices: the voice of God and the voice of the writers' pain and brokenness masquerading as the voice of God. That pain—accumulated over generations of slavery in Egypt and wandering in the desert—distorted, to varying degrees, the writers' ability to know and reflect God (just as our pain and brokenness do the same).

How might we discern between these two voices? Lerner suggests that the voice of God can be found in those parts of scripture that nurture hope about the possibility that we can join God in the task of healing the world from its domination by pain, oppression, patriarchy, and evil. God's voice is found in those parts of scripture which help us recognize the "other" as created in the image of God. Where scripture makes us doubt the possibility of human beings working toward a world in which we can live together in love and justice, it is not the voice of God.

However one explains "texts of terror," we would suggest several guidelines for Bible study. First, we should read *all* of scripture in order to discern its central truths. Jesus criticizes the biblical illiteracy of the religious establishment: "Is not this the reason you are wrong, that you know neither the scriptures nor the power of God?" (Mark 12:24). "Have you not read in the book of Moses...?" (12:26).

Second, we should read the Bible in community. The truth of scripture is revealed in the interaction between the Word, the reader, and the faith community—both our local faith communities and a much broader community that includes brothers and sisters from different times, places, and social locations. We do not fully hear the Word if we do not hear it from the perspectives of "others," most particularly those on the underside of history. Our knowledge of Jesus who walked with the outcasts is crippled if we do not begin to see him through the eyes of peoples who have been "outcasts" in our world today.

Third, we should try to attune ourselves to the cultural contexts in which the Bible was written, and seek to discover the world views and situations of the writers and their communities.

Fourth, we should not embrace any one interpretation as the singular correct interpretation for all time. The Word we encounter in the Bible is not static; it is the Living Word—creating and breathing life with God. We are to be in living relationship with it, wrestling with it, to learn who we are and how we are to serve God. In the context of a long-term honest relationship with God in scripture, we gain the wisdom to reinterpret the "texts of terror."

The beauty of this approach to scripture is that it does not eliminate abusive biblical texts. Rather, it allows them to enhance our faithfulness, offering glimpses of where our forbears' quest to be faithful ran aground on their own pain, fears, and needs to protect identity, security, or privilege. These texts, then, have an indirect kind of authority, not as models we should follow but as mirrors in which we can recognize, understand, and choose to change parallel behavior in our own context (see James 1:22-25).

Chapter 20

Revolutionary Patience
Mark 13:3-37

The Text in Context

Background: The Judean Revolt

Jesus' second great sermon (13:5ff) alludes to events in Mark's own historical moment: the Judean Revolt of 66-70 C.E. In June of 66, an insurrection against Roman rule began in Jerusalem, the culmination to decades of widespread social unrest and percolating armed insurgency. Temple sacrifices on behalf of the emperor were halted, both the Judean clerical aristocracy and Roman cohorts were driven out of the city, and the public archives (including records of debt) were burned. The rebellion spread to the surrounding provinces. In November, the Roman counterattack began under Gallus, the Roman Legate of Syria. But the imperial forces were successfully repelled by the nationalist fighters, and for a few short years many parts of Palestine were liberated from Roman rule.

A provisional government was set up, despite fierce internal power struggles, and the rebels began preparing for the next siege on Jerusalem that would surely come. A massive Roman counterinsurgency commenced the following summer, immediately retaking most of Galilee and moving south in a vicious scorched-earth campaign. Because of civil war in Rome, however, the military effort stalled, so that the final assault on Jerusalem was not begun until the spring of 70 under Titus. In the meantime there were internal coups and counter-coups between the radical anti-clerical and moderate rebel factions.

To those Palestinian Jews loyal to the Temple-state, the terrible social and political upheaval of the war with Rome no doubt portended "signs of the end" (see 13:4). But from Mark's perspective, the rebellion merely represented the "beginning" of yet another

cycle of violence (13:7f). With the Roman siege of Jerusalem imminent (13:14a), rebel recruiters were going throughout Palestine summoning patriotic Jews to Jerusalem's defense (13:6, 21f).

For Mark, only one voice could compete with their persuasive
call to arms—that of Jesus. His apocalyptic sermon, with its cau-
tionary refrain to "Watch out!" (13:5, 9, 23, 33) suggests that Mark's
community was critical of both imperial collaborators and nationalists. Its nonviolent stance, refusing to cooperate with either the Jewish guerrillas or the Roman counterinsurgency, earned it persecution from both sides of the war (13:9-13). The disciples, representing
the anxious concern of a community caught in the war, pose a double question to Jesus (13:4):

> When will this be
> and what will be the sign
> that these things are to be accomplished?

The sermon's two parts provide Jesus' response accordingly:
The first half (13:5-22) addresses the "time," the second the "signs"
(13:23-37). Both parts reiterate the counsel of the prophet Daniel,
who two centuries earlier during the Maccabean revolt had urged
the faithful to resist both the imperial beast and the delusions of
militant nationalism (Daniel 7-11). At the heart of the sermon is
Jesus' call to abandon Jerusalem (Mark 13:14b-20) because of the
apocalyptic conviction that a truly just social order cannot be established by the sword. The disciples are instructed to "wait and
watch" for the fall of the powers (13:23-27) and a genuine transformation of the world (13:28ff).

Read Mark 13:3-23

The first half of the sermon is structured in two parts around the exhortation to critical awareness:

> When you hear of wars and rumors of wars... (13:7)
>   ...the one enduring to the end will be saved (13:13).
> When you see the desecrating sacrilege... (13:14)
>   ...unless those days were shortened, no one would be
>   saved. (13:20)

Of particular concern are the seductive claims of those calling for
the final Messianic struggle:

> Watch out that no one leads you astray. Many will come in my name, saying "I am he!" and will lead many astray. (13:5f)

> If anyone says to you, "Look, here is Messiah!" ... do not believe it. False messiahs and false prophets will arise and show signs and wonders to lead astray, if possible, the elect. Watch out, for I have told you all this beforehand. (13:21-23)

The Christian community should not be sucked into the fevered vortex of "wars and rumors of wars" and the promises that this armed struggle will put an "end" to the old order (13:7). Jesus parodies these claims, asserting that they represent "only the beginning" of troubles (13:8; see Isaiah 26:17; Jeremiah 22:23; Hosea 13:13; Micah 4:9f).

Next comes specific instruction to a community enduring fierce persecution from both sides of the war. Jesus confirms that his followers will be "delivered up" both to Judean synagogue councils and imperial governors (13:9). In the midst of this holocaust, disciples must remain focused on the good news of God's sovereignty, and trust that the Spirit will accompany them in their trials (13:10f). Mark's realism recognizes that this persecution will split families and that the community will suffer defections (13:12f; see Micah 7:6). But Jesus is not asking his disciples to undergo anything that he will not himself face in this story: He too will be "delivered up" while his own "family" betrays him.

The "desecrating sacrilege" (see Daniel 11:31, 12:11) and Mark's cryptic editorial comment ("let the reader understand") in 13:14 refer to the final Roman siege of Jerusalem. In the tradition of Jeremiah (Jeremiah 21), Jesus calls for his followers to abandon the defense of the Temple-state as a lost cause. The conditions described in 13:15-18 certainly reflect the plight of wartime refugees. The so-called "liberation war," in Mark's opinion, is a disaster, serving only to victimize everyone (13:19f). With a final exhortation to endurance, the first half comes to a close (13:21-23; see Daniel 12:1).

Read Mark 13:24-37

The second half of the sermon employs the language of high apocalyptic symbolism in order to address the request for "true signs" of the end of the world. The apocalyptic vision looks for the end, not the mere recycling, of the politics of violence. Things will change, Jesus argues, only when the principalities and powers are pulled from their "heavenly thrones" (13:24f). But how will this be accomplished?

Cosmic unraveling is a traditional prophetic symbol of judgment (13:26; see Isaiah 13:10, Ezekiel 32:7f, Amos 8:9, Joel 2:10). In 13:24f (and in 13:28), Mark is alluding to Isaiah 34:4:

> All the host of heaven shall rot away, and the skies roll
>   up like a scroll,
> All their host shall wither like a leaf on a vine, or fruit
>   withering on a fig tree.

But Mark specifically identifies the darkening sun with the revelation of the Human One (13:26). This is now the second allusion in Mark's narrative to the dramatic "advent" of the Human One:

> ...of that one the Human One will be ashamed when he comes in the glory of his Father with the holy angels. Truly I say to you, there are some standing here who will...see the sovereignty of God come with power. (8:38-9:1)

> Then they will see the Human One coming with the clouds of heaven with great power and glory. And he will send out the angels... (13:26f)

The third instance occurs at the trial of Jesus:

> You will see the Human One seated at the right hand of Power and coming with the clouds of heaven. (14:62)

Traditional theology has assumed these refer to a time beyond the bounds of both story and history—the "Second Coming." But in fact this moment is narrated in Mark's story.

The three "predictions" of the Human One's advent parallel the three "portents" of the Human One's death at the hands of the authorities (see Chapter 11). Moreover, they each assert that someone "will see" this spectacle: the disciples, the powers, and the Sanhedrin, respectively. As we shall see, "some of the disciples" (15:40) and the authorities (15:31) do in fact "see" the crucifixion of Jesus (see Chapter 24). Do the powers witness it as well? As Jesus hangs on the cross, at least one of the cosmic signs of 13:24 is indeed realized: "There was darkness over the whole land" (15:33; see Chapter 24).

This is the heart of Mark's apocalyptic argument. The Human One's death and his revelation "in power and glory" are the same moment. It is through his demonstration of the nonviolent power of the cross that the powers are overthrown. But it takes the bi-focal vision of apocalyptic faith to "see" this (see Chapter 11). Although the early church understood this "mystery" of the cross (see 1 Corinthians 2:7f, Colossians 2:13-15), the modern church has not.

The sermon ends with two parables. The first returns to the fig tree image used earlier (11:13, 20; see Chapter 16). Jesus proposes the leafy (fruitless) fig tree as a sign of the apocalyptic "harvest" (13:28f; see Amos 8:1f, Joel 3:13). "These things taking place" in turn refers back to Jesus' exorcism of the Temple (see 11:28). Thus the world of the Temple-state is coming to an end. "This generation" will witness this eclipse (13:30), an allusion back to Jesus' first prediction of the Human One's advent (8:38f). Jesus' "words" (of the cross, 8:32, 38) will not pass away (13:31). This is the "lesson of the fig tree" we must "learn" (13:28).

In the second parable, God's true "lordship" over the "house" is reasserted (13:34-37). Though we do not know when history will finally be liberated from the grip of the powers (13:32f), we have been told how. The warning to "watch out" now becomes a command to "stay awake." These exhortations will be heard again in Gethsemane—the moment in which Jesus does (and his disciples do not) choose the Way of the cross (14:32-41; see Chapter 22). And the "watches of the night" (evening, midnight, cock crow, morning, 13:35) will be narrated during the Passion story.

In other words, the world has become Gethsemane. We all (13:37) must stay awake through the dark night of history, "watching" for possibilities of genuine transformation.

THE WORD IN OUR WORLD

What does it mean for us to discern the signs of the times today, and to retain hope in the face of so much violence and discouragement?

War, famine, refugees, debt, environmental destruction, poverty, arms trade, drug trade, economic instability. Imagine a map of the world overlaid with words or symbols indicating the reality of life in different countries or regions.

How well the text from Mark 13 mirrors our global reality! Every continent on the face of the earth is racked with desperate conditions of hunger, poverty, violence, and strife. In our own times, we have witnessed a growing disparity between the rich and the poor—while a very few live in comfort, the world is becoming uninhabitable for a majority of the human family. The environment itself reflects this human upheaval with pollution, despoliation, and cataclysmic change. What kind of future are we leaving for our children and grandchildren?

It is hard to believe that history has any redemptive purpose. Things seem to be getting worse, not better. The emotional cost of living in such a chaotic world is enormous. Sadness, awe, rage, fear, and a feeling of overwhelming powerlessness are the constant companions of thinking people.

Because we so often find these negative feelings intolerable, we are constantly tempted to displace them with aggressive behavior toward an "enemy" who becomes the object of all our fear and rage. Or we turn our frustration inward in self-destructive behavior —deadening the pain with alcohol or food or drugs. Or we respond to the complex and disturbing challenge of our world with panaceas, simplistic solutions that excuse us from deep or nuanced analysis. But the most dangerous temptation of all is not to look, to narrow our awareness, to enter into psychic numbness, to become passive and withdrawn.

The pervasive habit of our culture is to take refuge in denial, to hide from the world in the "business as usual" of our private lives. We close our eyes to avoid facing the reality around us by surrounding ourselves with the mind-deadening escapes of modern society. Yet the gospel calls us to look at reality and to acknowledge our feelings of sadness and despair that surface when we feel the pain of the world.

From the perspective of the gospel, to experience this pain and sadness is to enter into the agony of Christ. In communities of faith these feelings can be validated and channeled. Together we name the pain of the world and lift it up to God in prayer. By finding the strength together to face the brokenness of our world we encourage each other to move through it.

In prayer we rediscover that the human family is connected by more than just currents of matter and energy; by more than just electronic networks, information systems, markets, and policies; by more even than our common human instincts and longings. As children of God we are intrinsically connected to the Divine Being who created us and who is moved with compassion in the face of our suffering.

But the reign of God will go far beyond a revolution of the soul. The reign of God will bring about a radical transformation of the social order itself. All hierarchies of unjust privilege will be overturned: The first shall be last and the last shall be first. The gentle will inherit the earth; those who mourn will celebrate. The margin becomes the center: the despised outcast now sits at the seat of honor at the divine banquet. The crippled and sick are healed; the homeless and sojourner called home; the orphan and widow are reunited. The abused child will dwell in safety; the poor and the hungry will be given abundance. The oppressed will taste the precious liberty of God. And the rich, the indifferent, the powerbrokers, and the oppressors of this world will weep and gnash their teeth.

The Kairos USA document was written by communities of Christians in the mid-1990s. It was modeled on other Kairos documents, most notably that written in South Africa in the height of apartheid. The U.S. document, *On the Road: From Kairos to Jubilee,* names the signs of crisis around us but also names visible signs on the horizon in our own society of the inbreaking reign of God:

- the many people who are choosing to value relationships and family over material goals;

- small, active communities, where the undergirding of faith sustains principled actions for justice;

- the emergence of young urban leaders dedicating their lives to ending violence in our cities;

- neighborhoods and families accepting responsibility for rebuilding and sustaining principles of personal, interpersonal, and social morality;

- a burgeoning anti-racism movement;

- new and vibrant theologies arising from the experiences and life stories of people of color, women, and other peace-with-justice communities;

- the movement of Native peoples reclaiming land, culture, and sovereignty;

- the resilience of movements of people of color reclaiming their culture, heritage, languages, and rights to community self-determination;

- the struggles of gay and lesbian Christians who testify to the church that they too thirst for the living waters of God's love, affirmation, and grace;

- efforts to link demilitarization issues with those of economic justice;

- the clamor for a modern-day Jubilee to break the cycles of poverty and indebtedness through practices of reparation;

- the movement exploring economic alternatives such as land trusts, worker ownership, cooperatives, community-based economics;

- the growing concern over environmental issues and alliances forming to counter environmental racism; and

- the movement for universal health care.

(adapted from *On the Way: From Kairos to Jubilee*)

Even as God created us once out of nothing, so again shall God, in her mercy, reach into the nothingness of death and the entire world will be recreated. The *no* of divine judgment will give way finally, overwhelmingly, to the *yes* of divine grace and mercy that fills the cosmos with joy and laughter. This *yes* floods the universe with a healing and unifying light.

Negation will yield to an expansive affirmation of life itself. All the distinctions that define history now—barriers between rich and poor, black and white, oppressed and oppressor—will disappear as life is swept up in the divine embrace. In the midst of our historical crisis, then, we are called to watch and wait for this promise.

We do not know when the end will come. We are called to be prepared, to accept the risk that comes with true discipleship, to read the signs of the times. This is what it means to live in the end times: to put our faith in that reality which is as yet hidden in history, yet which breaks out in the most unlikely places.

OUR DISCIPLESHIP JOURNEY

This part of Mark's gospel narrates those charged and tense moments after Jesus entered Jerusalem until the time of his arrest. We have witnessed the scene in which Jesus cleansed the Temple by overturning the banking tables and forming a blockade to stop all traffic. We watched the confrontation in the public space of the Temple continue in Jesus' war of words with various representatives of power—the scribes, the Pharisees, the Sadducees, and the Romans.

Jesus queries us: Why are you afraid? Can you be baptized with my baptism? Could you not keep watch? Do you have eyes that see? Do you not remember? Is it not written? Who do people say that I am?

Open your life to these same hard questions posed by Jesus. Develop the habit of hard questioning, critical thinking—not only at a personal level, but also within the communities and institutions of which you are a part. Deliberately place yourself in situations that give you a perspective on life from the margins—in soup kitchens, shelters, on the street, in poor neighborhoods, poor schools, with refugee or immigrant communities. If you ever travel outside of your own region, move beyond the tourist places to see real life. Live attentively, with your senses alive to the people around you. Open your heart and your mind to Jesus' questions:

> Who is my mother and who are my brothers? What do family and community mean in a broken and divided world? What response does community demand in this situation?

> What is the reign of God like? Where do I see it around me now? How can I nourish its inbreaking?

> Could you not keep watch? Am I indifferent to the suffering around me? Am I asleep concerning the damage being done to other people or to the earth by our patterns of life? How can I be awakened?

V

THE WAY OF THE HUMAN ONE

OPENING MEDITATION

"Truly I tell you, wherever the good news is proclaimed in the whole world, what she has done will be told *in remembrance* of her." (Mark 14:9)

Several years ago sculptress Judy Chicago produced a powerful work of art titled "The Dinner Party." Her project was a beautiful triangular table with place settings for dozens of women from ages past whose stories were never adequately told, whose memories were faded and distant. The names of hundreds of other exceedingly important, but nearly forgotten, women were inscribed on the floor under and around the table. The place settings were heavily symbolic, with fabric and pottery, embroidery and weavings describing the lives and characteristics of the women.

Inspired by Judy Chicago's work, the Center for New Creation, an ecumenical project for peace and justice in Arlington, Virginia, from 1979 through 1994 scripted a daylong celebration of women that included a ritual meal. Over the course of several years, hundreds of women and men from different cultures and many walks of life participated in different settings in "Woman: A Celebration of Herstory."

Imagine that you are invited to such a celebration "in remembrance of her" (Mark 14:9)—especially in honor of the woman who anointed Jesus in preparation for his death, but also remembering the rich and beautiful heritage of women who have shaped history and our lives, women who are models for our discipleship today.

What possessed this woman to cross the boundaries that defined proper relations between men and women in her society? Why would we celebrate her? What were the implications of this compassionate act by a woman? What did the discipleship community make of it? More important, what did Jesus himself make of this moment of intimacy in the midst of a struggle that would soon cost him his life? Mark's Jesus said that the story of this woman would be told for all time.

But it has not been told. She has not been identified as the one who understood. She has not been named as the faithful one who seemed to know in her soul the cost of discipleship.

As you anticipate this "celebration," recall other women in the gospel of Mark whose stories have spoken to you. We honor their stories of suffering and of courage, of oppression and resistance, of faithful discipleship. As they have welcomed us into a discipleship of equals, so we welcome them as guides and lights in our lives.

We welcome Simon's mother-in-law, the Syrophoenician woman and her daughter, the hemorrhaging woman and Jairus' daughter, the woman who was divorced, the poor widow, Mary Magdalene, Mary the mother of James and Joses, and Salome (Mark 15:40). We welcome too the unnamed and unmentioned women in Mark's gospel. Take a moment to consider the many women never mentioned in the story, who are as critical to it as the many male characters. Name some of them aloud: the wives and daughters of the men killed in the parable of the wicked tenants, the many unnamed female disciples of Jesus.

Recall also other women—of history or of special importance in your personal heritage—whose memories you would hold up. Consider women of all races, listening with particular care to the voices of women living in worlds of poverty and injustice, to the voices of Third World women in this country and elsewhere whose struggle is wedded to the timeless struggle toward the Reign of Love.

Memory and ritual are crucial in sustaining the identity and courage of an alternative community. We walk with Jesus now to the cross. He himself drew our attention to the wisdom of the woman who seemed to understand the radical message he brought and the tremendous cost it would exact. In our own times, her voice is emerging in the voices of those previously unheard and unheeded who also understand quite well the story and its implications for our world. May her memory be retrieved, and the memories of other wise ones guide us, as we too try to follow.

Chapter 21

Intimacy and Betrayal
Mark 14:1-25

THE TEXT IN CONTEXT

We now begin reading our way toward the tragic denouement, and surprise ending, of Mark's story. Mark's double plot line converges. Jesus' struggle with the authorities reaches its consequence: arrest. On the other hand, the inability of the disciples to understand and embrace the Way reaches its logical conclusion: desertion.

Jesus' second sermon exhorted us to be ever vigilant for that apocalyptic "moment" in which the powers are toppled by the Human One (13:24-37). But when Mark narrates that moment we, like the disciples, will be caught off guard.

The "Passion narrative" is an intensely political drama, filled with conspiratorial back-room deals and covert action, judicial manipulation and prisoner exchanges, torture and summary execution. Yet these raw themes, perhaps because they are so uncomfortably persistent in our own world, tend to be suppressed by our traditional theological interpretations and pious liturgical reproductions of "Holy Week." We cannot understand the hope this story bears, however, unless we come to terms with its terrible realism.

Mark begins the Passion narrative with two stories that present Jesus as "king": an anointing (14:3-9) and a banquet (14:17-25). Each prepares the reader for the tragic turn the plot is about to take, in which this "messiah" does not lead the people to military triumph but is defeated. He also opens and closes the Passion narrative with stories of women who wish to ritually anoint Jesus for burial (14:3-9; 16:1ff). The function of this bracketing is to give the reader hope that, even though the male disciples will abandon the Way of the cross, there are female disciples who understand and accept it.

Read Mark 14:1-9

In 14:1, we are plunged back into the heart of the Judean social order: Jerusalem on the high holy days of Passover. These feast days always occasioned political turmoil in colonial Palestine, for it was a time when the people reflected on the Exodus story of liberation. It is in the context of this concern to keep public order that Mark reintroduces the government conspiracy against Jesus (14:2).

Jesus meanwhile is at table with a leper, practicing solidarity with the "least" to the end (14:3). He is interrupted by yet another anonymous woman who, judging by her bold approach and the expensive perfume, probably was a prostitute. Once again those with Jesus object, this time out of a concern for "wasteful spending" (14:4f). It is of utmost irony that the same concern for cash will shortly lead Judas to defect to the authorities (14:10f).

In her defense Jesus first addresses her critics' alleged commitment to the poor. The saying of 14:7, so notoriously used in the history of the church to justify the existence of poverty, is a statement not about the poor but about the social location of the discipleship church: "You will always be among the poor and can do the right thing for them at any time." He then interprets her action as a "beautiful thing" (14:6) and calls it an "anointing" (14:8). Jesus dramatically recasts her pouring oil over his head in terms of Samuel's prophetic anointing of both Saul and David as king (see 1 Samuel 10:1, 16:12ff). Obviously this story subverts traditional ideas of both kingship and male leadership!

"Let her be! Why do you make trouble for her?" shouts Jesus (14:6). In Mark, it is women who, because they embrace the Way of the cross and servanthood, can act as true leaders. This is an embarrassment to a patriarchal church that has long "made trouble" for women. "Wherever the good news is announced in all the world, what she has done will also be told in memory of her!" (14:9). This extraordinary commendation of the woman is also an unambiguous instruction that places the struggle against patriarchy at the heart of the message of the church. It has, however, gone unheeded in Christendom, past and present.

Read Mark 14:10-25

The authorities now decide to go "undercover," recruiting Judas as a mole (14:10f). Apparently the campaign against Jesus alluded to in 14:1 means that he is in hiding, for their strategy is intelligi-

ble only if the discipleship community has gone "underground."
This is precisely the impression we get from the elaborate instructions given by Jesus to his disciples in 14:12-16. A "runner" (iden-
tifiable in the crowd as a man carrying water, normally a woman's
job) leads the fugitive community through the city to a "safe
house," where they enter with a "password" (14:13f). There, in an
attic, they will celebrate the Passover feast truly "as those in
flight" (Exodus 12:11).

From the outset this "banquet" is fraught with anxiety, as
Jesus announces that he is aware of the infiltration (14:18). He underlines the breach of trust with an allusion to the lament of Psalm
41:9. The community, reacting with self-doubt, begins to unravel
(14:19). Jesus will reveal only that it is "one of the twelve," but his
condemnation is a sobering reminder about the cost of betrayal
(14:20f; see 8:34).

Despite all this Jesus affirms his solidarity with his companions, and breaks bread with them (14:22f). The extraordinary meaning of this ceremonial meal lies in Jesus' interpretation of it, which
he offers in lieu of the traditional Passover homily. He boldly applies the elements of the meal not to the Exodus story but to himself. He is the "paschal lamb" (Exodus 12) who renews the "blood
of the covenant" in his death (Exodus 24:8).

This banquet reinterprets the central ritual of the nation in
terms of giving one's life for the people. In place of the official Temple sacrifice, Jesus offers his "body"—that is, his practice in life and
death. This implied Temple/body opposition will become explicit
in Mark's narrative of Jesus' execution (see Chapter 24). Jesus finally announces that the feast has become a fast—until justice
should prevail (14:25; see 2:21f).

Mark's portrait of the Last Supper is also significant for what
it omits. "Do this in remembrance of me" were the words of "institution" (1 Corinthians 11:24f; Luke 22:19). But Mark does not use
them here, having already cited them in the commendation of the
woman who anointed Jesus. Instead of memorializing Jesus, Mark
wants us to remember discipleship practice.

Jesus, who exhorted us to "remember" the wilderness feedings (8:18), here at the Last Supper "blesses and breaks" the bread
as he did among the wilderness poor (6:41). And the "memory" of
his kingly anointing "as for burial" by the woman is invoked by the
cup, Mark's symbol for suffering at the hands of the powers (see
10:39, 14:36). So Mark's eucharistic moment is about remembering—not the mystical past but the ongoing practice of discipleship.

THE WORD IN OUR WORLD

A familiar story from the life of Salvadoran Archbishop Oscar Romero gives contemporary flesh to the intersection of intimacy and betrayal, community and conflict, in the context of Eucharist.

When Romero was appointed auxiliary bishop of San Salvador, he was noted for his conservatism. He was extremely nervous about the increasingly confrontational stance of many Salvadoran Christian communities over against the repressive government in the 1970s. More and more catechists, priests, religious, and members of parishes and communities were becoming involved in the resistance.

Meanwhile, the reign of terror was well under way. Already, lives had been taken by death squads and security forces supported by the wealthy classes. The National University had been closed and occupied by the military—with the approval of Romero as secretary of the Bishops' Conference. The public association of Bishop Romero with the oligarchy was extremely upsetting to the base communities. One parish at Zacamil in San Salvador invited the bishop to celebrate Mass with them and to engage in honest dialogue across what seemed to be profound distance and difference.

Instead of a homily, the community insisted on a dialogue with Bishop Romero. The debate became extremely heated. As recorded by Maria Lopez Vigil in *Piezas Para Un Retrato,* one priest who was a member of that community finally shouted at Romero, "And you come to speak to us about the option for the poor? What do you think? That we are crazy and that we haven't seen every day photos of you and the nuncio shamelessly drinking champagne with the rich?"

At last Father Pedro Declerc, who was concelebrating the Mass with Romero, said, "In this situation of distrust, although you and we are the Church, we do not have the conditions to celebrate Mass. I know it is finished; there is no Mass. . . . We do not have the conditions to pray together." Romero responded, "Here, one is able to celebrate nothing, nothing!"

The intimate moment of community gathered to break bread and share the good news of liberation and hope was broken by the threat of terrible betrayal. Bread could not be broken; Eucharist could not be shared. The community dispersed sadly.

Sometime later the breach was healed. Archbishop Romero returned to Zacamil when war and repression had honed the role of the church and its commitment to justice and the poor. He had by then gazed at the bullet-riddled corpse of his dear friend, Jesuit Rutillo Grande, executed with two parishioners by a death squad for choosing the side of the poor. On the Sunday following Rutillo's assassination, Romero refused again to allow any eucharistic celebrations, except for Rutillo's memorial Mass, in order to highlight both the tragedy of the murder and the unity of Salvadorans in their grief.

Romero had begun to understand the meaning of betrayal and crucifixion—in the body of his friend he had seen the body of Christ. From that moment on he began to walk a different path. He opened his eyes, his ears, and his heart to the suffering of his people. He embarked on a journey that helped him bridge the gap between the man he was—a shepherd on the verge of betraying his flock—and the community that so longed for his accompaniment.

Finally, he became a true shepherd to his people, denouncing the violence, calling for repentance on the part of the military and the powerful oligarchy, calling the church to courage and conversion, offering pastoral support to the poor and to those who struggled with the poor for justice. And he, like the One he followed, was martyred.

Chapter 22

Prayer as Staying Awake
Mark 14:26-52

THE TEXT IN CONTEXT

Read Mark 14:26-42

Jesus' presence on the Mount of Olives has previously signaled the beginning of a dramatic march (11:1) and a dramatic sermon (13:3). Now, however, it signals an escalating series of defections (14:26). Mark's tragic story line approaches its climax as Jesus turns to his disciples and reports: "You will all fall away" (14:27).

Jesus again appeals to Zechariah's shepherd parable (Zechariah 13:7; see Mark 6:34). In this oracle the prophet, despairing over Israel's corrupt leadership "who trafficked in sheep," himself becomes "the shepherd of the flock doomed to slaughter" (Zechariah 11:7). But as a counterpoint to this depressing news, Jesus assures them that the collapse of the discipleship community will not be the end of the discipleship story (Mark 14:28; see 16:7). In this "foreshadowing" of the surprise conclusion to his own gospel, Mark may have had in mind Ezekiel's version of the shepherd parable that spoke not only of scattering but also regathering:

> As shepherds seek out their flocks when they are among their scattered sheep, so will I seek out my sheep.... I will seek the lost and bring back the strayed and bind up the injured and strengthen the weak, but the fat and the strong I will destroy. I will feed them with justice. (Ezekiel 34:12, 16)

As we have come to expect, Jesus' realism about his destiny is immediately refuted by Peter (14:29). But as surely as Peter sets himself apart as the exception, Jesus counters that he above all will characterize the desertion (14:30). The whole community echoes

188

Peter's vehement protestations of loyalty (14:31), showing that they are all complicit in self-delusion.

Remarkably, Jesus calls one more time for solidarity from his inner circle, withdrawing to pray (14:32f). Jesus' inner turmoil (14:34) alludes to the anguish of Jonah, a reminder that God's "will" is the redemption of those who "do not know right from left" (see Jonah 4:9-11). The "cup" is now revealed as the Way of the cross (14:36; see 10:38f), and Jesus encounters it with genuine human terror, not contemplative detachment. There is no romance in martyrdom.

Though profoundly shaken, Jesus demonstrates true prayer, which takes us to the heart of Mark's theological argument. All things are possible for God, but the first concern of prayer is not to remedy personal distress but rather to seek the One whose will is the healing of our broken history (14:36).

Jesus shares our human desire that this might come about without cost to us (14:36). But he also understands that this is the great "temptation" (14:37). So he exhorts his followers to "watch" (14:34, 38). The "hour" Jesus spoke of in his apocalyptic parable is drawing near (see 13:32-37). Can the disciples "stay awake"? They cannot—Mark underscores three times that they sleep (14:37, 40f). Peter, who moments ago was boasting of his courage, does not have the "strength to stay awake one hour" (see 1:13; 9:18). So the "hour" arrives and only Jesus, praying at the heart of darkness, can summon the courage to go the Way of the cross (14:41).

Read Mark 14:43-52

Jesus now turns to face the music that has been playing in the background since the beginning of his mission. The terrible dialectic of intimacy and betrayal that has laced the Passion narrative climaxes in Judas' kiss, and Jesus is seized (14:45f). The arrest scene reeks of the overkill characteristic of covert state operations against civilian dissidents. The coded signal, the surprise ambush in the dead of night, the heavily armed escort, and the instructions for utmost security measures imply that the authorities expected armed resistance (14:43f). Yet the tone of Mark's report does not condemn the "bystander" who skirmishes with the police (14:47), but the sordid character of the whole operation that provokes the very violence it purports to prevent.

Jesus taunts his captors with the fact that their operation only unmasks their political weakness: "So, you have come to arrest me with swords and clubs, as if I were a robber?! Every day I was among you in the Temple, and you didn't dare seize me!" (14:48f). "Robbers" is the first of several references in the Passion narrative to the activity of "social banditry" in the Palestinian countryside (see 15:7). Peasant leaders formed guerrilla bands to harass their colonial oppressors in the manner of Robin Hood or Pancho Villa (see Horsley). They were routinely caught and executed by the Romans for treason—and they will share Jesus' fate in this story (see 15:27).

As he is being led away, Jesus calls upon the "script" of biblical radicalism (14:49; see 9:12f). This is the third time since the meal that Jesus has invoked the scriptural destiny of the true prophet, perhaps as Mark's counterpoint to the downward spiral of events (see 14:21, 27). It is this "script" that the authorities cannot understand and that the disciples cannot follow. The latter now realize that Jesus does not intend to abandon this script, and they flee for their lives (14:50). The sheep have scattered, and the discipleship narrative has collapsed. Yet as the reader buckles under the weight of this ignominious end, Mark tells a curious story.

In a parenthetical comment, we learn about a "young man" who flees with the other disciples (14:51). This naked flight symbolizes the shame of the discipleship community, leaving behind a "linen cloth." The garment will reappear as the burial wrap of Jesus (see 15:46), and the young man will reappear in Jesus' empty tomb, fully clothed in white robes (see 16:5). We shall see that this transformation of clothing, as in Jesus' transfiguration (9:3ff), represents both a promise and a challenge to the reader (see Chapter 25).

But at this point all we know is that everything has gone sour. The discipleship community, as has so often been the case in the history of the church, has abandoned Jesus at the first flush of conflict with the authorities. Dreams of a new social order are once again shattered by the brute force of state power. Jesus, now alone, goes to stand before a kangaroo court with no hope of justice. There his final struggle with the powers for the soul of history will be played out.

THE WORD IN OUR WORLD

As with Jesus' disciples, the challenge of walking the road of suffering with the Lord remains with us in the question of how we relate to the poor. People of faith have dealt with it in surprising, even paradoxical, ways.

For some years "staying awake" centered on North Americans getting out of the way, stepping aside, so that the oppressed majorities of the world could carry out their own liberation. A popular book of that period reflected on a "theology of letting go" and made the case for this attitude with some effectiveness.

Later the notion and practice of solidarity on the part of the non-poor toward impoverished areas and peoples gained currency. We could see a complementary task alongside the gritty struggles of the poor—one in which we could speak and even act in their names in places where they would never be heard.

Lately another way of positioning ourselves vis-a-vis oppressed peoples has emerged, this time from those peoples themselves. "Accompaniment" is the way this positioning is described, and it includes an entire range of attitudes and actions that bring to a certain fruition both of the earlier notions of letting go and of solidarity. The poor choose whether or not they will be accompanied. And it seems that in the process of accompaniment, both those who ask it and those who respond move to a new place in human experience.

For example, in Washington, D.C., a white evangelical grass-roots church strove for years to incorporate minorities into its ranks. After oft-repeated failures, a new model suddenly and providentially appeared, thanks to the invitation of an African-American, inner-city congregation. The entire framework reversed and instead of the whites inviting and including the blacks, it was the latter who offered to be accompanied by the white community.

Not all oppressed peoples want accompaniment, and for good reason. For example, in African America a debate rages about accompaniment. For decades the call was for "integration," for whites to move over and "allow" the African-American people a place at our table. But now blacks ask: Integration into what? Into all of the injustice and confusion of white America? Perhaps separation is better.

Nevertheless, it is encouraging that people of faith and so many others of good will are answering the call to accompaniment:

> – the growing Latino immigrant population in the United States has indicated its need for and willingness to be accompanied, inviting others to learn their language, understand their culture, and walk with them in their struggles to remain here and prosper;

- Native Americans, as they rediscover their traditions, invite others to learn their ways, especially with regard to ecological justice, and to put those customs into practice;

- the increasing numbers of U.S. citizens living below the poverty line understand the need to narrow the gap between them and an increasingly affluent class through a transformation of the economy;

- peoples in places like Haiti, Bosnia, East Timor, and earlier in South Africa, El Salvador, and Nicaragua invited accompaniment in their well-publicized political and social struggles for freedom.

In the developed, affluent world where boredom and the loss of a sense of purpose threaten to rot societies from the inside, accompaniment emerges as an antidote and a vision. Walking with the marginalized gives to the jaded and overly satisfied portion of humanity a new beginning and a part in the struggle. Once again it is the poor who gift us with their invitation to "walk with us a while." This echoes Jesus' request of his disciples in the Garden of Gethsemani: "I am deeply grieved, even to death; remain here and keep awake" (Mark 14:34).

Chapter 23

Denial and Confession
Mark 14:53–15:20

THE TEXT IN CONTEXT

It has often been argued that Mark's trial narrative intends to place culpability for Jesus' death squarely on the shoulders of the Judean high court. Such an interpretation is problematic not only because it has been used to justify a long legacy of Christian anti-Semitism, but also because it is suspect on both literary and historical grounds.

First we must explain why Mark records a change in the charge against Jesus, from blasphemy (14:64) to sedition (15:2). Both were capital crimes in their respective juridical spheres, but in occupied Palestine the Judean client government did not have the authority to execute criminals. Did the Sanhedrin "use" Pilate for their own ends, as has been the traditional portrait? Not likely. Extra-biblical sources make it clear that of all the procurators stationed in Palestine during the Roman colonial period, Pontius Pilate was one of the most ruthless. There is simply no historical evidence to suggest that Pilate could have been manipulated by the Judean leadership—much less the "crowds" (see 15:15).

On the contrary, he was expert at playing the native aristocracy off against each other for his political ends. Historically, therefore, the fact that Pilate signed off on Jesus' crucifixion, which was the Roman penalty reserved for those convicted of insurrection, can only mean that he judged Jesus to be a substantial threat to imperial security.

A literary analysis of Mark's account, moreover, reveals that he has constructed a careful parallelism between Jesus' two trials. Each consists of four aspects:

	Judean trial	Roman trial
1) trumped-up charges that are ironically fitting	14:58	15:2
2) two-fold interrogation	14:60-62	15:2-5
3) presiding judge "consults" and convicts	14:63f	15:6-15
4) final ridicule/torture scene	14:65	15:16-20

The function of this parallel composition was not to exonerate the empire. Rather, Mark wished to portray the Judean and Roman authorities as fully cooperative in their railroading of Jesus, whom they perceived as a common enemy. Indeed, there are strong elements of political parody in Mark's grimly comic caricature of these proceedings.

Read Mark 14:53-65

The first part of Mark's political cartoon pictures the highest court throwing out due process in favor of a rigged hearing. Twice the prosecution's attempt to coordinate the testimony of hired perjurers fails (14:56, 59). His accusers have obviously confused Jesus' statements concerning himself with his judgment on the Temple (14:58). Yet this fabricated charge reflects accurately the Sanhedrin's concern, since Jesus' repudiation of the Temple-state in fact poses a threat to their status quo. It also anticipates Mark's later juxtaposition of Jesus' body and the Temple (see 15:37f).

Jesus makes no attempt to refute these allegations because he understands that this is a political trial in which legal arguments are moot. The double interrogations in the two trials are almost identical. Jesus either refuses to respond or returns the sarcasm of the prosecutor's "naming":

High priest: "Have you no answer to make? What is it that these men testify against you?"

Jesus: He was silent and made no answer.

High Priest: "You are Messiah, Son of the Blessed?"

Jesus: "Am I?!" (14:60ff)

Pilate:	"You are the king of the Jews?"
Jesus:	"You say so?!"
Pilate:	"Have you no answer to make? See how many charges they bring against you."
Jesus:	He made no further answer... (15:2-5)

But Jesus convicts himself before the Sanhedrin by his confession of the Human One (14:62). This is not a defense but an exercise in apocalyptic bi-focal vision (see Chapter 11). According to Daniel's vision of the heavenly courtroom, the Human One is the prosecutor of the beast (see Chapter 11). Indeed the Human One throughout Mark's gospel is on the offensive, against the local authorities (2:10, 28) and ultimately the powers themselves (13:26). In order to deflect Jesus' indictment, the high priest charges blasphemy, a capital offense (14:63f; see Leviticus 24:26). He then turns to the Sanhedrin in order to secure the conviction, and turns Jesus over to be tortured (14:65). The goons' insistence that their prisoner "prophesy" is the ultimate irony, for Jesus has embodied both prophetic truth and consequences.

Read Mark 14:54, 66-72

Wrapped around the first trial is the pathetic cameo of Peter, whose denial stands in stark contrast to Jesus' faithful confession of the Human One. Having managed to slip into the courtyard incognito, Peter is trying to fulfill his vow to follow Jesus "to the end" (14:54; see 14:29). One can feel his despair as he stands powerless just outside the courtroom where Jesus is being arraigned. Gazing into the coals, numb with shock, he is no doubt terrified at the swift and brutal descent of metropolitan justice.

Then suddenly, at the very moment Jesus is summarily condemned to death inside the palace, Peter's cover is blown outside in the courtyard. It is a servant to the high priest who recognizes him, no doubt from earlier Temple skirmishes (14:66f). Inching slowly backward toward the gate, squeezed by conflicting loyalties, Peter makes the fateful choice to seek refuge in the shadow world of denial: "I do not know what you are talking about!" (14:68). In the end his country drawl betrays what the flickering shadows had hidden (14:70). Unable to follow Jesus, neither can he pass as an innocent bystander.

"And he began to curse his life" (14:71). Cornered and cowering, Peter swears his oath of dissociation. And as a rooster's hoarse cry drifts hauntingly in the sudden stillness, Peter's soul begins to implode, and he breaks down in bitter weeping (14:72). This story, too, is part of Mark's dark political cartoon, the dramatic enactment of Jesus' warnings about the Faustian bargain of self-preservation (8:34).

Read Mark 15:1-20

Following another consultation, which implicates the entire ruling class ("the chief priests, the elders and scribes and the whole council"), Jesus is turned over to the Roman procurator (15:1). The third part of Mark's political cartoon is his caricature of Pilate, who correctly identifies the issue as one of political authority (15:2). But to Pilate, Jesus is merely "King of the Judeans," as opposed to the nationalist title "King of Israel" (15:32). The former designation, held by Roman client-rulers such as Herod, was a contemptuous reminder that the Judeans were not sovereign in their own land.

Mark's Pilate is a sketch of pragmatism at work. In a shrewd public relations ploy aimed at playing the unruly crowd's patriotism off against itself, he grants amnesty to a convicted terrorist (Barabbas) in order to keep Jesus (15:6-11). Pilate would strike such a deal only if he understood Jesus to be the greater political threat. It is also historically inconceivable that Jews would ever have called for the Roman crucifixion of one of their own (15:12f). Mark is satirizing the Roman Colosseum tradition, in which the crowd was given the choice as to whether a wounded gladiator (usually a war prisoner or condemned criminal) should live or die. The "sheep without a shepherd" (6:34) are caught between the conflicting revolutionary claims of the violent urban guerrilla Barabbas and the nonviolent Galilean.

The fickle masses are central characters in the farce and important to Mark's political message. In a matter of days, the crowd has gone from "hearing gladly" Jesus' criticisms of the priestly elite (see 11:38) to being manipulated by them to lobby for his demise (15:10f). In the Colosseum parody, the tragedy is that the masses again succumb to the will of their political and class opponents (who fear them! see 14:2). That is why the shrieks of the crowd (15:13f) simultaneously echo the wails of the demons in Mark (see 3:11, 5:5, 9:26) and the cries of the oppressed (see 9:24, 10:47f, 11:9).

The scene with Pilate's security forces makes the parody complete: Jesus is dressed up in a Roman military cloak and a "laurel wreath" of thorns, symbolizing the very militarism and imperialism he has resisted (15:16f). Mocking the whole notion that the Jews could be self-governing, the centurions subject Jesus to the humiliation reserved for political prisoners (15:18f). Only when they tire of their sadistic games do they turn to carry out Jesus' sentence: death by crucifixion.

THE WORD IN OUR WORLD

Peter's inconsolable lament when he realizes the full, tragic weight of his denial still echoes through the ages, resonating whenever we believers betray the vision we hold dear.

The writer Dostoyevsky created a scene in his novel *The Brothers Karamazov* that has haunted the church ever since. In this scene, Jesus returns to earth at the time of the Great Inquisition in Spain, a time when thousands of heretics are being burned at the stake by the Grand Inquisitor, the most powerful ruler of the church. Christ returns quietly, humbly, but is immediately recognized by the people for who he is. In his interrogation of Jesus, the Inquisitor says: "I do not know who you are and I don't care to know whether it is You or only a semblance of him, but tomorrow I will condemn you and burn you at the stake as the worst of heretics. And the very people who today kissed your feet, tomorrow at the faintest sign from me will rush to heap up the embers of your fire."

The Inquisitor explains to his prisoner that his teachings are unrealistic; that he expects too much from humankind. The church has a more realistic view of humankind, as sheep to be managed. Christ's return is unwelcome—dangerous, in fact—because it threatens to upset the established social order which the church controls.

What about Dostoyevsky's story, or Peter's denial, haunts us today? Perhaps Peter's denial reflects most accurately our situation as disciples of Christ living in the United States in the last decade of the twentieth century. In the gospel there are only two ways of being in the world: discipleship or denial. Let us reflect here on denial.

What is denial? Human consciousness itself is a form of denial. We would find it very difficult to function at all without the ability of our consciousness to limit what we experience. This very function of human consciousness which allows us to focus on what we need to do also sometimes shuts out realities that we find overwhelmingly painful. The problem with denial comes whenever we use this defense mechanism exclusively. And that is what has happened: Denial has become the fundamental way that we as individuals and as a people respond to difficult realities.

A good example is our response to the reality of death and dying. Something in us goes into shock and lets in the reality only little by little, in measures that we can handle. But what if we never face the reality of our loss; what if we refuse to move through the grieving that we must do? Today, our whole culture seems to be organized around this kind of denial.

Another example is how family systems deal with the alcoholism or drug dependency of a member. Typically, co-dependent family members pretend that the problem isn't there. As the addiction increases, it takes increasing amounts of psychological energy for the addict and for the addict's family to maintain denial.

Just as denial can become unhealthy and dangerous for an individual or family, so it can be when a whole society refuses to acknowledge a painful contradiction between self-image and reality. We know that a nation can be in denial about its past, opting for a grandiose story of progress, prosperity, and righteous conquest while denying its own complicity in evil. A people can be in denial as well about its future, as, for example, when it continues to lay waste the environment.

Each time we resort to such denial our humanity as individuals is distorted and our character as a nation is eroded. Denial can so disconnect us from reality that we call death life and life death. Here we cannot escape the disturbing irony of Jesus' entry into Jerusalem: The same people of Jerusalem who welcomed him as the Messiah with Hosannas a short time later were demanding that he be crucified.

The story of Peter's denial asks disciples to face up to the ways in which we have denied the suffering Christ who is present in the world. Where have I seen the Christ and pretended that I did not know him? When have I broken faith with the Human One to save face, to stay safe, to guard my own life?

Chapter 24

The End of the World
Mark 15:21-46

THE TEXT IN CONTEXT

A story that began heralding a Way through the wilderness (1:2f) now ends on the Way of the cross. The cross: In Mark's time it could have scarcely been further from a religious icon. To restive imperial subjects, it conjured the fate awaiting those who dared challenge Caesar's sovereignty. To the civilized, it was a form of punishment so inhumane that Cicero once urged that it be "banished from the body and life of Roman citizens." But to Jesus it symbolized the cost of discipleship. And in Mark's story, it is portrayed as the great apocalyptic moment in which the powers are overthrown and their world comes to an end.

Read Mark 15:21-38

Jesus is marched, in the grand tradition of Roman conquest, to the site of execution (15:21f). This spectacle functioned as a deterrent to would-be subversives and as an aggrandizement of the Roman military presence. The prisoner would normally carry his own execution stake, but presumably Jesus is too weak from torture. "Simon of Cyrene from the country" is drafted for the task. This closes the circle of the Jerusalem narrative: Jesus entered the holy city amid a triumphant crowd of rural peasants (see 11:8), but leaves it accompanied by a sole farmer. There is irony, too: Jesus' first companion was another "Simon" (see 1:16), but he has renounced Jesus, so this stranger must suffice.

After the admonition of Proverbs 31:6, Jesus is offered wine to deaden the agony, but he refuses (15:23). Mark's simple phrase "and they crucified him" would have conjured in his audience's mind horrific images of flesh being nailed to wood. His clothes are divided up, the first of three allusions to Psalm 22's great lament (15:24; see Psalm 22:18). He is nailed up at the "third hour" (the first of Mark's three "watches" of the cross), and left to asphyxiate under Pilate's sardonic identification sign (15:25f).

Gathered at Golgotha like a tableau are representatives of the whole spectrum of Palestinian politics. Guerrilla rebels flank him, the very positions of "honor" for which the disciples earlier competed (15:27; see 10:37). Passersby, representing the uncommitted crowd, ridicule him with the false trial accusations (15:29f). This is the second allusion to Psalm 22 (see Psalm 22:7f). Even the chief priests and scribes are there, joining the chorus of contempt (15:31f). Presiding over the sordid scene is a Roman centurion, while watching in horror from afar are a few disciples, most of them women (see 15:39f).

There is an ironic, imploring tone to the taunt that Jesus "save himself." Even his opponents desire a less ignominious end to this tragedy. Their plaintive cry is the pitiful culmination to the struggle for faith in Mark's story. If only Jesus would come down from the cross so that we might "see and believe" (15:32)! Yet this is the moment in which our blindness will be most consequential, for to understand what happens next truly requires "eyes to see" (see 4:12; 8:18).

The thirst for last-minute intervention leads a bystander to misinterpret Jesus' last anguished gasp as a desperate petition to Elijah, the eschatological prophet who was supposed to rescue Israel from judgment (15:34f; see Malachi 4:5f). Mark makes it clear that this Aramaic phrase is instead the third allusion to the psalmist's lament (Psalm 22:1).

This is the third "apocalyptic moment" in the story. In the first, the heavens were "torn" and God's voice affirmed Jesus at baptism (see 1:10f). In the second, God's voice again affirmed Jesus, dressed in martyr's costume (see 9:3-7). This time there is no voice from heaven; only the silence of God. But there are two "signs" that Mark gives us. From the sixth to the ninth hour the sun is darkened (15:33). This recalls the time when Israel's God blotted out the sun for three days over Pharaoh's Egypt to aid Moses in his struggle against an imperial order presided over by the sun god Ra. But here it symbolizes the apocalyptic unraveling of the whole cosmic order of domination, an unraveling promised by Jesus (13:24f).

Jesus spoke three times of the advent of the Human One, assuring respectively the disciples (8:38f), the powers (13:26f), and the

High Priest (14:62) that they would see this moment (see Chapter 20). Sure enough, Mark has gathered these same witnesses around the cross. But what do they "see" in this cosmic darkness? Is it Jesus reviled, bringing the story to an end? Or is it the Human One revealed, bringing the world to an end—that is, the world over which the powers preside?

To help us, Mark narrates a second "sign." As Jesus' body expires in a great death-rattle, we are told that the Temple curtain is "torn" in two (15:37f). This torn curtain confirms the fundamental conflict between Jesus' "body" (symbol of the discipleship community, 14:22) and the "sanctuary made with hands" (the legal-cultic-political system of oppression), to which his opponents had unwittingly testified (see 14:58). Even in death Jesus has subverted the Temple-state. The "strong man's house" (3:27) has been ransacked. If we have eyes to see.

Read Mark 15:39-46

The immediate aftermath of Jesus' death provides no evidence that anything has changed, however. We are given three reactions: that of the centurion (15:39), that of the council-member Joseph (15:42-46), and that of some female followers of Jesus (15:40f, 47). Contrary to traditional interpretation, two of these three cannot be considered discipleship stories!

The Roman soldier's utterance is indistinguishable from that of the demons who are forever trying to control Jesus by "naming" him (see 1:24, 3:11, 5:7). After all, the centurion does not respond in discipleship, but remains in his role, dutifully reporting back to Pilate about Jesus' death (15:44f). In Mark it is only the divine voice that provides a reliable witness to Jesus as "Son" (1:11, 9:7). The centurion's words must be seen as the triumphant conclusion of the soldiers' mockery begun in 15:16-20.

Joseph's mission is to beg the body from Pilate—evidence of how firmly in control of events the procurator was (15:43, 45). This is not done out of compassion, but in order that the corpse not profane the Sabbath (15:42). While Joseph may have been "looking for the sovereignty of God," he is also a "wealthy member of the council" that condemned Jesus (15:43). Nor are his actions that of a disciple. He hastily wraps Jesus' corpse in the linen cloth of "betrayal" (see 14:51). He then throws it in a tomb, disdaining even the most rudimentary obligations of a proper Jewish burial (15:46). Like the centurion, this steward of the Sabbath seems to have had the last word over the "Lord of the Sabbath."

It appears, then, that the authorities have prevailed after all! It was not "Elijah" who took Jesus from the cross, but a member of the Sanhedrin. The rolling of the stone over the tomb entrance symbolically closes the story (15:46). Jesus is dead, the powers have taken over the narrative, and the disciples are nowhere to be seen. Except for some women.

Mary, Mary, and Salome now represent the lifeline of the discipleship narrative. These three women have replaced the male "inner circle" of James, John, and Peter, who are long gone. They are given a remarkable description: "When Jesus was in Galilee they followed him and served and, with other women, came up to Jerusalem with him" (15:40f). In other words, from beginning to end these women, unlike the men, understood the vocation of discipleship as servanthood. That is why they are here, "witnesses" to the terror of the cross. But they are about to witness something even more disturbing.

THE WORD IN OUR WORLD

In his crucifixion narrative, Mark switches to the historical present tense, drawing the reader into the drama, as if to ask us where we stand. Is there not a part of us in each character here? A part that, like the male disciples, is wholly absent, having long ago abandoned Jesus at the first whiff of confrontation? A part that, like the women, can only hold vigil, incredulous and numb with sorrow? And even a part that, like Jesus' detractors, joins in the protest against this ending? "Who indeed can believe" (Isaiah 53:1) that things have turned out this way?

We might legitimately approach this cross with all those who have dared hope for a better world, especially those who have been crushed struggling for a justice that seems forever deferred, and demand an explanation. For who of us is prepared to accept that *this* is the way to liberation?

Attempting to face that question, many Christians who struggle for human rights have appropriated the ritual of *Via Crucis* (Way of the Cross) in new and creative ways. Whereas traditionally the "Stations of the Cross" offered the believer personal meditations on Jesus' trial, suffering, crucifixion, death, and burial—all designed for spiritual contemplation—now the same "Stations" are given a much broader scope.

These alternative liturgies have as their goal a linking of Jesus' journey to Golgotha with the enormous suffering, both personal and social, represented in public places. Those who lead such modern variations of this ancient ritual are often themselves either victims or healers of the social evils being cited. Let us walk through a typical *Via Crucis*, which might be held in the U.S. capital city:

Station One: Jesus is condemned to death. The pilgrimage begins at an inner-city park where the homeless sleep, and the analogy is clear. Many of our brothers and sisters are condemned to a sub-human existence by an affluent society which has judged them to be disposable.

Station Two: Jesus takes up the cross. The procession moves to the city jail where day after day the condemned begin their own *via crucis* in a penal system that robs them of all dignity.

Station Three: Jesus falls. Outside an abandoned housing project, the pilgrims reflect on one more failure to provide adequate housing for the poor. This structure once stood as a symbol of social welfare, but now its broken windows and rotting floors testify to the indifference of society in the face of the down and out.

Station Four: Jesus meets his mother. In a particularly crime-infested area of the city a grandmother speaks of the children she has known who have had their lives cut short. She breaks into tears as she slowly names the boys and girls she has seen die from the greed and violence that result from drug trafficking and addiction.

Station Five: The cross is laid on Simon of Cyrene. A national coalition to abolish the death penalty takes responsibility for this stop on the way. They wage an incredible uphill battle to spare the lives of those condemned to die and to turn our society away from "killing to prevent killing."

Station Six: Veronica wipes Jesus' face. In the vestibule of a hospice for people with AIDS, a nurse recounts his experience with a dying patient on a previous Good Friday. He recalls holding the man in his arms during the last hours of his life, soothing his sores and assuaging his thirst.

Station Seven: Jesus falls again. On the sidewalk facing the Department of Justice, a public defender offers his reflections on the number of young people whom he has seen sent to jail after they fell back into crime. The lawyer points out that the criminal justice system too often aggravates the situation of ex-offenders by imposing on them the "two strikes and you're out" criterion.

Station Eight: Jesus meets the women of Jerusalem. The procession winds its way to the doorway of a bar that features "adult entertainment." Women lead the prayer for other women; sisters weep for their exploited sisters; men examine their consciences with respect to their attitudes toward wives, daughters, indeed toward all women.

Station Nine: Jesus falls a third time. The procession moves to the offices of the World Bank and the International Monetary Fund. Analysts catalog the repeated failures of these institutions to remedy the devastating poverty of nearly two-thirds of the world's population. They cite statistics on the growing debt owed to these institutions by poor nations and ask why so many sisters and brothers around the world continue to fall deeper into poverty, misery, and hopelessness.

Station Ten: Jesus is stripped of his clothes. Spanish becomes the language now as prayers ascend on behalf of refugees whose dignity, sense of purpose, and humanity often disappear in the struggle to cope with a foreign culture.

Station Eleven: Jesus is nailed to the cross. Outside of the health clinic where she works a doctor reflects on the endless line of patients nailed to a health care system that has forgotten those who cannot pay. She speaks of the needless suffering caused by the insurance industry and about a medical establishment whose greed drives nails of pain even further into human flesh.

Station Twelve: Jesus dies on the cross. The pilgrimage moves to an upscale part of the city, to the corporate headquarters of a transnational corporation. The meditation focuses on the countless people crucified each day, both at home and overseas, because of the profit motive of such companies. Jesus' crucifixion took a slow three hours; the crucifixions attributed to corporate selfishness last lifetimes.

Station Thirteen: Jesus is taken down from the cross. The *Via Crucis* makes its next-to-last stop at the embassy of a country that has recently executed a group of its human rights activists. A courageous citizen of that country speaks in halting English of the murdered activists and their permanent place in the collective memory of her compatriots.

Station Fourteen: Jesus is laid in the tomb. Finally, this *Via Crucis* comes to a military cemetery, where policies of the powerful have cost young men's and women's lives. One is lulled by the silence of this gravesite until the speaker, a conscientious objector to war, reminds the pilgrims that in many parts of the world youths kill other youths for reasons none of them understand.

Chapter 25

The Third Call to Discipleship
Mark 15:47–16:8

THE TEXT IN CONTEXT

Mark's first interpretive epilogue reviewed the main symbols of the first half of the gospel, and ended with a question to the reader (8:11-21; see Chapter 10). Similarly, in this second epilogue, Mark's narrative reaches its resolution, yet again leaves the reader with a question. Will we be spectators to this drama? Or will we be "spec-actors"—those who see and begin to enact in our own lives the ongoing narrative of radical discipleship?

Read Mark 15:47–16:3

When Joseph rolls the stone against Jesus' tomb, the discipleship narrative slams shut with the stupefying crunch of a prison door. The only lifeline we have now is Mark's simple indication that the same three women who observed Jesus' crucifixion (15:40) also "saw where Joseph put him" (15:47). Included is a Mary who is presumably Jesus' mother (see 6:3), though it is significant that she is not so identified here, perhaps in conformity with the teaching of 3:31-34. The fact that women, in the background throughout the entire story, suddenly emerge as the true disciples (15:41) is perhaps Mark's most radical social reversal.

Yet for the moment their actions are quite conventional, even expected. Charitable guilds of Jerusalem women were known to be present after executions in order to assure proper burial. This is the scene presented in 16:1-4. The three women are attempting to salvage some dignity by re-burying Jesus according to custom. As Joseph bought a linen in which to wrap Jesus' corpse, the women buy spices in order to properly anoint it. As he threw the corpse into a tomb before the Sabbath, they go there early in the morning after the Sabbath (16:1f).

Like so many scenes from the gospels, this one has been all too romanticized by the church. It would have been a risky act for these women to demonstrate solidarity with so notorious a political dissident. But it was hardly a triumphant one. This dawn brought them only the numb duty of last respects and that aching, unconsolable emptiness that comes from hope crushed. This seems merely the last, pitiless leg of Mark's discipleship journey, ending at the cemetery of our dreams for a new world.

Cruelly, even the therapeutic ritual of weeping over Jesus' corpse and mustering brave eulogies is denied. The entrance to the makeshift tomb is sealed shut by a boulder that "was very large" (16:4). They halt in their tracks, pulled up short. "Who will roll away this stone?" they cry to no one in particular (16:3). Is there not in this anguished question an echo of Sisyphean tragedy? This stone blocking their way terminates, without explanation, the discipleship journey. What an abrupt and bitter closure to the story! But there is one more scene in Mark's gospel, and upon it hinges the possibility of the Christian church.

Read Mark 16:4-6

The depressing narrative inertia of Jesus' trial and execution, which culminated in Joseph's sealing of the tomb with this stone, now suddenly begins to be reversed. "When they looked again, they saw that the stone had been rolled away" (16:4). The verb "to see again" was used by Mark in his stories of the two blind men (8:25, 10:51f). It is now revealed here as the expression of "bifocal vision" that characterizes apocalyptic faith (see Chapter 11). To the world of the Judean Temple-state and Roman colonialism, Jesus is just another imperial statistic. To those who "look again," the great stone of impediment has been removed.

But how? Neither by human muscle, nor technology, nor any Promethean scheme. The verb here expresses the perfect tense and the passive voice—the grammar of divine action. This stone has been rolled away by an ulterior leverage, by a force from beyond the bounds of story and history with the power to regenerate both. This intervention comes from outside the constraints of natural or civic law and order, from the One who is unobligated to the state and its cosmologies, radically free yet bound in Passion to us. Mark continues the biblical argument with Sisyphus and Prometheus: Nothing we can do could move this stone. By grace it has already been rolled away for us. We need only have eyes to see it.

Improbably the tomb, and with it the story, has been reopened. Tentatively the women move forward—but only to find that their noble mission of mourning is no longer needed. Peering around in the dim light of the cave they make out the figure of a "young man" sitting alone (16:5). Is this the same "young man" who, along with all the other male disciples, fled naked and ashamed when the authorities came for Jesus (14:51f)? Apocalyptic symbols proliferate. This mysterious young man is "sitting at the right," the place of true authority which the male disciples had coveted (see 10:37, 12:36, 14:62). And he is "dressed in a white robe," the apparel of martyrdom (9:3; see Revelation 7:9, 13).

"Don't be incredulous," he says to the women. "You're looking for Jesus of Nazareth, the one they executed? He is risen. He's not here where they put him. See for yourself" (16:6). The authorities thought this annoying episode of messianic pretension had been laid to rest. But it is just the beginning. The women look around frantically, their heads swimming, their hearts grinding to a halt. Don't be incredulous?! Incredulity does not begin to describe their confusion at this inconceivable news, this absurd contention. Is it possible that neither the executioner's deathgrip nor the imperial seal have prevailed?

Read Mark 16:7f

Then comes one last word from this enigmatic messenger: "Get up, go tell his disciples and Peter that he's going on ahead of you to Galilee. There you will see him, as he told you" (16:7). This young man—the symbol of the transformation from betrayal (nakedness) to discipleship (white robe)—has issued the third call to discipleship (see 1:17, 8:34). It is a prospect the women—the reader—never considered.

Our knees buckle at this invitation to resume the Way—for now we know its consequences all too well. From deep within us, from that unexplored space beneath our profoundest hopes and fears, roars a tidal wave of "trauma and ecstasy" (16:8). Terrified, we race with the women out of that tomb as if we have just seen a ghost. And so we have. For in Jesus' empty tomb is nothing but the ghost of our discipleship past and our discipleship future.

In Easter's first light, Mark's story ends as it began:

"He is going before you…" (16:7)

"Behold, I send my messenger before you who will construct the Way…" (1:2)

We are promised that we will see Jesus again in Galilee—which is where the disciples were first called to follow! The narrative is circular!

This epilogue presents us with the most dangerous of memories, a living one; the most subversive of stories, a never-ending one. Mark's resurrection tradition offers no visions of glory or triumph. It leaves us only with a God who hears our brokenhearted cries before the stone of impediment, and with the executed-but-risen-Nazarene who calls us to discipleship as many times as it takes.

The third call is specifically directed to those whose discipleship became mired in the dead-end of denial: "Tell the disciples and Peter..." (16:7). There is no wayward journey that cannot be redeemed by new beginnings. That is why Dietrich Bonhoeffer insisted that the church must "recover a true understanding of the mutual relation between grace and discipleship."

"And they said nothing to anyone, for they were afraid" (16:8). What an ambiguous conclusion! From earliest times it has troubled readers of the gospel, leading to several attempts to append "happier" endings (the patently non-Markan "longer endings"). Others have contended that Mark's ending means that the women, too, betrayed their commission, in which case the gospel is finally a tragedy after all. But fear does not imply desertion in Mark. On the contrary, throughout the story fear has accompanied those who journey with Jesus, whether on the dangerous crossing to "the other side" (4:41, 6:50) or on the fateful march up to Jerusalem (9:32, 10:32).

The narrative strategy of "they said nothing" has something else in mind. The genius of this "incomplete" ending, like a painting lacking the finishing stroke, is that it demands a response from its audience. Mark leaves us not with a neat resolution but with a terrible ultimatum. Who will tell this "good news"? For it is not only the women who "know"—we know now as well. If we wish the story of discipleship to continue, we cannot remain mere spectators.

Will we respond? If we are honest, we will admit that the cross is so intimidating, and our blindness so pervasive, that we can only answer, "We believe; help us in our unbelief!" (9:24). We are somewhere between the "young man" who flees naked and the "young man" clothed in martyr's garb. Even our best efforts at faithfulness seem inevitably to founder. But all that is part of the story, too. For it is at the point of failure and disillusionment that the invitation comes again. Then our discipleship journey either truly ends or truly begins.

Jesus is risen! But where has he gone? He is neither entombed (as the Romans think) nor enthroned (as the longer endings imagined). Mark refuses to "show" him to us. If we wish to "see" Jesus, we too must journey to Galilee. Jesus has gone on ahead of the church. Only by responding to the invitation to discipleship can we join him where he already is: on the Way.

THE WORD IN OUR WORLD

"To see again" is Mark's master metaphor for a faith that looks more deeply into reality in order to see what could be. We might translate it literally: "to revision." In Mark's Easter narrative, the weary old story of the world, in which the powers always win and the poor always lose, is radically revised. But we can "see" this only in "Galilee," the symbolic site of discipleship. Mark's story began in the wilderness, far from the centers of power and privilege. To that location the disciples are urged to return.

"The women looked again and found that the stone had been rolled away" (16:4). We too are invited to look again and see that a way has been opened up—a way that carries us toward life. A way was opened for the women to prepare the body of Jesus and to follow the risen one to Galilee. A way has been opened for us as well to bind the wounds of our world. In a place of death, a new beginning is offered. As in Peter's case, our failed discipleship can be redeemed by grace.

Death and resurrection, brokenness and healing, marginalization and empowerment, sin and reconciliation, injustice and transformation all shape the very pattern of the Christian life. Resurrection is gratuitous—a pure, unearned gift of God. It is the ultimate test of and the only hope for a disciple's faith. At the same time, we are called by the Spirit to eke out the resurrection bit by bit, step by step on the Way. Sometimes our experience of resurrection is glorious and clear. But most often it is the fruit of long, painful labor—birthed, but needing nurture.

Francine's is such a story. She is an African-American grandmother living a difficult life in an inner-city neighborhood of Washington, D.C. She is a strong matriarch, a survivor determined to make her family survive, a rock-solid foundation. Francine is determined to carry her children and grandchildren over the rocky terrain of drug-infested alleys and gunfights and disillusionment that is the landscape of her neighborhood. Francine has never given up on her children or her neighbors or herself. She simply loves them back to life.

Francine's family is not likely to be used as a model to illustrate "family values," though it should be. She is a single parent. At least one of her children is a drug addict, suffering from all of the abuse and irresponsibility that affliction entails. At least one of her children has spent time in jail. Francine is largely dependent on public assistance. She has enormous health problems and survives on the fragments of help she can derive from the public health care system.

The context in which Francine lives all but undoes her most valiant efforts. A lack of opportunity for quality education, little preventive health care, poor living conditions, few neighborhood recreational facilities, and a continual threat of violence exacerbate her problems.

With great skill and passion, Francine tells and retells the stories that help her children and grandchildren know who they are. With clarity and patience, she tries to pass on to her loved ones the value system that guides her own exemplary life. She is responsible and demanding. She is not perfect, but she is faithful. She is an active contemplative, constantly reflecting on the will of God in her life and having no choice but to test that will in her struggle to survive.

Francine's love for her family is first and foremost. But she is as likely to take a neighbor's child under her wing as one of her own grandchildren. She is counselor and organizer and advocate for her neighborhood, her extended family. Without a doubt, she breathes life into everyone she meets.

We are all "threatened with resurrection," as Julia Esquivel put it. Only the courage to embrace it is lacking. The Francines of this world offer the rest of us the inspiration to reach for resurrection.

The story is ours to conclude. How will it be written in the narrative of our own lives? Mark's story of resurrection invites each of us to journey to Galilee in the geography of our own faith. Where do we see signs of new life in ourselves and our world? How can we nurture and celebrate those signs of life?

OUR DISCIPLESHIP JOURNEY

> At the very center of Christian faith lies the assertion that
> Jesus of Nazareth, the Son of God, died by crucifixion.
> ... Curiously enough, however, theological reflection on
> the cross of Jesus is very infrequent; and when it is carried
> out, it rarely reaches the level of showing that the cross
> and the proclamation of a "crucified God" embody the
> authentic originality of the Christian faith. Such reflection
> usually remains on the level of pious contemplation..., a
> more or less magical conception of redemption, one
> which ends up eliminating the element of scandal in the
> historical cross of Jesus.... In recent times theology... has
> sought to elaborate a theology of the resurrection, look-
> ing to it as the paradigm of triumphant liberty and the
> joy of living which was lost in the cross. In short, theol-
> ogy has tended to sidestep the task of reflecting on the
> cross itself.
>
> —Jon Sobrino, S.J., *Christology at the Crossroads*

In our observance of Holy Week, do we tend to skip over Good Friday, moving quickly in our thoughts from the remembrance of the
Lord's Supper on Maundy Thursday to Easter Sunday? Does Jesus'
journey to Golgotha make us uncomfortable? Strike us as anti-
quated? Puzzle us? Do we find any connection between the inevitable sufferings of our human existence and Jesus' passion and
death? Do we ever link the cross of Jesus with the crosses borne by
two-thirds of humanity in the world of the poor?

Have we reflected on the analogy between the reasons for
Jesus' condemnation and execution and the reasons why there are
oppressed women, men, and children throughout the world? Can
we see the same forces of evil that conspired to eliminate Jesus conspiring in our world? Can we look squarely at ourselves to see if we,
personally or societally, might form part of that same conspiracy?

211

We offer one final reflection from an artist friend of ours. She has portrayed what she calls "Crux Americanus," the American Cross. It depicts a balding, slightly paunchy, middle-aged man on a soft-looking cross. He is dressed in jogging clothes. Rather than nails his hands are fastened to the cross beam with velcro cloth, and his feet rest upon a small platform protruding from the cross. There is a slightly clerical look about him, suggesting a priest or minister about to go for a leisurely trot. Indeed, he looks for all the world as if he is about to say: "OK, this is enough. I think I'll just hop down now." Crux Americanus?

We are all on a journey. There is little more important than how we understand that journey. A story from Native American tradition describes how one tribe learned to find its way on long journeys. These travelers navigated by singing a song as they journeyed, a song that was a kind of roadmap by which they could remember changes in direction and key landmarks.

This tradition reminds us of the life of Christian community. We travel along in a world that is constantly changing and uncertain. To chart our course, we have a story that we sing as we go. We are a community that charts its course through time by telling the sacred story of the people of God. We hope that this reading of Mark's discipleship story will enable you to take up with joy your own discipleship journey.

APPENDIX 1
Mapping Mark's Narrative

One of the greatest barriers to Bible study in North American churches today is the alienation we feel from scripture. This distance is attributable to many things, such as feelings of reverence or revulsion, experiences of ambivalence or irrelevance, or just too much boring Bible study. But at the root of this problem lies our perceived inability to interpret scripture. That perception is explicitly and implicitly reinforced in pulpits, theological books, and seminary classrooms, where biblical interpretation is assumed to be the privileged domain of intellectual or clerical elites. The authors of this book believe, in contrast, that because the Bible was written by, about, and for non-elites, it therefore belongs to *all* the people of the church. But for us to reclaim the Bible as ours we must not only assert our right and ability to interpret it; we must *also practice!*

We need to work "hands on" with scripture. Treating a biblical text in a tactile manner, taking it apart and putting it back together like the puzzle it is, helps reduce the distance we feel from it. As we handle a text ourselves, rather than relying upon secondary theories or interpretations, we begin to grow familiar and even intimate with it. Learning about the character and internal dynamics of a text does not require advanced degrees—only our attentiveness, willingness to work patiently, and common sense. It is the authors' experience from working with groups that the more we handle the text the more it comes alive to us—and in turn the more we become open to what it has to say to us.

We would do well to remind ourselves that these ancient texts are stories, and that storytelling is not so foreign to us. We all possess what Robert Funk, in *The Poetics of Biblical Narrative,* calls a "native competence" in narrative. Funk contends that just as people routinely form and interpret sentences, whether or not they are trained in the rules of grammar, so too do we naturally tell and interpret stories, with or without consciousness of "narratology." Story is part of our native tongue.

Test this hypothesis yourself. Ask someone to talk about what she did yesterday. Quite spontaneously she will become a storyteller: setting up and deconstructing scenes, plotting time, leaving certain people or events out in order to emphasize others, perhaps even lending a dramatic twist or two to the story. We know intuitively how to "read" plots, characters, and settings that are narrated within our own cultural universe. We need only to become more conscious of our competence and to strengthen these muscles in order to apply them to texts generated in a very different historical and cultural universe.

Below is a very basic type of narrative analysis that focuses on the fundamentals of text-handling: the structure, dynamics, and fundamental elements of a narrative world. One axiom is that form and content are intimately related to each other. Careful attention to *how* the narrative is structured is an indispensable key to interpreting a text. The building blocks of literary structure are familiar:

i)   **Sentences:** multiple words arranged according to grammatical and syntactical rules and conventions. Attention to sentence structure (e.g., placement of the verb or use of adjectives) is crucial to determining the meaning of a text.

ii) **Episodes:** a series of related sentences around a common event or theme, often defined by changes in plot, character, and/or setting in space or time. Episodes are basic units of narrative with their own internal structure.

iii) **Sequences:** episodes that are linked around themes or plot development. A sequence has an internal structure of its own, as we will see in the prologue to Mark studied below. It also stands in structural relationship to the overall narrative.

iv) **Major Sequences:** a "sequence of sequences" articulating a major plot line of the story as a whole. Major sequences are "structural pillars" upon which the story is built, and also have an internal design of their own.

v)   **Architecture:** takes into account all four of the above, looking for coherence and pattern. An overall architectural pattern can sometimes be called a *genre*.

A building is a helpful analogy for understanding the structure of texts. A window (= *episode*) usually has its own design (= *sen-*

tences), yet is also part of the design of a wall (= *sequence*). Both the window and wall must cohere with the overall design of the room (= *major sequence*), which in turn must cohere with the master floor plan (= *architecture*). Analyzing texts is much like the process of examining a house, moving back and forth in perspective from close-up to medium-range to a view of the whole.

The text with which we will introduce these tools is Mark's prologue, the gospel's first sequence (see Chapter 1). The exercises referred to appear at the end of this appendix.

Exercise 1: Identifying Episodes

The best place to begin handling the text is to lay it out on a worksheet, with plenty of room for notes. Photocopy texts from a Bible, or—better yet—type them out on a piece of paper (an exercise that increases your intimacy with the text). The first step is to break down the text into workable units. This we can do by looking for natural episodes, using our common narrative sense. Episodes can usually be determined by changes in setting, voice, or action. Exercise 1 below has placed breaks between episodes and numbered them for easy reference. This sequence is comprised of six episodes.

Exercise 2: Sequence Architecture

The next step is to see if we can loosely label the episodic units according to their respective themes. Then we can see if and how the units are linked, the most common indicators being verbal/thematic repetition or overlap. If these themes reoccur elsewhere in the sequence, we should look for a pattern. The results of such an analysis are in Exercise 2 below. Labeling the units by theme indeed reveals a pattern that is concentric in structure (A B C / C' B' A'). This form has three possible functions. First, the outer frame (which is "unlinked") defines the sequence as a whole, bracketing the prologue with the assertion that the gospel *both proclaims* Jesus (v 1) and *is proclaimed by* Jesus (v 15). Second, the architecture introduces several themes that will be revisited throughout Mark's narrative:

gospel:	8:35; 10:29; 13:10; 14:9;
wilderness:	1:35; 6:31f; 8:4;
baptism:	10:38f; 11:30

Third, the concentric structure focuses attention upon its architectural center: the relationship between John and Jesus. The entire narrative will be woven around these two *personas:* John as "Elijah" (6:15; 8:28; 9:11f; 15:35f) and Jesus as the "stronger one" (3:27; 5:4; 9:18; 14:37). Both these characters survive in the wilderness and preach repentance. A relatively simple structural analysis thus tells us a great deal about how this section sets the stage for the rest of the story. Having determined the form of the sequence, we begin to look more closely at its contents.

Exercise 3: Settings

The basic elements of a story, as every cub reporter knows, are:

> *time and place* ("when/where"), or <u>setting</u>;
> *actors* ("who"), or <u>characters</u>; and
> *events* ("what"), or <u>plot</u>.

Taking the time to catalogue all the elements will pay dividends in interpretation. This is a second axiom of narrative analysis: Because authors are in full control of their material, every detail is there for a reason! After identifying these elements as they appear, note what information the story world gives us about each element. Then ask what the element might have connoted in the cultural context that produced the story. Exercise 3 below looks at settings, paying particular attention to whether these coordinates are given positive or negative value in the story world: whether the protagonists feel safe or threatened, whether good or bad things happen there. Note the spatial tension between center and margins both by the "suppression" of Malachi's Temple as the site of God's intervention and the movement of the people from Judea/Jerusalem to the wilderness. These concrete sites representing the political status quo are opposed by indeterminate symbolic sites (Way/kingdom/heaven), which are "rupturing into" history (1:10).

Exercise 4: Characters

The next step is to focus on characters and other symbolic components. We can clearly begin to identify protagonists and antagonists. But pay close attention to how Mark portrays characters in terms of their relative social "power" (both John and Jesus are heroes, but are located on the margins). Mark will, for example, dramatically contrast Jairus and the bleeding woman in order to make a sharp social point (see Chapter 7). One should also trace patterns of characterizations throughout the story as a whole: Jesus clashes with the Pharisees around issues of table fellowship, the scribes emerge as his arch-opponents, and the male disciples go from being sympathetic to antipathetic to the Way of Jesus. See how much can be learned without even yet focusing upon "what happened" in the story! Patient analysis gives us more data with which to interpret meaning carefully.

Exercise 5: Plot

The final step is to look at plot development and dynamics. Note how the plot of Mark's prologue is driven by "predictions" and their fulfillment. Note also how "Isaiah" introduces John, John introduces Jesus, and Jesus introduces the sovereignty of God.

Such step-by-step exercises can and should be done for each episode and sequence in Mark, preferably *before* beginning each chapter in this book. To be sure, our natural narrative competence cannot solve all the interpretive mysteries presented to us by an ancient text such as the gospel of Mark. But it can get us "into" the story deeply enough for other kinds of analytical work to take place.

Mark's story will yield its depth and richness only through an investment of time and patience by the reader. This will not be easy for North Americans, for the culture industry is a powerfully corrosive force upon our willingness and ability to make this investment. Most forms of contemporary media are engineered for a passive audience. They leave no room for critical reflection — that is their power as propaganda. We have been socialized into instant narrative gratification by overwhelming special effects, trite characters, and predictable plots that resolve in happy endings just in time for commercial breaks. All of these things contribute to our lack of patience with complex narrative, our short attention-spans, and the atrophy of our storytelling muscles.

Rediscovering and exercising these muscles will not only facilitate more engaging Bible study. It is culturally subversive to recover our *ability* and *responsibility* to reflect critically upon the cultural texts around us that compete for our hearts and minds. Critical literacy in the narratives of the Bible *and* those of the culture around us is crucial if we are to become "spec-actors" — those who "see" what is happening and respond in discipleship.

EXERCISE 1: IDENTIFYING EPISODES

TEXT	ANALYSIS

¹The beginning of the gospel of Jesus Christ.

1) This appears to be a relatively freestanding clause; we can see it as a kind of "title."

²As it is written in Isaiah the prophet: "Behold I send my messenger before your face who shall prepare your Way; ³the voice of one crying in the wilderness: Prepare the Way of the Lord, make God's paths straight."

2) This citation, a kind of "offstage" voice (no actual setting), is a discrete episodic unit with "Isaiah" as its main character.

⁴John the baptizer appeared in the wilderness, preaching a baptism of repentance for the forgiveness of sins. ⁵And there went out to him all the country of Judea, and all the people of Jerusalem; and they were baptized by him in the river Jordan, confessing their sins. ⁶Now John was clothed with camel hair, and had a leather girdle around his waist, and ate locusts and wild honey. ⁷And he preached, saying "After me comes he who is stronger than I, the thong of whose sandals I am unworthy to stoop down and untie. ⁸I have baptized you with water; but he will baptize you with the Holy Spirit."

3) The appearance ("onstage" now) of a new character in a distinct setting signals a new episode. This unit includes John's action and the people's response (vv 4f); Mark's description of John (v 6), sometimes called "showing a character"; and John's words (vv 7f), sometimes called "the character's telling." This episode opens with a description of John's general preaching (v 4) and closes with an account of his specific message (vv 7f). Note how this message serves to introduce two characters who will be key to the story: the "stronger one" and the Holy Spirit.

⁹In those days Jesus came from Nazareth of Galilee and was baptized by John in the Jordan. ¹⁰And when he came up out of the water, immediately he saw the heavens opened and the Spirit descending upon him like a dove; ¹¹and a voice came from heaven, "You are my beloved Son; with you I am well pleased."

4) The appearance of new characters (Jesus, a voice from heaven and the Spirit/dove) signals a new episode. Again the unit consists of description, action, and "dialogue."

¹²The Spirit immediately drove him out into the wilderness. ¹³And he was in the wilderness forty days, tempted by Satan; and he was with the wild beasts; and the angels ministered to him.

5) The relocative verb ("drove him out") signals a change in episode. As here, episodic units can be as short as one or two sentences in Mark.

¹⁴Now after John was arrested, Jesus came into Galilee, preaching the gospel of God, ¹⁵and saying, "The time is fulfilled, and the Kingdom of God is at hand; repent, and believe the gospel."

6) This episode is defined by a specific time ("after John's arrest") and place (Galilee). It is separated from 1:16 by the change in scenery and the shift from general to specific action.

EXERCISE 2: SEQUENCE ARCHITECTURE

ANALYSIS

TEXT

A = Outer frame [theme = gospel/Jesus]

[1]The beginning of the gospel of Jesus Christ.

No link—<

B = Inner frame
[theme = wilderness]

[2]As it is written in Isaiah the prophet: "Behold I send my messenger before your face who shall prepare your Way; [3]the voice of one crying in the wilderness: Prepare the Way of the Lord, make God's paths straight."

Link: wilderness —<

C = Structural Center
[theme= baptism,
relationship between John
& "stronger one"]

[4]John the baptizer appeared in the wilderness, preaching a baptism of repentance for the forgiveness of sins. [5]And there went out to him all the country of Judea, and all the people of Jerusalem; and they were baptized by him in the river Jordan, confessing their sins. [6]Now John was clothed with camel hair, and had a leather girdle around his waist, and ate locusts and wild honey. [7]And he preached, saying "After me comes he who is stronger than I, the thong of whose sandals I am unworthy to stoop down and untie. [8]I have baptized you with water; but he will baptize you with the Holy Spirit."

Link: baptism —<

C' = Structural Center
[theme = baptism,
relationship between John
& Jesus]

[9]In those days Jesus came from Nazareth of Galilee and was baptized by John in the Jordan. [10]And when he came up out of the water, immediately he saw the heavens opened and the Spirit descending upon him like a dove; [11]and a voice came from heaven, "You are my beloved Son; with you I am well pleased."

Link: Spirit—<

B' = Inner frame
[theme = wilderness]

[12]The Spirit immediately drove him out into the wilderness. [13]And he was in the wilderness forty days, tempted by Satan; and he was with the wild beasts; and the angels ministered to him.

No link—<

A' = Outer frame [theme = gospel/Jesus]

[14]Now after John was arrested, Jesus came into Galilee, preaching the gospel of God, [15]and saying, "The time is fulfilled, and the Kingdom of God is at hand; repent, and believe the gospel."

EXERCISE 3: SETTINGS

TEXT	ANALYSIS

[1]The beginning of the gospel of Jesus Christ.

[2]As it is written in Isaiah the prophet: "Behold I send my messenger before your face who shall prepare your Way;

scripture will be a site of contention in this story.
Way will be a positive coordinate symbolizing discipleship.

[3]the voice of one crying in the wilderness: Prepare the Way of the Lord, make God's paths straight."

wilderness will be a positive coordinate, but also a site of struggle (1:12f); symbolic and literal margin; vs. Temple (Mal 3:1 citation), a site suppressed here

[4]John the baptizer appeared in the wilderness, preaching a baptism of repentance for the forgiveness of sins. [5]And there went out to him all the country of Judea, and all the people of Jerusalem; and they were baptized by him in the river Jordan, confessing their sins. [6]Now John was clothed with camel hair, and had a leather girdle around his waist, and ate locusts and wild honey. [7]And he preached, saying "After me comes he who is stronger than I, the thong of whose sandals I am unworthy to stoop down and untie. [8]I have baptized you with water; but he will baptize you with the Holy Spirit. "

movement from Jerusalem/Judea to wilderness Jordan =
from center to margin = spatial/political tension

Jordan = "boundary" of Jewish Palestine (cf 3:8;10:1)

stoop down = posture connoting deference in honor culture

[9]In those days Jesus came from Nazareth of Galilee and was baptized by John in the Jordan. [10]And when he came up out of the water, immediately he saw the heavens opened and the Spirit descending upon him like a dove; [11]and a voice came from heaven, "You are my beloved Son; with you I am well pleased."

Nazareth=obscure place, "Nowheresville"
Galilee = margin, symbolic of alienated northern Israelite tribes, will emerge as narrative center of gravity
into/out of = implies process of immersion/engagement
descent from ruptured heavens = apocalyptic symbol; movement from heaven to earth

[12]The Spirit immediately drove him out into the wilderness. [13]And he was in the wilderness forty days, tempted by Satan; and he was with the wild beasts; and the angels ministered to him.

out into wilderness = site of apocalyptic struggle between good (Jesus & angels) and evil (Satan & beasts)

[14]Now after John was arrested, Jesus came into Galilee, preaching the gospel of God, [15]and saying, "The time is fulfilled, and the Kingdom of God is at hand; repent, and believe the gospel."

Kingdom of God = liberated political space positive coordinate referring to old tribal confederacy

EXERCISE 4: CHARACTERS

TEXT	ANALYSIS
[1]The beginning of the <u>gospel</u> of <u>Jesus Christ.</u>	<u>gospel</u> = *Roman propaganda, expropriated by Mark* <u>Jesus</u> = *main character of story; designation as "Christ" will, however, be contentious (see 8:29ff)*
[2]As it is written in <u>Isaiah</u> the prophet: "Behold I send my <u>messenger</u> before <u>your</u> face who shall prepare your way; [3]the voice of one crying in the wilderness: Prepare the way of the Lord, make God's paths straight."	<u>Isaiah</u> = *scriptural authority important in Mark (see 2:25; 7:9ff; 12:26, 36)* <u>messenger</u> = *indirect introduction of John* <u>you</u> = *may refer to God or Jesus but also to readers who are here invited into the story (see 16:7)*
[4]<u>John</u> the baptizer appeared in the wilderness, preaching a baptism of repentance for the forgiveness of sins. [5]And there went out to him all the country of Judea, and <u>all the People of Jerusalem;</u> and they were baptized by him in the river Jordan, confessing their sins. [6]Now John was <u>clothed with camel hair. and had a leather girdle around his waist.</u> and <u>ate locusts and wild honey.</u> [7]And he preached, saying "After me comes he who is <u>stronger than</u> I, the thong of whose sandals I am unworthy to stoop down and untie. [8]I have baptized you with water; but he will baptize you with the <u>Holy Spirit.</u> "	<u>John</u> = *direct introduction; minor on-stage role but major story-presence, representing prophet's vocation and destiny (see 9:11-13)* <u>people of Jerusalem</u> = *Those from the center need liberation* <u>Elijah</u> = *persona identified by costuming (see 2 Kg 1:8); living off land = free of dominant social order* <u>stronger one</u> = *Jesus' apocalyptic persona (see 3:27)* <u>Holy Spirit</u> = *appears elsewhere only in 3:29, 13:11; though we are told Jesus will baptize <u>with</u> it (see 10:38-40), we are shown him being baptized and impelled <u>by</u> the Spirit (vv 10, 12)*
[9]In those days Jesus came <u>from Nazareth</u> of Galilee and was baptized by John in the Jordan. [10]And when he came up out of the water, immediately he saw the heavens opened and the Spirit descending upon him like a dove; [11]and a <u>voice</u> came from heaven, "You are my beloved Son; with you I am well pleased."	<u>from Nazareth</u> = *a hero of unmiraculous and obscure origins* <u>voice</u> = *a "mask of God" (provides reliable testimony to Jesus, see 9:7)*
[12]The Spirit immediately drove him out into the wilderness. [13]And he was in the wilderness forty days, tempted by <u>Satan;</u> and he was with the <u>wild beasts;</u> and the <u>angels</u> ministered to him.	<u>Satan</u> = *Introduction of arch-enemy (see 3:23; 4:15; 8:33)* <u>wild beasts/angels</u> = *opposing forces in apocalyptic struggle (see Dan 7:3)*
[14]Now after <u>John was arrested.</u> Jesus came into Galilee, preaching the gospel of God, [15]and saying, "The time is fulfilled, and the Kingdom of God is at hand; repent, and believe the gospel."	<u>Herod</u> = *implied here, though he won't be introduced until flashback account in 6:14ff*

EXERCISE 5: PLOT

TEXT

ANALYSIS

[1]The beginning of the gospel of Jesus Christ.

the beginning (mythic time)
- *old story (Genesis) = creation*
- *beginning of new story = re-creation*
- *expectation[1] generated (messenger coming?)*
- *prophetic voice regenerated*
- *Exodus journey regenerated (see Ex 23:20)*
- *Mal 3:1ff "Day of Lord" = end of world?*
- *Is 40:3 = Israel's renewal = new beginning?*

[2]As it is written in Isaiah the prophet: "Behold I send my messenger before your face who shall prepare your way; [3]the voice of one crying in the wilderness: Prepare the way of the Lord, make God's paths straight."

[4]John the baptizer appeared in the wilderness, preaching a baptism of repentance for the forgiveness of sins. [5]And there went out to him all the country of Judea, and all the people of Jerusalem; and they were baptized by him in the river Jordan, confessing their sins. [6]Now John was clothed with camel hair, and had a leather girdle around his waist, and ate locusts and wild honey. [7]And he preached, saying "After me comes he who is stronger than I, the thong of whose sandals I am unworthy to stoop down and untie. [8]I have baptized you with water; but he will baptize you with the Holy Spirit."

John's ministry (generalized past)
- *expectation[1] fulfilled*
- *Exodus/Isaiah confirmed by wilderness site*
- *Malachi disconfirmed by wilderness site*
- *mass popular response = "revival"?*
- *"Elijah" = Mal 4:5 confirmed = judgment?*
- *"After me " = plotted succession: John → Jesus → disciple → reader*
- *expectation[2] generated (stronger one coming?)*
- *expectation[3] generated (Spirit baptism coming?); though unfulfilled in the story, it is alluded to again in 10:38-40, and implies a "future" to the narrative (see 13:11)*

[9]In those days Jesus came from Nazareth of Galilee and was baptized by John in the Jordan. [10]And when he came up out of the water, immediately he saw the heavens opened and the Spirit descending upon him like a dove; [11]and a voice came from heaven, "You are my beloved Son; with you I am well pleased."

Jesus' baptism = (first action "shown " in story)
- *expectation[2] fulfilled? Unsure; the one to whom John vowed submission submits to John*
- *Public scene issues in private vision.*
- *Fulfillment of condition for expectation[3]?*

[12]The Spirit immediately drove him out into the wilderness. [13]And he was in the wilderness forty days, tempted by Satan; and he was with the wild beasts; and the angels ministered to him.

Temptation (mythic time)
- *40 days = Exodus motif confirmed*
- *represents overall theme of story: Jesus' struggle against the Powers*

[14]Now after John was arrested, Jesus came into Galilee, preaching the gospel of God, [15]and saying, "The time is fulfilled, and the Kingdom of God is at hand; repent, and believe the gospel."

Jesus preaches (kairos moment)
- *expectation[2] fulfilled: Jesus is John's successor because he preaches repentance*
- *Why is John arrested? See "flashback," 6:14ff*
- *expectation[4] generated (kingdom coming?)*
- *"kairos" time introduced (see 11:13; 13:33)*
- *time fulfilled = old story "resolved"*
- *Kingdom at hand = new story imminent*

APPENDIX 2
Mapping Our Family History

It is more than coincidental that for many North Americans the family Bible has been a primary repository for genealogical information such as births, baptisms, marriages, deaths, and sometimes even political affiliations and migrations. It is as if some deep intuition has led families to preserve their stories within the covers of the sacred story. The authors of this book believe that our family histories are a primary text that should be read alongside the gospel.

Wendel Berry in *Fidelity* gives us a sense of the potential of such an exploration: "The man who was my grandfather is present in me as I felt his father to always be present in him. You work your way down...into the interior of the present until finally you come to the beginning." An archaeology of our origins is important because our ancestors' history remains within us.

We discover in our family story how our ancestors participated in and were impacted by the historical experience of the nation. Connecting with that collective history may in turn help us get to the root of our national problems and may help us stop repeating the mistakes of the past. We may discover how historical traumas or liberative heroism shaped our own family system, and thus our own lives. If we wish to heal the wounds of past generations we must grieve the tragedies and celebrate the goodness.

Marginalized communities are often more aware of their history than European-Americans because they have had to struggle to preserve a sense of ethnic identity within a hostile dominant culture. Yet the stories of European-Americans are much more culturally and ethnically complex than the myths of assimilation have led us to believe. They may include experiences of displacement, flight from war, victimization by prejudice or religious persecution as well as stories of prosperity or class and race privilege. European-

American stories include episodes of resistance and hope as well as of conformity and upward mobility.

What do we want to affirm and celebrate in the stories of our families, and what cries out for healing and transformation? What values and behaviors do we wish to preserve and what do we wish to leave behind as we move into the future? We invite you to reflect on your family history and the ethnic-cultural traditions that are your birthright in your Discipleship Journal as you journey through a reading of Mark's gospel.

The geneagram is one tool that can help you begin to construct a family tree as a basis for deeper reflection on your story. At the top of a large sheet of paper place symbols representing your grandparents on both sides of your family, using a square for the male and a circle for the female. Underneath them place your parents and their siblings, and underneath your parents place yourself and your siblings. Continue on down the page if you have children or grandchildren. See the sample skeleton chart below.

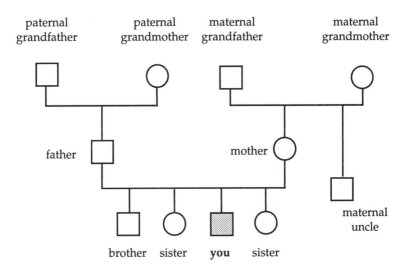

Once you have sketched out the basic family genealogy, make notes concerning significant information alongside each symbol. Include approximate dates of birth and death and any outstanding life events such as migration, illness, employment and unemployment, war, land ownership, economic status, etc. Now try to go back further than your grandparents' generation. Can you identify the generation(s) that first came to the U.S.? From where did they come, and under what circumstances? What were they leaving—socially, economically, and politically? What did they come to in the New World? How did women fare? What were the class and race relationships of each generation?

You will probably notice areas where you do not know very much about your family history, particularly the farther back you go. This may be because this information has not been shared with you or is not immediately available. There may be layers of family legend to sort through. What has been idealized, scapegoated, or covered over in your family's narrative of itself, and why?

You may feel frustrated in this inquiry. Is there a desire in you to know more about your family history? If so, how might you address the obstacles that you face in trying to uncover your family story? Consider other possible sources of information both inside and outside your family. What do you feel about what you know—and do not know? You may wish to share your response to this exercise with a study group. Are you indifferent, curious, filled with pride, shame, grief, or wonder? You may discover in your family story the presence of traumatic content that is emotionally disturbing. You are in charge of how much you share.

Keep this geneagram with your discipleship journal. In a number of chapters in this book you will be offered questions concerning your family history for reflection, discussion, and/or journaling. To begin, think about the two questions below.

1) Name three significant larger historical events (e.g., war, economic depression, labor strikes, racial unrest) that shaped your grandparents. Do the same for your parents. How did these events alter and shape the aspirations of your ancestors? How might they have shaped certain values, attitudes or biases that you carry?

2) Where did your grandparents live and work? Where do you live and work? Is there any relationship between the two?

APPENDIX 3

Mapping Our Social, Economic, and Political Contexts

The gospel of Mark was written within a specific social, economic, and political context. So too, different communities interpret the gospel according to their particular contexts. Understanding these contexts involves the tools of social analysis. Social analysis is the task of breaking open the conglomerate reality around us in order to learn about the history of the present situation as well as the current balance of power and its underlying structures and systems, social and political dynamics, economic relationships and cultural forces.

Many of the Word in Our World sections suggest different tools for doing social analysis. The center-margins concept used in Chapter 1, for example, helps us think about the ways in which some groups are closer to the places of power and decision making, while other groups are excluded. Social analysis often involves graphically mapping the information we have, or determining the right questions to ask in order to get the information. Consider the following "champagne glass" graph, from a 1994 report of the United Nations Development Program, that illustrates the distribution of wealth around the world:

(Each horizontal band represents 1/5 of the world's population)

Richest 20% control 82.7% of
total global income

Next 20% control 11.7% of the
total global income

Next 20% control 2.3% of the
total global income

Next 20% control 1.9% of the
total global income

The poorest 20% control 1.4%
of the total global income

Another example is the simple grid of what is called in Spanish a "coyuntura." In this exercise we plot out essential aspects of power as it is manifested in different spheres. For example, begin to plot how wealth and power are constructed in the U. S.:

Sphere	Neighborhood	Municipality	State	Nation
Economic				
Military				
Political				
Cultural				
Religious				

To fill in such a chart you may ask questions such as:

- What are the main economic resources of the sphere?

- Who owns and controls them?

- Who works?

- Who benefits and who loses from this pattern of work and ownership?

- Who has greatest access to resources, and who least?

- What effect does this have on family life in the different classes?

- In what ways is the earth and its local flora and fauna being nurtured or destroyed?

- Who has power to make decisions, and how is this power obtained and maintained?

- How is this power backed up by armed force? Who makes laws and who benefits from the laws?

- What does the local society believe about itself?

- What are its chief stated values, and who promotes them publicly?

- What contrasting or minority values are expressed and among whom?

- How do each of these spheres shape the others?

We should remember that such analysis should not pretend to be value-free. We must explicitly acknowledge where we ourselves stand and what values and biases we hold. It is best to begin with a simple outline of the data so we can grasp the big picture before looking more closely at detail. And examining the relationships between all the factors and spheres is key.

Some of the specific areas to be examined in social analysis of a given area include:

- *social sphere:* demographics; ethnic and racial make-up; cultural factors; class structure; social problems; religious groups and their involvement in public issues.

- *economic sphere:* natural resources; technological and industrial practices; agricultural practices; ecological health.

- *political sphere:* power groups; voter turnout; positions of elected officials; "informal" power brokers and outside political influences such as media, business groups, and labor unions.

The more we know about how government, education, the media, businesses, and the church all work and work together or at odds, the more clearly we will be able to understand why some in our particular social context are poor and others rich, what perpetuates inequity, who makes decisions and who is affected. Tools of social analysis can be found in Anne Hope and Sally Timmel's *Training for Transformation* and in Joe Holland and Peter Henriot's *Social Analysis: Linking Faith and Justice.*

APPENDIX 4
Liturgical Resources

These responsive readings—intended to supplement the chapters to which they correspond—may be used in a variety of ways. They might be particularly helpful as the opening of a study session or in the context of a worship service in which the corresponding text is read and preached.

The readings in this appendix may be powerful and moving. People may want to share their reactions with others. We recommend that time be allowed, at some point following the readings, for that sharing to occur.

A liturgical reading to be used with Chapter 6:

A PSALM FOR CASTING OUT DEMONS

Choir 1:　　We are possessed by demons.
　　　　　　All of us.
　　　　　　No matter how many times we pray, they won't go
　　　　　　away completely.
　　　　　　Moods, habits, devilish desires
　　　　　　inhabit the regions of our subconscious
　　　　　　and break out suddenly, inexplicably,
　　　　　　taking us over,
　　　　　　making us someone we would rather not be,
　　　　　　someone we really are not.

Choir 2:　　We are obsessed with demons,
　　　　　　surrounded daily by demonic forces:
　　　　　　drink, drugs, illicit sex,
　　　　　　money, power, acquisition;

they are taking control of our neighborhoods,
trying to break down the doors of our homes
and too often breaking our hearts....

Choir 1:   God can cast out demons.
             Through a rock-solid faith,
             the power of prayer,
             and unrelenting discipline,
             God brings demons down.

Choir 2:   Cast out the demons treacherously lurking within us
             and around us.

Choir 1:   Cast out the evil propensities
             that threaten our lives.

Voice: Drugs are demons.

All: Cast out the demons of drugs.
             Prevent them from overpowering us.

Voice: Drink is a demon.

All: Cast out the demon of drink.
             Let it not control our lives.

Voice: Rape and incest are demons.

All: Cast out the demons of rape and incest.
             Prevent them from overpowering us.

Voice: Violence and abuse are demons.

All: Cast out the demons of violence and abuse.
             Let them not control our lives.

Voice: Avariciousness and greed are demons.

All: Cast out the demons of avariciousness and greed.
             Prevent them from controlling our lives.

Voice: Uncontrollable anger is a demon.

All: Cast out the demon of uncontrollable anger.
            Let it not control our lives.

Voice: Envy is a demon.

All: Cast out the demon of envy.
            Let it not control our lives.

Voice: Injustice is a demon.

All: Cast out the demon of injustice.
            Let it not control our lives.

Voice: Oppression is a demon.

All: Cast out the demon of oppression.
            Let it not control our lives.

Voice: War is a demon.

All: Cast out the demon of war.
            Let it not control our lives.

Choir 1:   Let us put ourselves in the hands of God
            Who has overcome the demons.

Choir 2:   O God, Who destroys demonic forces,
            strengthen our determination
            and acknowledge our prayer.

All: We will not give in to demons.
            They will not overpower us.
            They will not control our lives.

            — Miriam Therese Winter
               WomanWisdom: A Feminist Lectionary and Psalter

A liturgical reading to be used with Chapter 7:

Rich Woman, Poor Woman—
A Dramatic Reading for Two People

1. I am a woman.
    1. I am a woman.

2. I am a woman born of a woman, whose man owned a factory.
    2. I am a woman born of a woman, whose man labored in a factory.

3. I am a woman whose man wore silk suits, who constantly watched his weight.
    3. I am a woman whose man wore tattered clothing, whose heart was constantly strangled by hunger.

4. I am a woman who watched two babies grow into beautiful children.
    4. I am a woman who watched two babies die because there was no milk.

5. I am a woman who watched twins grow into popular students with summers abroad.
    5. I am a woman who watched three children grow, but with bellies stretched from no food.

6. But there was a man:
    6. But there was a man:

7. And he talked about the peasants getting richer by my family getting poorer.
    7. And he told me of the days that would be better, and he made the days better.

8. We had to eat rice!
    8. We had rice!

9. We had to eat beans!
    9. We had beans!

10. My children were no longer given summer visas to Europe.
    10. My children no longer cried themselves to sleep.

11. And I felt like a peasant.
    11. And I felt like a woman.

12. A peasant with a dull, hard, unexciting life.
    12. Like a woman with a life that sometimes allowed a song.

13. And I saw a man.
    13. And I saw a man.

14. And together we began to plot with the hope of the return of freedom....
    14. I saw his heart beat with the hope of freedom at last....

15. Someday, the return of freedom.
    15. Someday freedom.

16. And then,
    16. And then,

17. One day,
    17. One day,

18. There were planes overhead, and guns firing close by.
    18. There were planes overhead, and guns firing in the distance.

19. I gathered my children and went home.
    19. I gathered my children and ran.

20. And the guns moved farther and farther away.
    20. But the guns moved closer and closer.

21. And then, they announced that freedom had been restored!
    21. And then, they came, young boys really....

22. They came into my home along with my man.
    22. They came and found my man.

23. Those men whose money was almost gone....
> 23. They found all the men whose lives were almost their own.

24. And we all had drinks to celebrate.
> 24. And they shot them all.

25. The most wonderful martinis.
> 25. And they shot my man.

26. And then they asked us to dance.
> 26. And then they came for us.

27. Me.
> 27. For me, the woman.

28. And my sisters.
> 28. For my sisters.

29. Then they took us.
> 29. Then they took us.

30. They took us to dinner at a small private club.
> 30. They stripped from us the dignity we had gained.

31. And they treated us to beef.
> 31. And then they raped us.

32. It was one course after another.
> 32. One after the other they came at us.

A liturgical reading to be used with Chapter 13:

A PARAPHRASE OF PSALM 22

(If this is read aloud by a group of men and women, both male and female voices should be in both sections.)

All: My God, My God, why have you forsaken me?
    Why do you not help me?
    O God, I cry to you by day, but you do not
    answer me.
    I cry to you by night, but find no rest.

Left side: I am scorned and despised,
    All who see me mock me and say,
    "She trusts in God, let God deliver her;
    Let God rescue her, since she believes in God."

Right side: I am minimalized and betrayed.
    My family, my friends, my minister say to me,
    "You must be exaggerating the abuse.
    It couldn't be that bad.
    It happened so long ago,
    Just forget it and get over it."

Left side: Many wild bulls surround me.
    They open their mouths like ravenous lions.

Right side: The legal system, society, and the church refuse
    to believe my story.
    They tell me I have a sick mind, and that I
    imagined the abuse.

Left side: I am poured out like water.
    My bones are dislocated.
    My heart is like wax and melts within me.
    My strength is gone; my tongue sticks to my
    teeth.
    I want to die.

Right side: I am at the end of my rope.
Memories and flashbacks engulf me.
My pain and my grief are tearing me apart.
I want to die.

Left side: Wild dogs surround me; evil people encircle me.
They have pierced my hands and feet;
I can count all my bones.

Right side: I am being engulfed by an uncaring system.
No one will listen to me.
The abuse I suffered has shattered the very
essence of my being.

Left side: My enemies gloat over me and stare at me.
They divide my clothes among them,
and gamble for my coat.

Right side: My perpetrator murdered my soul, but my
church protects him and covers up for him.
I am revictimized by a church that values silence
more than truth, and a good image more than
justice.

All: O God, don't abandon me, too!
Help and rescue me!

Left side: Deliver my soul from death, my life from vicious
dogs.
Save me from the lion's mouth,
Protect me from jackals,
Rescue my soul from hell!

Right side: Deliver me, O God, from those who protect the
system.
Save me from those who say I am lying.
Protect me from all who claim that I'm
responsible for my own abuse.
Rescue me from those who stonewall justice,
hoping that I'll go away quietly and not press
charges.

All: O God, hear my voice! Do not turn away from me!
      Listen to my plea!
      For still will I believe in your justice and
      truth,
      and the redemption of all your oppressed people.

This paraphrase of Psalm 22 was part of a worship service written by Susan F. Jarek-Glidden for the 1991 New England Area Pastors' Assembly of the United Methodist Church, at which the central topic was clergy sexual abuse. The intent was to help break down walls of silence and empower survivors of abuse to find their voices. The focus could be widened to include abuse of other kinds. It is reprinted in *Wellsprings: A Journal for United Methodist Clergy, Vol. 7, No. 1 (Spring 1994).*

BIBLIOGRAPHY

Bailie, Gil. *Violence Unveiled.* New York: Crossroad, 1995.

Beck, Robert. *Nonviolent Story: Narrative Conflict Resolution in the Gospel of Mark.* Maryknoll, NY: Orbis Books, 1996.

Birch, Bruce. *Let Justice Roll Down: The Old Testament, Ethics, and Christian Life.* Louisville: Westminster/John Knox, 1991.

Borg, Marcus. *Meeting Jesus Again for the First Time.* San Francisco: Harper & Row, 1993.

Brock, Rita Nakashima. *Journeys By Heart.* New York: Crossroad Publishing Co., 1992.

Ellul, Jacques. *Anarchy and Christianity.* Translated by G. Bromiley. Grand Rapids: William B. Eerdmans, 1991.

Equity Trust Inc., *Information for Prospective Participants* (539 Beach Pond Road, Voluntown, CT 06384), February 1994.

Fortune, Marie M. *Violence in the Family.* Ohio: Pilgrim, 1991.

Funk, Robert. *The Poetics of Biblical Narrative.* Sonoma: Poleridge Press, 1988.

Gottwald, Norman. *The Hebrew Bible: A Socio-Literary Introduction.* Philadelphia: Fortress Press, 1985.

Gutiérrez, Gustavo. *Las Casas: In Search of the Poor Jesus Christ.* Maryknoll, NY: Orbis Books, 1993.

Holland, Joe, and Peter Henriot, S.J. *Social Analysis: Linking Faith and Justice* (revised ed.). Maryknoll: Orbis Books, Dove Communications, and The Center of Concern, 1984.

Hope, Anne, and Sally Timmel. *Training for Transformation.* Zimbabwe: Mambo Press, 1984. (Available from The Center of Concern, 3700 13th St. NE, Washington, DC 20017.)

Horsley, Richard. *Bandits, Prophets & Messiahs: Popular Movements at the Time of Jesus.* San Francisco: Harper & Row, 1988.

Kairos USA. *On the Way: From Kairos to Jubilee.* (Kairos USA, 5757 Sheridan Road, #16A, Chicago, IL 60660.)

Lerner, Michael. *Jewish Renewal.* San Francisco: Harper Perennial, 1994.

Maiina, Bruce, and Richard Rohrbaugh. *Social-Science Commentary on the Synoptic Gospels.* Philadelphia: Fortress Press, 1992.

May, Gerald. *Addiction and Grace.* San Francisco: Harper & Row, 1988.

McIntosh, Peggy. "White Privilege: Unpacking the Invisible Knapsack," *Race, Class and Gender.* London: Wadsworth, 1993.

Mead, Loren. *The Once and Future Church.* Washington, D.C.: Alban Institute.

Neusner, Jacob. *A Short History of Judaism: Three Meals, Three Epochs.* Minneapolis: Fortress Press, 1992.

"Reaganomics and Women: Structural Adjustment U.S. Style," Alternative-Women in Development, c/o Center of Concern, 3700 13th St. NE, Washington, DC 20017.

Reems, Renita. *Just a Sister Away.* San Diego: Lura Media, 1988.

Ringe, Sharon H. *Jesus, Liberation, and the Biblical Jubilee.* Philadelphia: Fortress Press, 1985.

Segundo, Juan Luis. "Capitalism versus Socialism: *Crux Theologica.*" In R. Gibellini, ed., *Frontiers of Theology in Latin America.* Maryknoll, NY: Orbis Books, 1979.

Sobrino, S.J., Jon. *Christology at the Crossroads.* Maryknoll, NY: Orbis Books, 1978.

Sugirtharajah, R.S., ed. *Voices From the Margin: Interpreting the Bible in The Third World.* Maryknoll, NY: Orbis Books, 1991.

United Nations Development Program. *Human Development Report 1996.* New York: Oxford University Press, 1996.

West, Cornel. *Race Matters.* New York: Vintage Books, 1993.

Wink, Walter. *Engaging the Powers.* Augsburg Fortress, 1992.

Winter, Miriam Therese. *WomanWisdom: A Feminist Lectionary and Psalter.* New York: Crossroad Publishing Co., 1993.